Sufism
In India and Central Asia

Sufism
In India and Central Asia

Edited by
Nasir Raza Khan
Associate Professor
India Arab Cultural Centre
Jamia Millia Islamia (Central University)
New Delhi 110025 (INDIA)

LONDON AND NEW YORK

First published 2023
by Routledge
4 Park Square, Milton Park, Abingdon, Oxon OX14 4RN

and by Routledge
605 Third Avenue, New York, NY 10158

Routledge is an imprint of the Taylor & Francis Group, an informa business

© 2023 Contributors and Manakin Press

The right of Contributors to be identified as authors of their chapters has been asserted in accordance with sections 77 and 78 of the Copyright, Designs and Patents Act 1988.

All rights reserved. No part of this book may be reprinted or reproduced or utilised in any form or by any electronic, mechanical, or other means, now known or hereafter invented, including photocopying and recording, or in any information storage or retrieval system, without permission in writing from the publishers.

Trademark notice: Product or corporate names may be trademarks or registered trademarks, and are used only for identification and explanation without intent to infringe.

Print edition not for sale in South Asia (India, Sri Lanka, Nepal, Bangladesh, Pakistan or Bhutan)

British Library Cataloguing-in-Publication Data
A catalogue record for this book is available from the British Library

Library of Congress Cataloging-in-Publication Data
A catalog record for this book has been requested

ISBN: 9781032373584 (hbk)
ISBN: 9781032373591 (pbk)
ISBN: 9781003336617 (ebk)

DOI: 10.4324/9781003336617

Typeset in Times New Roman
by Manakin Press, Delhi

Dedicated

To my Father
Mr. Jafar Raza Khan
Who taught me invaluable lessons of life... to believe in myself

Acknowledgement

Sufism in India and Central Asia is a relatively less talked about area in South Asian scholarship. The historical importance of Sufism which linked the two regions by travel culture, religion and ideas going back a thousand years certainly deserves more attention. Much more so, in present times there is in need of an anchor for a way of life as an antidote to the multiple conflicts around the world. This volume aims to bridge a gap in the understanding and scholarship by bringing together a number of articles dealing with Sufism in Central Asia, the Caucus region and India.

The idea of bringing out a concise volume on Sufism in India and Central Asia came to my mind during my visit to various Sufi Dargahs in Central Asia, particularly in Uzbekistan and Kazakhstan, where I found many similarities in the rituals and customs, especially among the local people. My stay in Central Asia was a source of intellectual stimulus and self-discovery, and the memories will have a lasting impression on my life.

I would not have been able to bring out this volume without the support of many distinguished scholars who have contributed their article for this volume. As an editor I would like to thank the contributors to this volume, for their valuable contribution, patience and cooperation they have shown during the course of editing this book. I would also like to gratefully acknowledge and thank my colleagues in my University for providing intellectual support, valuable insights and sparing time for engaging in academic discussions, especially, Prof. Ajay Darshan Behera, Prof. Mohammad Ilias and Dr. Mathew Joseph C. I am also thankful to my research scholar, Jaffer who did a wonderful job in proof-reading the manuscript.

I am also grateful to my family members for their understanding, invaluable support, and encouraging words. I am very grateful to Shaista, my wife for being a source of inspiration, driven me to complete the task by selflessly giving her time and energies to our sweet and loving children – Areeba and Ariz, I would like to present this book to them and wish for their bright future.

A word of thanks goes to the publisher of Manakin Press, for agreeing to bring out this volume on time.

— Nasir Raza Khan

Contents

About the Editor and Contributors	xi

INDIA-CENTRAL ASIA: CULTURAL EXCHANGE

1. Introduction — 1–16
NASIR RAZA KHAN

2. Sufis in India and Central Asia During the Thirteenth and Fourteenth Century — 17–24
IQTIDAR HUSAN SIDIQUI

3. Sufism: Cementing Bonds Between Central Asia and Kashmir — 25–38
MUSHTAQ KAW

4. The Role of Sufis in Diplomatic Relations Between the Khoqand Khanate and India — 39–52
SHERZODHON MAHMUDOV

5. Khwaja Badruddin Samarqandi: Founder of Firdausi Silsiah in India — 53–70
NISHAT MANZAR

REGIONAL SUFI CENTRES AND THEIR INTER-CONNECTIONS

6. Sufis in Jammu and Their Cultural Impact — 71–84
JIGAR MOHAMMED

7. Kalimat al-Sadiqin: a Sufi Biographical Account — 85–100
GULFISHAN KHAN

8. Central Asia to India: Immigration of Sufis and Urbanization in Medieval Rajasthan — 101–112
JIBRAEIL

9. Sufism in Bengal: Interactions and Impacts Through the Ages — 123–140
MOHD SHAHEER SIDDIQUI

SUFI TRADITIONS IN CENTRAL ASIA AND CAUCASUS

10. Sufism and Religious Syncretism in the History of Central Asia   141–148
    LAURA YEREKESHEVA

11. The Style of Persian Sufi Prose XI - XIII Centuries   149–170
    MEHDI KAZIMOV

12. Significance of Abd-ur-Rahman Jami's Sufi-Poetic Discourse
    in the Literary Legacy of Medieval Persia   171–184
    G. N. KHAKI

13. The Understanding of Self and Others in Teachings of Sufism
    by Najmuddin Razi (1177-1252)   185–194
    USMONALI KAMOLOV

TEACHING OF SUFIS AND COMMUNAL HARMONY

14. Shaikh Sharfuddin Bu Ali Qalander Panipati's Contribution for
    the Development of Composite Culture in Panipat During 14th Century   195–208
    S.M. AZIZUDDIN HUSAIN

15. The Theme of Perfect Human in Sufism   209–222
    MUKHAYYO ABDURAKHMONOVA

16. Sufism in Karnataka: An Analysis of Shishunala Sharif   223–232
    VARADA M. NIKALJE

    Bibliography   233–240

    Index   241–248

About the Editor and Contributors

NASIR RAZA KHAN presently working as Associate Professor at the India-Arab Culture Centre, Jamia Millia Islamia, New Delhi, and former Director of the Centre for Indian Culture, Tashkent, Uzbekistan, under the Ministry of External Affairs, GOI. He regularly gets published research papers on cultural history and architectural conservation in Books and Journals. His recent publication includes; Central Asia and the World Powers, (Delhi: Primus Books 2013), Regional Sufi Centres in India: Significance and Contribution, (Delhi, Manakin Press 2015) and India and Central Asia: Geopolitics, Economy and Culture, (Delhi: Primus Books, 2016).

G. N. KHAKI is Professor and Director, Centre of Central Asian Studies, University of Kashmir, Srinagar. His area of research includes Central Asia, Islamic Studies and India Central Asia relation. He has contributed papers and articles in various books and journals.

GULFISHAN KHAN teaches Medieval Indian History at the Centre of Advanced Study, Department of History, In Aligarh Muslim University. Her publication includes Indian Muslim Perceptions of the West during the Eighteenth Century, (Oxford University Press, Karachi: 1998) Essays on Sayyid Ahmad Khan and Shaikh Muhammad Abdullah, (AMU Press, Aligarh, 2015) and Khwajah Shams al-Din Muhammad Hafiz Shirazi and the early British Romantics, (AMU Press, Aligarh, 2015)

IQTIDAR HUSAIN SIDDIQUI is retired Professor and ex-Chairman, Centre of Advanced Study, Department of History, In Aligarh Muslim University.

He is acclaimed Medieval Indian Historian having authority on Persian sources. He is author of several books included: Some Aspects of Indian history and culture, (1969), Modern writings on Islam and Muslims in India, (1974), Islam and Muslims in South Asia : historical perspective, (1987), Perso-Arabic sources of information on the life and conditions in the Sultanate of Delhi, (1992), Composite culture under the Sultanate of Delhi, (2012) Medieval India, (2013)

JIBRAEIL is working as Assistant Professor at Centre of Advanced Study, Department of History, Aligarh Muslim University; Aligarh. He has attended more than fifty National/International Seminars and Conferences and published thirty five research papers in National/International Journals and Proceedings.

JIGAR MOHAMAD is Professor at Department of History, University of Jammu. He has been associated with different Academic bodies; he has published number of research articles in reputed national journals.

LAURA YEREKESHEVA is Head, Central and South Asian Studies, Institute of Oriental Studies, Almaty, Kazakhstan. She is also UNESCO Chair Coordinator in Kazakhstan. She has attended many international Conference and Seminar and have contributed research article in national and international Journal, books etc.

MEHDI KAZIMOV is Professor and head of the department of Iranian Philology of Baku State University, Azerbaijan. He also looks after the department of study and publishing of written monuments of Oriental Studies Institute of the Academy of Sciences of Azerbaijan. M. Kazimov is credited with 11 books and more than 130 articles.

MOHAMMAD SHAHEER SIDDIQUI Who is presently working in Visva-Bharati (A Central University) Santiniketan, West Bengal. He has contributed papers and articles in various journals. He has edited Books, Philosophical Legacy of Education, 2014 Sufism and Indian Spiritual Traditions, (2015).

MUKHAYYO HAKIMOVNA is Associate Professor at Department of South Asian languages, at Tashkent State Institute of Oriental Studies (TSIOS), Tashkent, Uzbekistan. Apart from her publications in Uzbek Language she is co-author of translation Babur's Ghazals and Ruboyis from ancient Uzbek into Urdu, published by Delhi's Educational Publishing House, in 2002.

MUSHTAQ A. KAW is Professor and Head, Department of History, Maulana Azad National Urdu University (MANUU), Hyderabad, and formerly Director of Centre of Central Asian Studies, Kashmir University, specializes in South and Central Asian studies. He has authored/ co-authored four books, and published many articles in reputed national and international journals. His recent book included, Central Asia in Retrospect and Prospect (co-author), (2010).

NISHAT MANZAR is Professor in the Department of History & Culture, Jamia Millia Islamia, New Delhi. She specializes in Medieval Indian History and has published papers on mysticism, artisans and urban wage earners, landed aristocracy in pre-Mughal India and various other themes based on information contained in the Persian and European travellers' accounts of the sixteenth–eighteenth century. She has published a monograph entitled Social Life inside the English Factories in India during the Seventeenth Century.

S. M. AZIZUDDIN HUSAIN is Professor at Dept. of History & Culture, Jamia Millia Islamia, New Delhi. He has also served as Director, Rampur Raza Library (U.P.), Ministry of Culture, (GOI), former Dean, and the Officiating Vice Chancellor of Jamia Millia Islamia. He published many books and article in reputed Journal and edited volumes. His recent publication included, Hakim Kamaluddin Husain-Hayat Aur Ilmi Karname, (2012), Medieval Society & Culture, (2015)

SHERZODHON MAHMUDOV is Senior Researcher at the Institute of History of the National Academy of Uzbekistan, Tashkent, Uzbekistan. His area of research includes History of Central Asia, Sufism; he has published papers in Uzbek language.

USMONALI KAMOLOV is Senior Research Fellow of the Institute of Philosophy, Political Sciences and Law of Tajik Academy of Sciences, Dushanbe, Tajikistan.

VARADA M. NIKALJE is Assistant Professor (English) at the National Council of Educational Research and Training (NCERT), New Delhi, India.

Her work is related to qualitative improvement of English language education in terms of contributing academic support to states and UTs: in terms of syllabi and textbooks, graded reading series and teacher training. Her interests include folk literature and Sufism.

CHAPTER 1

Introduction

Nasir Raza Khan

Sufism in India and Central Asia is an attempt to put into perspective the relevance of Sufism. The concept and teaching of Sufism is to provide a realistic assessment of its role in the region. The vast regions which stretch from India (especially northern India), Iran, Afghanistan, Central Asia and Anatolia (Turkey) was had close interaction throughout history. The people of these regions with different ethnic backgrounds, cultures and languages have been intermingling for many centuries, as seen in the cross-current exchanges of religious ideas and belief.

The word Sufism, popularly known as mysticism is most likely derived from the Arabic word *suf* (meaning "wool") which means "the person wearing ascetic woollen garments". Sufism is deeply rooted in Islam and its development began in the late 7th and 8th centuries. The Sufis love their creator; they cherish the desire closeness and follow his path. According to Islam, there are two types of service in Sufism. First, throughout the night, they remain in prayer, meditation and contemplation of Allah and second, throughout the day, they serve his creatures especially human beings. Sufis help the people irrespective of caste, creed, religion, faith, belief and sex. They are broad-minded persons having the universal vision. They follow the path of Islam which found in divine love, universal charity and human compassion to enshrine righteousness, piousness, truthfulness and kindness.

Sufism greatly emphasizes the concept of humaneness which is more liberal in forgiving human weaknesses and more broad-minded on differences of belief. Sufism had a deep empathy for poetry and mystical music. It espoused the principle of allegiance to the *murshid* (Pir) thus enriching the religious experience of the followers. The Sufi saints should spread their message of peaceful coexistence between different communities through the relating of anecdotes and parades, living like ascetics to establishing Khānkāh where charity was given in the form of food, clothes, money, etc. Once Islam had entered in India and become popular among Muslims and Hindus then. sufism eschewed the notion of *Kafir* or non believers and called for respecting all forms of religious beliefs.

The teaching of the Sufi saints greatly influenced the Muslim rulers in India in Medieval period; they encouraged the rulers to respect the Hindu's Festivals as the part of India's culture. A great conqueror like Akbar wrote to his son Murad that he should keep peace with all religions and save himself from those who exploit religious differences for political ends. In the Deoband movement the personality of Imdadullah Muhajir Makki (1817- 1899 A.D.) was very prominent. He was a practicing Sufi who took part in the revolt of 1857 against the British Raj and become the head of the new government that was setup. After the revolt failed he took residence in Mecca and promoted moment to spread modern education among Muslims in India. In fact the Sufi moment became known for teaching in local languages which made its ethics more popular. It did not inculcate a severe colonial approach towards religious rituals or the ordainment of severe punishment. It had its own ethics which inculcated love towards all human beings and didn't look at romance as a contravention of any Islamic law. Sufis eschewed the use of *fatwas* to enforce religions law through compulsion. They had a more persuasive approach towards the preaching of Islamic ethics and influenced the prominent Hindu saints and poets like Kabir(d. 1518 A.D.) and Surdas (d. 1573 A.D.) who came from poor backgrounds but live like kings and even sections of the Sunni clergy. Their popularity rather than the assertion of mandatory authority to made them vital bridge builders among Hindus and Muslims promoting peaceful coexistence among them. By highlighting its humaneness the Sufis help to build the popularise tolerant image of Islam.

The contemporary relevance orders of the Sufi make them active till today is obvious. The Sufis supported India's freedom moment and inculcated nationalism as a positive value. Most of the Sufis remained in India, since they did not recognised the concept of Kufr. Some of the Sufi *Khānāhs* and Dargahs in India like; *Khaja Education Society* of Dargah Hazrat Khaja Bandanawaz,

Gulbarga and many more are now engaged in spreading modern education, healthcare, a rational life style and spiritual values. Sufi Khānkāh and Dargahs need more attention to highlight their social role, and be recognised as a part of national heritage which would strengthen the countries' national unity.

Since its arrival in the seventh century, Sufism has been integral part of Islam to defining the culture, political behaviour and economic interaction of Central Asians. Hence, its resurgence in the region is neither surprising nor unintelligible. Despite bans on unofficial religious activity, Sufism received widespread allegiance at the grassroots level during the Soviet period. Sufism remains an important strand as a calming influence in the context of violence and terrorism in the name of Islam. Their impact on many parts of the world is so deeply rooted that it forms a significant part of popular religious beliefs and practices.

Sufism has an illustrious history in India evolving for over 1,000 years. Sufi mystic traditions became visible during the Delhi Sultanate; the Persian influence flooded South Asia with Islam. Some Sufis and *Dervishes* of Samarqand, Bukhara, Arab and Syria came to different parts of India in the early eleventh century. Well-known names include Sheikh Ismail of Bukhara settled in Lahore in about 1005 A.D., Syed Nisar Shah travelled through Arabia, Persia and parts of North India and Deccan and finally settled in Trichinopoly during 964-1039 A.D. Hazrat Sheikh Abdullah, a Sufi of Yemen who belonged to Ismailia sect, came to India and preached Islam in Gujarat and Cambay region. Nuruddin Ismail Nur Satgarh, a Sufi from Persia, also came to Gujarat during the period of Siddi Raja (1094-1143 A.D.). Sheikh Husain Zanjani came from Azerbaijan and settled in Lahore. Hazrat Nizamuddin Aulia described his name in his *'Fawaid-ul-Fawad'* with a description that Ali Hujwiri and Zanjani both were the disciples of the same sheikh, Hazrat Abul Hasan Ali Hadrami. When Hujwiri reached to Lahore at the advice of his 'Pir', he found only the funeral procession of Husain Zanjani. Sheikh Ali Hujwiri came to Lahore and died in 1072 A.D. His tomb in Lahore is a place of world-wide attraction and it is treated as a door to Indian Sufism. He is popularly known as *Dataganj Bakhsh.* Sheikh Hujwiri's book *'Kashf- ul-Mahjoob'* is considered as an encyclopedia of Sufism. The book also throws light upon the types of Sufis, the origin of the term 'Sufi' and different Sufi cults developed through the ages.

There are detailed evidences of regular Sufi activities from Central and West Asia to India from 11th to 14th century A.D. during the period. Prominent names of Sufi Masters like Khwaja Moinuddin Chishti at Ajmer, Hazrat Nizamuddin Aulia at Delhi, Khwaja Qutubuddin Bakhtiyar Kaki at Delhi, Baba Farid in Punjab, Shihabuddin Suhrawardi etc. In north India four popular Sufi *silsilas* were established by different Sufi Masters viz. Chishtiyya, Qadriya, Naqshbandiya and Suhrawardiya. Many branches of the four major Silsilas developed in different parts of India by the vicegerents of the Sufi Sheikhs of these Silsilas as Regional Sufi Centres in Bengal, Assam, Bihar, Deccan and Far East and South.

The Chishtiya order played an important role in northern India. Baba Fariduddin Ganj Shakar, who was the disciple of Qutbuddin Bakhtiyar Kaki, worked in Punjab (Ajodhan and Pak Pattan). Baba Farid occupied a high place among Sikh community. In Delhi Hazrat Nizamuddin Aulia, the disciple of Baba Farid popularized the order by establishing his Khanqah and service to the people as basic principles of Sufism. He was called by the people of Delhi *'Mehbub-e-Ilahi'* due to his unvarying service and love for the mankind irrespective of caste, creed and religion. The last great Saint of this order at Delhi was Sheikh Nasiruddin Mahmood popularly known as *Chiragh-e- Delhi*. He died in 1336 A.D.

Chishti Saints in North India are known for their social contribution and empowering the public in social affairs by character building improving and moral strength to cope with the day to day problems. They were enriched the arena of Sufi Literature by composing *Malfuzat'* Literature (Collection of sayings) as well as *Maktubat* (Collection of Letters written to different people).

Unlike Chishti Sufis, Suhrawardi Sufis whose founder Sheikh Shihabuddin Suhrawardi were close to royal Court. Shihabuddin Umar Suhrawardi, author of *Awarif-al-Ma'arif* started his political career as a spiritual sheikh, the official Sufi Master of Baghdad, at the instance of Caliph Al-Nasir, (1179-1225 A.D.).

He wanted to revive the almost unconscious spiritual life throughout the Islamic world with a political ambition to reunite the Islamic kingdom against the Mongol threats. The Caliph dispatched the Sheikh as his ambassador to the courts of the Malik al-Adil'(1200-1218) of Ayyubid dynesty in Egypt and the Khwarazm Shah Ala Uddin Muhammad (1200-1220) of Central Asia. During his spiritual influence the capital city of Seljuk's became the new Centre of rejuvenated religious life and spiritual mysticism.

Sufism is deeply rooted with the History of Central Asia, and always played a significant role even in political development in central Asia. According to one scholar, 'Sufism was an influential vehicle for the spread of Islam in Central Asia because of its implicit tolerance, accommodations for the syncretisation of other religious and folk traditions and its stressed on charity, humility, simplicity and piety. Sufi leaders helped demarcate relations between the ruler and populace during the Timurid period.'

Sufism should also be encouraged in Central Asia to combat extremist ideologies countries like Uzbekistan, Tajikistan and Turkmenistan. It has been implementing this approach for many years by investing money in centuries on old shrines, publishing ancient Sufi manuscript and promoting Sufism in Islamic education. The reason being the transformative spiritual and political power of Sufism in the contemporary Muslim world especially in central Asia could not be underestimated or ignored. Sufism has implicit tolerance, accommodations for the syncretisation of other religious and folk traditions. It stresseson charity, humility, simplicity and piety makes an important philosophy and to be adhered into the contemporary scenario. Sufism is connected intimately to the history of Central Asia and it has often played a significant role in politics in the region. Sufi practice shrine visitation is a very strong vehicle for promoting tourism as well as means of cultural exchange between India and Central Asian countries.

Including the preservation of National tradition and encourage the visiting *(zeyarat)* of Sufi shrine are the clear indications that Central Asian republic supporting Sufism to combat Islamist trend by promoting a vision of directly link with Sufism. The Central Asian republics government has allowed Sufi practices which were the most of the part of their tradition like the visit of local shrine, reconstruction of Shrine to project as common Turkic culture. Uzbek, Tajik, Kazak, Kirgiz and Turkmen mostly followed *Hanafi* jurisprudence is considered the most liberal schools of Sunni Islam. *Naqshbandi* Sufism which in their opinion was the best reflects on the so-called traditions and Islamic history of Central Asia.

The present volume is a compilation of the fifteen chapters, which attempted to look for answer to questions and highlight the relations with Sufism in India and Central Asia and give a real assessment in contemporary period. The book has been divided into four main sections viz, India-Central Asia and Turkey Cultural Exchange through the Agencies of Sufis; Regional Sufi Centres and their interconnections; Sufi Traditions in Contemporary Central Asia; and Teaching of Sufis and Communal Harmony. In each section authors have given emphasis to discuss the different elements of Sufism in India and Central Asia.

The first segments of chapters in the present volume discuss the *Cultural Exchange through the Agencies of Sufi*s. I.H. Siddiqui discusses in his chapter *'Sufis in India and Central Asia during the Thirteenth and Fourteenth Century'* migration of Sufism from central Asia to the Indian subcontinent. He explained the Sufism from Afghanistan or Khurasan of Central Asian region and their cultural identities. Najibuddin Kubra played very significant role in the development of Sufism in this region. His paper is focused on the Sufi's work and contribution of Firdausi Silsila. In fourteenth century, the followers of Najibuddin Kubra established the Kubrawiya silsila. Sheikh Fakhruddin came to Delhi and developed the friendly relations with Chishti Sufis of Delhi region. Firdausi Silsila spread Sufism on Indian from Delhi to Bengal during this time. His arguments are based on the literary sources and translation of the Sufi Literature of Central Asia and India composed during the thirteenth and fourteenth centuries.

Mushtaq Kaw chapter deals with *'Tradition of Sufism as a Link between Kashmir & Central Asia'*. He explained the sources of Sufism from Kashmir and Central Asian region and their influence. Kashmir and Central Asia are closely related within the geographical distance about 100 km. only. This region has the geographical relations across the Pamir plateau and Hindukush region. The exchange of ideas had been transforming from Central Asian to Kashmir culture since ancient period. The Silk route had played the major role for this intellectual and cultural development. Such economic exchanges also opened the spiritual routes for the common people of both the regions. These regions had political and economic relations too. Number of Sufis came from the Central Asian region to Kashmir Valley. Sufis composed the folk literature and translated the orthodox traditional literature into Persian and regional languages. It represented the folk touch of Islam in Kashmir. *Rishi* cult, developed in Kashmir during 12th century gave the importance to the *Dhikr* practice and Vegetable meals within day to day life of society. The veneration culture also developed in Kashmir during those times. People from different religious background regularly come to *Dargahs* or Shrines for seeking solutions to their vows and problems from spiritual powers of the Sufi shrines even today.

Sherzodhon Mahmudov's chapter speaks on The Role of Sufis in Diplomatic Relations between the Khoqand Khanate and India; his papers highlighted and analyze the dynamic relations between the Khoqand Khanate and India in the light of Sufism. According to him despite the historical importance of this diplomatic relations, there is no study on this topic. In many of the 19th century sources there is proof that there was established relation between Khoqand Khanate and India. Historical compositions, official correspondences and archival documents were written in the 19th century shows that leaders of Sufi orders took an active part in establishment of these relationships. Sufi leaders got more effective results in their ambassadorial activities than merchants and statesmen. Written sources also contain information about embassy missions led by Sufi leaders. Miyan Khalil Sakhibzada was a descendant of one of leaders of the *Naqshbandiyya-Mujaddidiyya* Sufi order like Imam Rabbani Akhmad al-Sirkhindi. He was the leader of the Naqshbandiyya-Mujaddidiyya Sufi order and had a lot of *murids* not only in India and Central Asia, but also in Russia. This information was also corroborated by the "India Office Letters" stored in the British library. Miyan Khalil Sakhibzade arrive India to Khoqand in 1826 by the invitation of the ruler Muhammad Ali-Khan (1822-1841).

Nishat Manzar's chapter explores the importance of Kwaja Badruddin Samarkandi, Founder of Firdousi Silsilah in India. In her chapter she elaborately described about the hagiography of Kwaja Badruddin Samarkandi, who was the founder of one of the most unread and unnoticed *Silsilah* called 'Firdousi *silsilah*' in India.

The second section of this volume deals about the Regional *Sufi Centres and their Inter-Connections*' and discuss the development of Regional Sufi centres and their socio-cultural contributions. First chapter 'Sufis in Jammu and their Cultural Impact' is written by Jigar Mohammad, who discussed the contribution and the role of Sufis in making the History of the Hills of Jammu region. His arguments are supported with examples of other regional Sufi literature composed by eminent Sufis in southern parts of India as 'Chakkinama', 'Lorinama', Shadinama', Suhagnama' and Suhela'. Eulogistic literature was also composed in Bijapur region of South India. Similarly in Jammu Hills, there are 134 Sufi Shrines and unfortunately very few pieces of Sufi literature are available and most popular are 'Rauzatul Arifin by KishwarQadri. He also mentioned that Raja Jaisingh of Jammu accepted Islam by the influence of Sufism and Sufi Literature. In Jammu, Sufis came from Punjab. *Pir* (Sufi master) culture also developed in Jammu and Pir Miththa is very popular Sufi name in Jammu. He further emphasized that it is wrong interpretation that Sufis worked for the spread of Islam rather they worked for common people, served them and always spread the message of love and communal harmony irrespective of religion and caste.

Gulfishan Khan's chapters traced on Kalimat-us-Sadiqin (The discourse of the truthful): Jiyarat of the Sufis of Delhi: The city of Saints. She gave the historical account of Sufi saints of Delhi and their cultural contribution. She tried to differentiate between the official sources of Sufism and non-official sources of Sufism. She argued that the Sufis were the people or man of God. The official sources of Sufism are related to court culture. She also described briefly about the short biography and contribution of 17th century's one of the famous Sufi saints Abdul Hamid Lahori (died in 1655) in the major popular book *"Futhat-i-Malkuiya"*. She also described about the importance of Sufi saint Syed Jalal Bukhari (1595-1647). He was settled in Ahmedabad in present the state of Gujarat in India. Emperor Jahangir and Shahjahan invited Syed Jalal Bukhari in their Court, which lead to close association of Sufism and court culture. Her presentation briefly discussed about the role and contribution of Sufis and Sufism in the socio-cultural life of the common masses. She also analyzed the historical importance of Delhi and its close connection and linkage between Central Asia and India.

Jibraeil in his chapter 'Central Asia to India: Immigration of Sufis and Urbanization in Medieval Rajasthan discuss about the arrival of early medieval Sufis in India. The information about the Sufi saints and their activities in Rajasthan is available in abundance. They appeared in the region before coming of the Turks in India. They had started preaching activities on the western and northern outskirts of Rajasthan from the 8th century onwards. Among prominent Sufis who visited this desert region were Syed Roshan Ali, Syed Mohammad Tahir, Syed Anas Mashhadi and Hamiduddin Rehani. In last decade of the eleventh century A.D. Abul Fazl in his *Akbarnama*r records that Akbar visited Ajmer several times, and consequently developed the route of Agra to Ajmer. Large numbers of *sarais* were constructed for the benefit of traders. Nagaur had been a well-known centre of Sufis presently is considered as the heritage town of India in general and Rajasthan in particular. It is said that this *qasba* was reached at peak during the period of Shaikh Hamiduddin Nagauri (*Chishti Silsila*) and Qazi Hamiduddin Nagauri(*Suhrawardi Silsila*). After that it was developed as the big mart town and junction of trade and commerce.

Shaheer Siddiqui's chapter discusses the 'Sufism in Bengal: Interactions and Impacts through the Ages'. He explained the Sufism in Indian culture reoriented the spiritual thinking by amalgamating of ancient Upanishad pinnacle's virtues with the esoteric aspects of Islamic teaching. Most of the Sufi saints established their centres in India and started appreciating the teachings of Islam, though they were highly influenced by the social, religious and spiritual environment of the country and their ways of teaching and practices were also inspired by Indian spiritual tradition with the passage of time. In Bengal Sufism breathed though Sheikh Akhi Siraj, a great Sufi of *Chishtia* but it could not escape to be influenced by contemporary Bengali spiritual culture as *Bauls, Nathism, Tantric* elements and practices of Buddhism. The popular Sanskrit work on Yoga *'Amritkunda'* written by a Hindu Yogi Bhujar Brahmin was translated in Arabic first time in Bengal by Rukn- al-Din Samarqandi under the title *'Hauz al Hayat'* during 1210 AD.

The historical role and contribution of Sufi AkhiSiraj and Nur Qutb Alam, during 14th and 15th Centuries, shaping the spiritual atmosphere of Bengal cannot be neglected. Bengali songs of Qazi Nazrul and Rabindranath Tagore filled the spiritual firmament of Bengal with ecstasy. Tagore's Gitanjali is the epitome of spiritualism. Devendranath Tagore had memorized the *Diwan-e-Hafiz* by heart and used to recite in the *Upasana* Temple at Santiniketan Ashram.

There are four set of chapters in the third segment of the book, *Sufi Traditions in Contemporary Central Asia*. In this section distinguished scholars have given a deep analysis of Sufi traditions of Central Asia. Laura Yerekesheva's chapter 'Sufism and Religious Syncretism in the history of Central Asia', emphasized on the importance of local culture and belief in her deliberation. It is difficult to study and interpreter Islam without first talking about the tradition and culture of the region. Mehdi Kazimov in the chapter 'the style of Persian Sufi prose XI-XIII centuries', discussed some stylistic peculiarities of Sufi prose in Persian language, on the basis of the compositions of Hujviri, Ansari, Najm ad-Din Razi, Mohammad bin Munavvar and Fahr ad-Din Iraqi the literary components inherent to sufi prose, inserted stories, symbolic images and abstraction of narration are investigated.

Three chapter 'Significance of Abd-ur-Rahman Jami's Sufi-Poetic Discourse in the Literary Legacy of Medieval Persia' emphasizes to identify the role of Islam in the promotion of scientific ethos of Medieval Persia; unfold the literary legacy of the region to identify the place and status of Mawlana Jami. Also try to sketch the position and poetic vision of Jami and refer to the similarities' that exist between him and celebrated scholars of the world and explore the contribution of Jami in the Sufi-Poetic discourse of the region.

Usmonali Kamolov discussed 'the understanding of self and others in teachings of Sufism: Najmuddin Razi (1177-1252)'. Najmuddin Razi was one of the prominent representatives of Sufism of his time. According to Najmuddin Razi everything in the world was created for the sake of the person. If the person was not the purpose of the creation, the world and of all the multi-collared existence hardly would be created. And if to investigate thoroughly into existence, it is possible to notice that the creation purpose is hidden in the essence of existence of the person. The unique or sole way of clarification of the heart, the Sufi see in disposal of all not approved person qualities and blamed tempers. According to Razi, each succeeding person should counteract, first of all, to his soul (*nafs*)and under the direction of the leader (*Sheikh*) must to transform his blamed tempers and not approved qualities into worthy behaviour and approved qualities.

Last segment of this volume exclusively discusses the Sufis Teaching and Communal Harmony, while analysing how the contribution of Sufi saints are visible in the contemporary society, Azizuddin Husain's chapter trace the Shaikh Sharfuddin Bu Ali Qalander Panipati's Contribution for the Development of Composite Culture in Panipat during 14th Century. His paper opened new vistas of thinking; it gave new concept to the researchers interested in discovering unheard voices of the Sufi poets of India and their contribution towards spreading universal brotherhood and peace.

He argued that in general we know Panipat, because of certain historical wars but none of us know that the Sufis belonging to Panipat have immensely contributed towards Indian culture and tradition. If we talk about Bu Ali Qalander Panipati, we see that nothing much have been written or known about him but he was a towering personality who had very good relations with Delhi sultans. Though Qlandar settled in Panipat but he still holds his genealogy importance in Iraq from where he belongs. This shows his firm footing both at his birthplace and workplace. As far as his relations with other Chisti Sufis like Sheikh Nizamuddin Auliya is concerned that we do not come across any references. Whether he met Sheikh Nizamuddin Auliya or not but we get a tradition that Amir Khusaro visited Panipat and he recited a ghazal, response of which Ali Qalader also recited his new *ghazal* on this occasion. But As far as historical chronicles are concerned those sources are silent. As stated above he had good relations with Sultans of Delhi like Jallaladin Din Khilji, Alludin Khilzi, Qutabin –din Mubarak Shah, Ghiasudin Tughlaq etc. Historians believe that both Jallaudin Khilji and Alludin Khilji were ardent devotees of Qalandar. Qlandar composed *Mastnavis*. Manuscripts of those are preserved in Mulana Abul Kalam Library and Khuda Baksh Library. He further argued that it is a sad state of affair that we don't find much work done on his Masthnavis. Some scholars have done comparative study of Qlandar's masthnavi with Jhalludin Rumi's Masthnavi. Qlandar's successors have imbibed spirit of harmony, understanding of Indian religion and feeling of brotherhood. This is evident from the fact that one of his descendants Sheikh Sadquallah Panipati has done poetic translation of Ramayan in Persian.

He quoted one more instance depicting the spirit of brotherhood and fraternity. 18th century's sufi Mohammad Afzal wrote with pen name Gopal. He said Kurukshetra University, M. D. University Rohtak are teaching courses pertaining to foreign policies like America and Far East etc. but the historians as well as the students are totally unaware of the history of Panipat at a distance of about 45 Km. and also of the contribution of the Sufis of *Hansi, Amroha,* etc. He posed a question to the audience is this what we call and comprehend Progress? We are teaching history of America, and other Far East countries but the historians are not aware of the contribution of the sufis of their own areas. When will our universities include in the curriculum Sufis of places like Panipat, Nagor, Sarwar etc.

While explaining the *Perfect Human in Sufism* Mukhayyo Abdurakh-monova, explore the vibrant colour of Sufism with the regional impacts. Sufism developed in Arabian Peninsula but when it came to the region outside the Arabia to Central Asia, it mixed and grew with new colours of lifestyle and practices. *Salik* or the real Sufi *Murid* and disciple worked hard for the achievement of the real goal of this world and the life hereafter. The Qur'an and

Hadith are the real guides for the Sufi *salik* or the seeker of the path of Truth. The Central Asia and Indian subcontinent had the same way of thinking about the *Tasawwuf* and the Shrine visiting culture with *URS* festival celebrations. The Sufism made the spiritual synthesis between the different kind of classes and creeds within the society.

Last chapter written by Vardana M. Nikalje *Sufism in Karnataka: An Analysis of Shishunala Sharif's Songs* is an elaborated account of a saint Shishunala Sharif, the famous Sufi Saint of Karnataka through the deliberation of the songs composed by the Saint on Mystical themes. She also demonstrated some of the songs with rhythm in beautiful voice. In the songs of Saint Shishunala, a spiritual interpretation is hidden disclosing the mystery of the Universe but people can equally enjoy the ecstasy of the thoughts in beautiful rhyme and selection of words for the poetry. In her paper she has showed one video clip from a Kannada Movie in which a song of Shishunala was sung with ecstatic group dance which reflects the popularity of the saint in contemporary south India. She further raised a thought provoking question regarding the means and efforts to preserve such heritage in modern times. She also motivated by her appeal to make efforts for translation of such popular spiritual poetry in other Indian Languages so that the universal message of love and mystical union might reach to all and sundry.

In this present volume the distinguished scholars have attempted to emphasize the concept of Pluralism and Co-existence and the subsequent prospects for establishment of Pluralistic Society. In the global context vis-à-vis the role of Sufis has become an advanced discourse of contemporary academic activity. Appreciating and evaluating all discussions and conjectures about Pluralism and Communal Harmony if also gives a space to the definitions that are being assigned to it in the modern world, also to discover the roots and origin of Pluralism both as a concept and as a process in the early Islamic period. Most of the features of the current wave of pluralism and Communal Harmony, in fact, owe its origin to the basic tenets of religion. Most of the prominent Sufis in the far off lands, dissemination of knowledge and learning, establishment of *khankahas* and *maktabas,* the process of migration, Promotion of Sufi institutions and the concept of peace and justice are some of the features essentially with Islamic orientation to encourages Pluralistic viewpoint at doctrinal and practical levels. The volume illustrates the contribution of Indian Sufis to peaceful cosmopolitan civilization and cultural advancement in the promotion of communal harmony and co-existence in shaping the history of Sub-Continents noteworthy and unprecedented. Furthermore some of the papers attempt to evaluate the role of Sufis and their institutions to evaluations in secularising and harmonising the cultural and civilization ethos of Indian Society.

The present volume shows how in various ways the Sufis have played a comparable constructive social, economic and even a political role in their time. Sufi saints who travelled from Central Asia to India have been a vista of historical success in uniting diverse societies for progress and prosperous endeavour. The book present overall views of Sufism in India and Central Asia and discusses some of the vital issues in different chapters written by the distinguished scholars from India, Central Asia and other parts of the World.

Reference

[1] literally, "one who gives right guidance, rushd, irshād, in Sūfī mystical parlance, the spiritual director and initiator into the order (tarīka) of the novice or murīd [q.v.] who is following the Sūfī path; Encyclopaedia of Islam, Second Edition. Edited by: P. Bearman, Th. Bianquis, C.E. Bosworth, E. van Donzel, W.P. Heinrichs. Brill Online, 2015. Reference. 19 October, 2015 <http://referenceworks.brillonline.com/entries/encyclopaedia-of-islam-2/murshid-SIM_5548>

[2] A composite word of Persian origin meaning a building usually reserved for Muslim mystics belonging to a Sufi order."Khankāh." Encyclopaedia of Islam, Second Edition. Edited by: P. Bearman, Th. Bianquis, C.E. Bosworth, E. van Donzel, W.P. Heinrichs. Brill Online, 2015.

[3] T.B. Arnold, Preachings of Islam, London: 1896, p.153

[4] S.S.S. A Rehman, Bazm-e-Sufia', Azamgarh: 1971, p.40

[5] Nicholson, Reynold Kashf al-Mahjub of al-Hajvari, (2000).

[6] Annemarie Schimmel, Mystical Dimensions of Islam, Chapel Hill: Univ. of North Carolina Press,1975, p. 245.

[7] Rizvi, S.A.A. (1978) A History of Sufism in India, Vol.I, Delhi: Munshiram Manoharlal. p. 88

[8] Emily O'Dell, The Teaching, Practice, and Political Role Sufism in Dushanbe, National

Council for Eurasian and East European Research, University of Washington, 2011.

[9]Emily O'Dell, The Teaching, Practice, and Political Role Sufism in Dushanbe.

[10]"URS" is an Arabic word and its literal meaning is wedding. After the death of a Holy Saint, his disciples, descendant or Sajjadanashin usually begins to celebrate his annual Urs. That is the death anniversary of the saint.

CHAPTER 2

Sufis in India and Central Asia during the Thirteen and Fourteen Century

Iqtidar Husain Siddiqui

Shaikh Najmuddhin Kubra, a Thirteen century Central Asian Sufi (d.1220nAD) occupies an important place among the leading mystics in the history of Islamic mysticism. A highly educated man with brilliant thinking mind conceived fresh ideas that inspired his contemporaries as well as later generations of Sufis. He was not only a visionary Sufi saint but also processed qualities of leadership in worldly affairs. When the Sultan of Khwarizm fled away his capital on the eve of Chinggis Khan's invasion, the Shaikh stayed with the residence of Khwarizm city, organized defence and laid down his life fighting against his invader. After him his disciples elaborated their precept and ideas. Assessing the significance of Shaik Najmuddin Kubra's writings, Annemarie Schimmel observes:

(His) works shows an amazing insight into the spiritual progress on the sufi path. He was probably the first to write about the visions of the light in different colours and shapes which the seeker may encounter on his way towards the divine.

The Mongol conquest of Central Asia led the surviving murids of Shaikh Najmuddin Kubra to seek refugees in the neighbouring Muslim lands. During Sultan Shamsuddin Iltumish regime Delhi become the, safe haven for them. Amongst the refugees one of them was Shaikh Najmuddin Sughra who is said to have been one important link in the chain of Kubravi Sufis of India who lead the foundation of Firdousi Silsila in India.

Sultan Shamsuddin Iltumish who impressed by his learning and was the murid of Shaikh Najmuddin Kubra who entrusted to him the charge of the office of the Shaikhul Islam of the Sultanate of Delhi. It may also be added that Shaikh Najmuddin Kubra belonged to the Suhravardi Silsila (order) and, therefore, his immediate spiritual successors called themselves Suhravardi. It was, sometime, in the fourteen century they founded a separate Silsila and named it Kubravi Silsila after the great Shaikh. Long before its foundation in India, the Sufis of the branch was called Firdousi after Shaikh Ruknuddin Firdousi. The later was the disciple of Shaikh Badaruddin Samarkhandi, the murid of Saifuddin Baqarzi, the Khalifa of Shaikh Najmuddin Kubra. The aim of this essay is to have an argument on the impact of the teachings of the followers of the Shaikh Najmuddin Kubra in the Sultanate of Delhi.

The Firdousi record presents Shaikh Najmuddin Sughraas an important link in the chain of Firdousi Silsila saints, while the evidence available in other sources of information reveals him as a Shaikhul Islam jealous of fellow Sufis and presenting them probably, his dealing with fellow Sufis against their practices noting conformity with the Islamic sharia' embittered his relation with them. Stories were recorded that tarnish his image: Mir Khurd, the late Fourteen century Chishti writer would gave us a believe that the Shaikhul Islam Najmuddin Sughragrew jealous of Shaikh Khutbuddin Bhaktiar Khaki and accused him of gaining cheap popularity-through the disciple of Karamath (miraculous power). The sixteen century Suhravardi Sufi, Shaikh Jamali Dehlavi writes about Shaikh Jalaluddin Tabrizii, the leading Suhravardi Sufi who migrated from Bagdad and settled in Delhi during the reign of Sultan Iltumish. Being of charismatic personality he gained popularity within a short time. The Shaikhul Islam, Najmuddin Sughra became jealous of him and plotted to defame him. He hired Gauhar, dancing girl, to allege that Jalaluddin Tabrizi had illicit relation with her. The Sultan was informed and Mahzar (special tribunal) was ordered by the Sultan to enquire into the allegation. Shaikh Bahahuddin Zakaria was invited from Multan to act as the 'Hakam' (the arbiter). On Shaikh Zakaria's arrival in Delhi, the day was fixed to conduct proceedings and settle the case. When the Mahzar was held the Sultan also came to the Jama mosque to attend it. Gauhar, the dancing girl, who was presented as the main witness got nervous and then confessed that she, was bribed to malign Shaikh Jalaluddin Tabrizi. There upon the Sultan dismissed Najmuddin Sughra from the post of Shaikhul Islam and Shaikh Jalaluddin

Tabrzi was honourably exonerated. K. Nizami and Athar Abbas Rizvi accepted this story uncritically.

Probably, the statement by Shaikh Nizamuddin (Auliya) about the banishment of Shaikh Jalaluddin Tabrizi from Delhi escaped the notice of both the modern scholars. Attention made by Shaikh Nizamuddin Auliya of this episode turns to reveal that Shaikh Najmuddin Sughra continued to enjoy the confidence of Sultan and retained the post of Shaikhul Islam till his death. In the system of governance of the Sultanate the Sultan was expected out to interfere with the Shaikhul-Islam, and the sadr (chief justice) unless found guilty of miscreant. Shaikh Jalaluddin Tabriziwas banished by the Shaikhul Islam. According to Shaikh Nizamuddin Auliya, Shaikh Jalaluddin Tabrizi stayed in Badaon for sometime after that he had been exiled from Delhi. One day, when he was taking a walk along with his companions, he stopped, and said to them: let us prepare to offer funeral prayer for Najmuddin Sughra for he has passed away? Having offered the prayer in absentia, Shaikh Jalaluddin Tabrizi remarked: 'He (Najmuddin Sughra) banished me from Delhi, God has removed him from the world'.

As for the actual cause of Shaikh Jalaluddin Tabrizi's banishment from the Delhi our early sources are silent about it. The aforesaid statement by Shaikh Nizamuddin Auliya suggests that Shaikhul Islam exiled him on the basis of his suspicion private life. Besides these references to the Shaikh's banishment, other references contained in the Fawayid u-Fuad are indicating of the fact that Shaikh Nizamuddin Auliya considered him as a true friend of God. It is, however, worth recalling that picture of Shaikh Tabrizithat emerges ongoing through the malfazats of the chishti Sufi and Shaikh Jalaluddin Suhravardi, (known as Jahanian-I-Jahangasht) is that of a great spiritualist, distinguished for his selfless love of man and God. He was held esteemed and remembered by the leading chishti and Suhravardi Sufis respectfully, after his passing away. He was an example in renunciation and detachment from the worldly affairs.

As regards the other followers of Shaikh Najmuddin Kubra in India, who might have survived Shaikh Najmuddin Sughra, none is mentioned by the sources till the arrival of Shaikh Badaruddin Samarkhandi, sometimes during the latter half of the thirteenth century. Shaikh Badarudd in Samarqandi was the disciple and the Khaleefa of Shaikh Saifudd in said Bakharzi, the Khaleefa of Shaikh Najmudd in Kubra. He took abodes in Delhi and became a friend of Shaikh Nizamuddin Auliya. Both of them were fond of listening to sama. Since the followers of Shaikh Najmuddin Kubra belonged to the elitist SuhravardiSilsila, were careful enough to enroll those persons, murids whom they found seriously interested in their spiritual development. They were trained and guided in esotericism. That is why,a few amongst the disciples of Shaikh Badaruddin Samarqandi, exceeded only the name of Shaikh Ruknuddin Firdousi is mentioned. Firdousi was his family surname. As mentioned above, the murids(disciple) of Shaikh Ruknuddin Firdousi organized themselves into a separate fraternity and named it after their pir (preceptor) as Firdousi Silsila. Shaikh Ruknuddin Firdousi was succeeded by his step brother, Shaikh Najibuddin Firdousi whom he trained in exoteric and esoteric services to act as his Khaleefa(successor) after his death. Shaikh Najibuddin Firdousi's chief muridand Khaleefa was Shaikh Sharafuddin Maneri Firdousi who resided in Bihar town (Bihar state). It was under his leadership that Firdousi Silsila gained wide fame. The epistles composed by him in Persian prose on different aspect of Islamic mysticism (Tasawuf) lifted him to the rank of leading metaphysical thinker; their collection entitled Maktabat-i-sadi gained popularity during his lifetime and are still read by people who interested in Sufism.

Also worth mentioning is the fact that the early Firdousi Sufis practiced sobriety and considered the display by Sufi saints of miraculous power and irreligious practice, calculated to gain cheap popularity. They set traditions of austerity and emphasized its importance, so that their followers could also emulate them. Consequently, their influence remained confined to the elite in Delhi.

With the emergence of Shaikh Sarafudhin Yahya Maneri Firdousi, a new chapter opened in the history of Firdousi Silsila, in India. The reference contained in his Malfazat(collections of his utterances in several volumes) to his visitors Khanqah show how his influence and popularity had spread in different parts of Bihar's outside. We also find therein odd bits of information about the impact of the Indian environment on the Muslim elite. Certain Hindu yoga exercises seem to have been adopted by the Sufis of Indian, Khurasan and Transoxiana. For instance, Qazi Ashrafudhin, a learnt visitor, makes the query; "how many times did the prophet performed his spiritual prayer upside down (Salat-I-M'akus) and did he do this as an ascetic exercise or with some motive?" in reply the Shaikh says that the prophet did it only once in order to gain divine love and Sufis do it to follow his tradition. The translator of the Shaikh's Malfuzat, Khwan-i-Pur Nimatremarks "the influence of Yogi Practices current at the time is evident in the statement" Further his comment.

'It is hard to see how orthodox scholars from Arab land could possibly agree with this statement. It does tell us however, that the practices were not to Sharafudhin and his contemporaries, and he is one of the many examples of the influences of Hindu ascetical practices on the Sufis. Shaikh Sharfudhin feels obliged to offer an explanation of the practices which links into that of Mohammed.

It may be pointed out that in adopting this ascetic exercise Indian Sufis were not directly influenced by Yogis. Long before their arrival in India, Sufis had adopted this practice in Central Asia under Budhist influence. Shaikh Sharafudhin Yahya Maneri's source of information is Fawaidul-Fuad, wherein the eleventh century saint, Shaikh Abusaid Abul Kahir is reported as having performed it in the same anecdote. This tradition is linked to the prophet of Islam. Shaikh Sharafudhin seems to have accepted uncritically whatever he reads in popular works on Sufis.

Likewise we find useful material on the teachings of the Shaikh as well as his attitude towards society. A liberal-minded saintly person who always sided with those ulemas (clerics) and who took into account convenience of people before they issued a fatwa (decree) provided their judgement didn't violate the Quranic law. For instance, in Sonargaon people used to eat lime made of shellfish mixed in betel leaf. People objected that the shellfish was unlawful and the issue was referred to the ulema. The lime made of shellfish as it could cause inconvenience to innumerable people who were pan addicts. The Shaikh was pleased and said:

Things should be made easy for the people; because path of Islam is wide one. Whatever brings hardship upon the people is not permitted to be imposed upon them. Those things which have been prohibited by the text of the book (*i.e.* Quran) itself, even though people have accepted and become habituated to them, are not to be allowed simply to make things easy for the people.

As regards the Shaikh's commitment to social service has become his life mission. In his early life when he was in retreat and lived along with God in the jungle of Rajgir, he would come to the town on Friday every week and helped the people in need. Once he told his murid: "when I was in that old cave, there was a military governor there". He didn't have a very good way of dealing with the people, many of them were would to get one of intercede on their behalf. I used to do for each one of them. I would write down their request that a great number of people began to mob me for their purpose. From time to time my human nature asserted itself and I got annoyed. Shaikh Zada Chishti- It is happened that he had come to visit one in that place. He observed that this business proved vexatious for me on occasions that I grew annoyed. Afterwards he said: 'so you are annoyed, be careful not to get annoyed. Take upon yourself the affiliation of the people'.

Being metaphysical thinker himself, he was one of a few representative Sufis of India who could appreciate Inhal-Arab's doctrine of al- wujud (philosophy of being) from Abdul Kasim Jili' philosophy of wahdatul-wujud(unity in the essence of the creator and the created). Though Jili is regarded as a follower of Ihnal–Arabia he was an independent thinker and propounded his doctrine where in the Quranic concept of the transcendence of God is compromised. It is to the credit of the Ihnal-Arabithathe cleared Tasawuf of un-Islamic influences and worked not his philosophy in the light of the Quran and Hadis. The epistle on the Quranic concept of tanhid (thing of God) laid to show contained in the Maktulat-i-Sadithat which was deeply impressed by Ihnal-Arabia. The epistle reads:

'Sufimasters's opinion in the fourth statge, such a surfeit of the dazzling divine light becomes manifest to the pilgrim. They said every single existing particle that lies within his vision becomes concealed in the very lustre of that light which particles in the air are lost to the sight on the account of the brightness of the light emanating from the sun. (This occurs not because the particles have ceased to exist but rather because the intensity of the sun light makes it impossible that anything other than this concealment should result.) In the same way, it is not true that a person becomes God for God in infinitely greater than any man-nor the person really ceased to exist; for ceasing to exist is one and becoming lost to view quite another.

Finally, a word may be added about Shaik Sharafuddin Maneri's attitude towards the state, unlike the great Chishti saint, he did not consider cooperation between the Sufi and the state. He extended the cooperation to the state for the benefit of people. He agreed to settle down in the state Khauqah built by the order of Sultan Muhammed bin Tuglaq and spent money, accruing from the land grant made by the state for the upkeep of charity house, feed the travellers and distribute money to the poor on behalf of the Sultan. On Muhammed bin Tuglaq's death the Shaikh relinquished the post of Shaikhul Islam because of his relation with Sultan Firoz shah had become strained. However, he showed love and regard to the Sultan of Bengal. As a matter of fact, sincerely devoted to the cause of religion and aware of the importance of the cosmic consciousness for man, the Shaikh took up his mission towards the work of medicating and the divine temper in every one who turned to him for religious guidance. It may also be added that the Shaikh didn't think righteousness to be the quality of a Muslim alone. He appreciated the deep religious spirit processed by Hindu recluses. He considered the conversion of a non-Muslim to Islam through inducement immoral. Once, a Yogi who was so much impressed by him decided to embrace Islam. He stayed with Shaikh Khauqah for three days and then allowed to depart. The murids enquired the Shaikh why he was not converted to Islam. The Shaikh's response was that as the Yogi become believer in the oneness of the God, he did not require to stay any longer and that was alright.

References

[1]Annemarie Schimmel, Forword to the Malfuzat Khwan-i-PurNimat, compiled by ZainBadrArabi and translated in English by Paul Jackson S J, Delhi, 1986, pp.xi-xii.

[2]Shoeb Firdousi, Manaqibul-Asfia, Culcutta, A. H. 1313, pp. 2-8, 124, Also Hasan Sijsi, Fawaidul-Fuad, Lahore, 1966, p.245.

[3]Mir Khurd, Siyarul-Auliya, pp. 54-55.

[4]Shaikh Jamali Dahlavi, Siyarul-Arifeen, Delhi, A. H.1311, pp. 165, 167-168.

[5]Ref, Khalid Ahmad Nisami, Some Aspects of Religion and Politics in India During the Thirteenth Century, Aligarh, 1961, pp.163-64.

Athar Abbas Rizvi, History of Sufism in India, vol.1, pp.200-201.

[6]HasanSijzi, Fawaidul-Fuad, Neval Kishore Press, Lucknow, A. H. 1885, p.144.

[7]Hamid Qalandar, Khairul-Majalis, ed. K. A. Nizami, Aligarh, 1959, p.185.

[8]Khwan-i-PurNimat, eng.tr, p. 9.

[9]Ibid., p.11, F.n,2.

[10]HasanSijzi, Fawaidul-Fuad, Lahore, 1966, p.7.

[11]Khwan-i-PurNimat, eng.tr, p. 18.

[12]He belonged to the town of Chist in Afganistan where the Chisti Silsilastemmed.

[13]Khwan-i-PurNimat, eng.tr, p. 57.

[14]Makhtubat-i-Sadi, eng.tr, Paul Jackson, entitled "Letters from Maneri", New Delhi, 1990, pp. 13-15.

[15]Ref, Paul Jackson, Shaikh Sharafuddin Yahya MAneri;The Way of A Sufi, Delhi, 1987, pp. 153-54.

CHAPTER 3

Sufism: Cementing Bonds between Central Asia and Kashmir

Mushtaq A. Kaw

Introduction

Besides a shared historic-cultural past, Kashmir and Central Asia had a common political history under the Indo-Bactrian Greeks (190 BC), Sakas (Scythians) and Parthians (90 BC–64 AD), Kushanas (1st–2nd century AD) and Hunas (5th century AD), Karkotas of Kashmir (8th century), Mughals and the Afghans (16th-19th century). Even they were strategic partners to the ancient Silk Route network across the Himalayas, the Pamirs, and the Hindukush mountains. Hoards of monks, Sufis, saints, scholars, businessmen, artists and adventurers periodically traversed them for fame, fortune and missionary and philanthropic pursuits. Till the Partition of Indian sub-continent into India and Pakistan in 1947, such trans-surface connections, symbolised economic prosperity, cross-cultural and fertilization fertilisation and mutual diaspora, lost relevance with the discovery of the Sea Route and the Great power rivalry for regional influence and commercial leverage.

Sufism and religio-cultural exchanges

Obviously, both regions experienced mutual and diversified influences on each other, which is proved by their religio-cultural compatibility and sharing of two popular religions of Buddhism and Islam during the BCs and ADs respectively. Notably, Sufism, as an inner mystical dimension, was the dominant expression of Islam in both regions. It emerged as a sustained philosophy based on direct God-man spiritual relationship; hence, a selfless experience seeking for actualisation of truth (God) not necessarily through any structured scheme of logic and reason but through individual's acts of love and devotion to God. Consequently, Sufism attained the distinction of a mystical the way of life in which mystics/ascetics, both male and female, sacrificed the world herein for the world hereafter. They opted for a life of indigence and celibacy for eternal peace and salvation. Such a human behaviour, usually uncommon to expressed through certain practices like Zikr, folk, poetry, music, hymns, etc. and for purifying the body and merging into his being.

The genesis of Sufism in the region is allied to the evolutionary process of Islam and the local influence on its growth and consolidation. Historically speaking, Islam was introduced in the region by the Arabs during the 6-7th century. However, it could not retain its egalitarian character. For local resistance, it had to be an inevitably compromise with the region's pagan, nomadic and tribal traditions. As a result, Arab Islam shaped into the "folk Islam" having strong social support from political, cultural, economic and religious elite. It was deeply entrenched into the Central Asian landscape notwithstanding certain well-thought out reactionary movements against it. Thus, mystical or Sufi Islam in Central Asia is the natural concomitant of the local-alien religio-cultural synergy- a speciality that Frederick Starr and other scholars eulogise for characterising the golden heritage of the region.

Central Asian Islam and Sufism entered Kashmir roughly around the 14th century: courtesy the contribution of revered religious missionaries like Saiyyid Sharafuddin or Bulbul Shah, Saiyyid 'Ali Hamadani, Saiyyid Muhammad Hamadani and other Sufis of Suhrawardi and Kubrawi orders. Subsequently, Islamization process in Kashmir was supplemented by the local brand of Sufis called the Rishis in local parlance. Its assimilation was possible due to its compatibility with the similarly situated religio-cultural prefecture of Kashmir. True, some of its manifestations were ultra-virus to the basic faith and its monotheistic belief in "No God but God." Nonetheless, the Sufis and clerics adopted it for religious expediency. They allowed Sufism to sustain as Islamization process in Kashmir was at an embryonic stage of its growth in Kashmir. This explains why, the early neo-converts continued to visit temples, perform Hindu ritual yajna, dress in Hindu attire and invoke stones, idols, images and deities for blessings. They did not perform the Islamic practice of circumcision and instead perpetrated acts of un-Islamic innovations.

No doubt, in due to the course of time, they refrained from observing the Hindu practices. But they did not abandon the mystical form of Islam and rather upheld it strongly on the Central Asian analogy. Both literature and folk vindicate the facts of mutual influences and the role of Sufis in welding Central Asia and Kashmir together into an unbroken spiritual knot. As a matter of fact, the Sufis and saints, contributed immensely to the establishment, consolidation and promotion of Islam and the universal values of human-coexistence, peace and endurance in both regions. Their saying and doings assumed significance next to real faith in the region as they transcended all borders of caste, creed, colour, region and religion.

Quite precisely, whole Central and South Asian region including Kashmir, India, Afghanistan, Iran etc. is dotted with cluster of tombs and mausoleums dedicated to the popular Sufis, saints and other legendries. During his empirical studies, the author noticed large number of tombs situated in villages, towns and cities of five post-Soviet Central Asian states. While some seem to have survived the Soviet on slaught, others were newly constructed by the post-Soviet Central Asian states to boost supra-nationalism and revive region's glorious past.

Despite the 21st century scientific temperament, the people of the region are gravitated to the Sufi-centric cults of personality and shrine worship. Indeed, these cults are so deeply entrenched in the human psyche that even visiting the tombs of local rulers and military chiefs has routinely become their part, in Central Asia. The titular heads enormously patronise such cults for these, their believes in accord with national heritage are strategically feasible to dilute violent trends, safeguard authoritarian regimes and wean away the masses from what is said to be the reactionary and revolutionary Islam in academic parlance.

The devotees regularly visit the tombs and mausoleums, throng them, tie tags and lit candles for blessings in the attainment of their spiritual and mundane ends, and for curing ailments, bearing children, auguring bumper harvests, seeking jobs or marriages, passing examines, to name only a few. They comprise people of all shades, age and gender groups including men, women, and children. Peasantry, in particular, constitute the larger group who visit tombs and donate in cash and kind, and even slaughter animals at the shrines for blessings. During my periodical visits, I came across large number of devotees paying obeisance at the shrines in Samarqand, Bukhara (Uzbekistan), Kashghar, Yarkand and Ilchi in Xinjiang (China), Khojand, Kulya'ab and Dushanbe (Tajikistan), Bishkek and Isykul (Kyrgyzstan), Almaty and Turkistan (Kazakhstan) and Turkmenistan for considering it as a rich legacy and important as next to original Islam. Thus they take the tomb as a symbol of Islamic identity, which though is not as per the original scriptures.

The same holds true of Kashmir Valley where Muslims esteem the Sufi saints of Naqashbandi, Kashani, Badakhshani, Bukhari, Geelani, Andrabi, and Sayyid families from Central Asia. Most of them arrived Kashmir in the train of proselytization project of revered Sufi saint Saiyyid Ali Hamdani. In course of time, they married local women, settled and made Kashmir as their permanent abode. In the mean time, Kashmir produced its local brand of Sufis called as the Rishis who are distinguishable from the immigrant Sufis for vegetarianism and their reservation to garlic and onion in their food.

They are venerated for their celibacy, non-violence and super natural powers, which the devotees believe to resolve their problems in this and their afterlife. Great public gathering are marked on the eve of their anniversaries. Besides other things, group dhikr or collective chanting of religious literature in the chorus is organised on the festive occasions. The practice of reciting Aurad-e Fatiya (containing 99 names of God) in group form is evenly organised at Saiyyid Ali Hamdani's shrine at Kuliyab in Tajikistan. It suggests spiritual commonalities between the two regions and the considerable Central Asian influence on the minds, thought, belief and practice of the Kashmiris. A noted Kashmiri historian rightly maintained that history of Islam in Kashmir can't be comprehended "without the study of historical development of Sufism in the valley called as the "Resh/PirWaer" meaning "abode of Rishis or Saints."

Sufism and its allied shrine cult are quite popular in the region for these, as is generally believed, tend to: (*i*) promote close-knit relations between individuals and groups; (*ii*) guarantee social security against men-made and God-made forces; (*iii*) imbibe a sense of peace and harmony; (*iv*) distinguish between sacred and profane values; (*v*) guard people from calamities and other threats; (*vi*) brace them to spiritually meet the challenges of life; (*vii*) console them in the event of stress and strain; (*viii*) and nurture ethico-moral code, human inter-mixing and exchange of rural-urban commodities on festive occasions. Smith's remarks are apt: "by the ritual performance and rehearsal of ceremonies and feasts and sacrifices, by the communal recitation of past deeds and ancient heroes' exploits, men and women have been enabled to bury their sense of loneliness and insecurity in the face of natural disasters and human violence by feeling themselves partake of a collectively and its historic fate which transcends their individual existences."

Reaction and Response

However, Sufi spiritual movement was periodically challenged by certain forces on intellectual, ideological and other grounds in Central Asia. It's so happened with the onset of the Saudi and Soviet-sponsored Wahabi and Jadidist Movements in 1912 and 1924 respectively. In effect, the Soviets (1918-1991) deleted Islam including its Sufi traditions from their nationalist. They regarded it as an "ideological enemy" of Marxism-Leninism, and "an alien, conservative, and reactionary faith which offered nothing short of intolerance, fanaticism, primitivism and barbarism." However, the post-Soviet Central Asian States revived it soon after their independence in 1991. They legitimised Islam and Sufi traditions under their nationalist narrative and declared it as a catalyst to secularism, inter-ethnic, inter-cultural and inter-faith dialogue and the scientific temperament. Therefore, they incorporated their "spiritual past" into their national or state-agenda and declared it as a rich national heritage, oltinmeros (golden heritage) for representing universal humanism. Hero and saint cults were identified with symbols of worship and blessing. Historical monuments and folk were glorified within the nationalist frame.

Thus, while Tajik President Rahminov extolled the great Sufi saint Sayyid Ali Hamdani and his mausoleum at Kuliyab, President Karimov monumentalised the 13th-14th century Sufi saint, Baha-ud din Naqashbandi by renovating his grave and naming one of the streets after his name in Bukhara proper. His tomb and that of Imam Abu Hanifa at Samarqand in particular are eventually visited by large number of devotees for divine intercession as was observed by the author at both places in 2008 and 2009 respectively. As on date, Sufi cult predominates the life of the Central Asian Muslims for, they are led to believe, that it combines faith and tradition and symbolises legacy that was handed down to them since generations together.

Of late, however, Sufi traditions are susceptible to inextricable threats from violent and non-violent Islamist groups in Central Asia. Sequentially, it has triggered, for varying perceptions, a serious religious conflict between the state "from above" and the Wahhabis, Salafis, Devbandhis and others "from the below." The Islamists invariably espouse return to the universal or Islam of the Prophet's times and press for a strict, orthodox, puritan and all-encompassing practice of Islam. They strive to rejuvenate Islam and address Muslim (Ummah) degeneration, poverty and "humiliation at the global level." They terminate all traditions including Sufism as irreligious for being outside the Islamic scriptural framework and attribute the state policy on religion as a calculated move to save "authoritarian" or "discursive" regimes and swoon the masses in amnesia. They react against the state failure, socio-economic marginalisation, political deprivation and denial of human rights. Olivier Roy rightly argues that since fundamental Islam is a response to all social excesses, the titular state heads of Central Asia, as such, find in Sufism a safety value for their respective regimes; hence, incorporate its literature in the educational content of the region. Quite precisely, the Islamists condemn their Islamic perception and view it simply as the "official" or "state Islam" than the one based on original scriptures. They maintain that Central Asian Muslims are deliberately drawn into a dichotomous situation on its account. They are so moulded that they find not a little difference between "to be" and "not to be" ["faith" and "tradition"] obviously for the stiff state conditions on their personal right to religion. As a result, the masses are so profoundly indoctrinated with secular thought that they innocently understand that "Islam by birth is as good as Islam by choice." Eventually, they have no escape from the tradition based "state" or "Official" Islam. They are not, exceptions apart, inclined to the Wahabi/Salafi or what is termed as the "political" Islam in academic parlance. By choice, they prefer to have the medieval Islam for it combined on both faith and tradition.

Anyhow, for their sharp reaction, both violent and non-violent, against the secular or traditional Islam, the Islamists undergo unprecedented repression at the hands of the state. In his aired message on May 1, 1998, President Karimov of Uzbekistan bluntly announced that "Such people [Islamic extremists] should be shot in the head. If necessary, I shall shoot them myself." He enacted laws whereby he declared them country's enemies and their Islam as "an alien, fanatic, obscure and backward thought as compared to the Uzbek national traditions." His other counterparts also passed laws to admonish the Islamists in their respective states. Most of the Islamists are caged, killed and expatriated as is regularly reported by the Forum 18 and International Crisis Group in Central Asia. However, in retaliation, many of them joined the Hizb-utTahrir (HeT), Islamic Movement of Uzbekistan (IMU) and Islamic Movement of Central Asia (IMCA)type radical Islamist organisations for regime change and the establishment of theocratic states in the Central Asian space. While, non-violent groups carry out underground activities to drive the Muslims to the thought and organisation. The violent ones seek training, plan and organise militant attacks from across the borders in Afghanistan. Their association with Taliban is well established.

The given religious stand-off persists with horrendous implications for the region and its rich tradition of mysticism. It could complicate if Taliban return to power through peace settlement or force either. Taliban may not directly plunge into Central Asian affairs. They could, however, back up the Islamist groups for their designated mission. The newly-emerging Daesh or IS group of Islamic insurgents could also pose a potent threat to the rich mystic past of the region.

Like Central Asia, Kashmir mystic thought experienced challenges from time to time. It began with a social reaction organised by an eminent scholar, Abhinav Gupta and the most able King Harsha during the early and late 11th century respectively. It was supplemented by a Saiva Yogini, Lalla, and a revered Kashmiri saint Sheikh Noor-ud Din Rishi or Nund Rishi during the 14th century. Lalla openly preached monotheism and belief in "oneness of God" and condemned, like her Indian Bhakts, stone worship in all its forms and manifestations: "He is here, there and everywhere. The idol is nothing but a stone. The temple is nothing but a stone. From top to bottom all is stone." Even the Sufi saint Sayyid Ali from Hamadan preached monotheism and impressed upon the masses to worship none but God. His prescription of Aurad-e Fatiya

Sufism in India and Central Asia

[containing ninety nine names of God] is self-explanatory. On the issue of the statehood, he cautioned the rulers to take the throne as the symbol of responsibility than power and their base on statehood and conduct public affairs on the Shari'ah [Islamic Law] and Din [Islamic Faith]. His literary masterpiece of Zakhirat-ulMuluk provides the proof in this behalf. Similarly, North India-based Ahli-Hadis movement was against Sufism or the non-traditional forms of Islam. As on date too, it continues its tirade against the Sufistic legacy.

This does not suggest that the Sufi traditions do not live in modern Kashmir. Its followers regularly pay obeisance at the Sufi shrines especially on the festive occasions pre-supposing thereby their unceasing belief in the living and non-living things. They believe that it furnishes such a sheet-anchor to them as holds them tied to the shrines as well as to the fundamentals of Islam. This naturally nullifies the opinion of those who consider "Sufism" as an alien part to Islam and who dismiss Sufism as an "aberration or a development outside the pale of Islam."

Of late, however, a counter-trend exists due to the widely-distributed Islamic literature and the enormously growing influence of the Tabligh-i groups: the Jamaat-e-Ahli-Hadis, Jammat-i Islami etc. Consequently, many shrines are going into the oblivion. Those in place, quantitatively speaking, draw a little number of the visitors when compared to the past. The well-educated youth, in particular is disinclined to the Sufi and shrine culture as they are oriented to search for the real truth in Islam and prefer scriptural to the traditional Islam.

Conclusion

Islam and Sufism have been co-related ideological and spiritual processes experienced by Central and South Asians during the medieval times. These processes evolved historically within a local or regional than universal context; hence, these were different from the egalitarian and monotheistic character of Arabian Islam.

Notwithstanding the unceasing conflict on the issue of the "folk Islam" and "puritan Islam," Sufi traditions live strongly in Central Asia either because of the generational influence and ignorance of the masses about Islam or else the extraordinary patronage of the post-Soviet Central Asian States under a well-thought out regime-saving and supra-nationalist agenda. Even in Kashmir, the tradition lives exactly under the state support. However, it is losing its grip on the masses, youth in particular, with every passing day. It seems likely that this rich heritage will extinct, if not immediately forces the new market and the widely spawning influence of neo-liberalism or globalization.

References

[1] India-Tajikistan Cooperation, Perspectives and Prospects, pp. 8–20; Mushtaq A. Kaw, "Kashmir and Chinese Turkistan-A Study in Cultural Affinities", HamdardIslamicus, XXVII (3) (Karachi), July–September, 2004, pp. 41–50, and Journal of Pakistan Historical Society, LII (3) (Karachi), July–September, 2004, pp. 63-80; Mushtaq A. Kaw, "Tajik and Kashmiri Weddings: Differences among Commonalities", Greater Kashmir, 16 June, Srinagar, 2007; Mushtaq A. Kaw, "Central Asia and Kashmir: A Study in Common Tajik and Kashmiri Rituals", Mir'aas: Reflecting the Heritage of Kashmir (A Quarterly Publication of Kasheer Foundation), Vol. I (I) New Delhi, January–March, 2008, pp. 31-34.

[2] The Greeks in Bactria and India, p. 155; Chronicles of the Kings of Kashmir, Vol. I, pp. 109, 116-47; R. C. Kak, The Ancient Monuments of Kashmir, London, 1933; Bridget & Raymond Allchin, The Rise of Civilization in India and Pakistan, New Delhi, 1989.

[3] Percy Brown, Indian Architecture (Buddhist and Hindu Periods) (Bombay, 1959), p. 34; G .S. Gaur, "Semthan Excavations-A Step towards Bridging the Gap between the Neolithic and Kushanas", in Essays in Archaeology and History in Memory of Shri. A. Ghosh , (eds.) B. M. Pande and B .D. Chattopadhyaya, New Delhi, 1987, pp. 327–37; Kashmir History and Archaeology through the Ages., p. 122; Elizabeth E. Bacon, Central Asians under Russian Rule, A Study in Cultural Change (London, reprint 1994), pp. 3–5.

[4] For details see, Kalhana'sRajatarangni, Chapter III, Verses 486-97; Chapter IV, Verses 8, 132, 150, 163, 186, 207, 216, etc.; Chronicles of the Kings of Kashmir, Vol. I.

[5] Sayyid Ali, Tarikh-i Sayyid Ali, Per .ms (R & P Deptt., Srinagar), ff. 2–4; Baharistan-i Shahi, (Anonymous), Per .ms (R & P Deptt., Srinagar), ff. 9–10; AbulFazl, Ain-i Akbari, Vol. II, Nawal Kishore edition (Lucknow, 1869), p. 385; Muhammad Ashraf Wani, Islam in Kashmir(Fourteenth to Sixteenth Century), Srinagar, 2004, pp. 55–58: The Agrarian System of Kashmir, pp. 295-301.

[6] MushtaqA.Kaw, "Restoring India's Silk Route Links with South and Central Asia across Kashmir: Challenges and Opportunities," The China and Eurasia Forum Quarterly, Vol. 7(2), May/June, 2009: 59-74.

[7] Mushtaq A. Kaw, "Trade and Commerce in Chinese Central Asia (19th-20th Century)," In

Central Asia: Introspection (eds.) Kaw &Bandey, Srinagar: Centre of Central Asian Studies, University of Kashmir, 2006, pp. 47-61.

[8]YaacovRo'I, Islam in the Soviet Union, London: Hurst & Company, 2000, p. XII.

[9]Petra Steinberger, "Fundamentalism in Central Asia: Reasons, Reality and Prospects," In Central Asia: Aspects of Transition, London, 2003, pp. 223-24.

[10]MushtaqA.Kaw, "Turkey's Relations with Central Asian Republics," Journal of Central Asian Studies, Vol. XVIII (1), Srinagar: Central Asian Studies, University of Kashmir, 2009.

[11]Frederick Star, Lost Enlightenmnet: Central Asia's Golden Age from the Arab Conquest to Tamerlane, London: Princeton University Press, 2015.

[12]Surat Ibrahim 14, Ayat 29-30; Surat 16, Ayat 22; Surat Ta-Ha 20, Ayat 98; Surat Al-Ikhlas 112, Ayat 1-4:The Holy Qur'an, eng. tr. of the Meanings and Commentary, Revised and Edited by the Presidency of Islamic Researches, IFTA, Kingdom of Saudi Arabia, 1413 Hijra/ 1988 AD., MadinahMunawarah.t

[13]Muhammad Ashraf Wani, Islam in Kashmir, New Delhi: Oriental Publishing House, 2005.

[14]MushtaqA.Kaw, "Central Asian Contribution to Kashmir's Tradition of Religio-Cultural Pluralism," Central Asiatic Journal, Vol. 52 (2), autumn, 2010: 237-55 .

[15]MushtaqA.Kaw, "Rethinking Islam in Contemporary Central Asia," In Central Asia Today: Countries, Neighbors, and the Region (eds.) SunatulloJonboboev, MirzokhidRakhimov and ReimundSeidelmann, Germany: CUVILLIER VERLAG Gottingen, 2014, pp. 393-418.

[16]H. W. Bellow, Kashmir and Kashghar: A Narrative of the Journey of the Embassy to Kashghar, 1873-74,Delhi, reprint, 1989, pp. 302, 310, 324-5, 327; Bayard Taylor, Travels in Cashmere, Little Thibet and Central Asia,1876-81,New York, 1892, p. 228; Robert Shaw, Visit to High Tartary and Kashghar, 1867-69 (New Delhi, reprint, 1996), p. 460; Chinese Central Asia, pp. 177-8, 182-4; P. S. Nazaroff, Moved on from Kashmir to Kashghar,London, 1935, p. 26.

[17]Mushtaq A. Kaw, "Chinese Turkistan and Kashmir- A Study in Cultural Affinities," HamdardIslamicus, XXVII (3), (ed.) Sadia Rashid, Karachi, July–September, 2004, pp. 41-50 & Journal of Pakistan Historical Society, LII (3), Karachi, July–September, 2004, pp. 63-80.

[18]Surat Ibrahim 14, Ayat 29-30; Surat 16, Ayat 22; Surat Ta-Ha 20, Ayat 98; Surat Al-Ikhlas 112, Ayat 1-4:The Holy Qur'an, eng. tr. of the Meanings and Commentary, Revised and Edited by the Presidency of Islamic Researches, IFTA, Kingdom of Saudi Arabia, 1413 Hijra/ 1988 AD., MadinahMunawarah.

[19]For details see, MohibbulHasan, Kashmir Under the Sultans (Srinagar Kashmir, 1959) and Islam in Kashmir (Fourteenth to Sixteenth Century), pp. 231-73.

[20]Rishis formed a group of ascetics and folk heroes who abstained from meat, planted trees and performed such rituals as were an amalgam of diverse cultures: J. J. Modi, "Religious Ceremonies", Journal of the Bombay Branch of the Royal Asiatic Society (HereafterJBBRAS), vol. XIX, December, 1895, pp. 236-8; Hassan Shah, T'arikh-i Hassan, Urdu tr., Moulvi Ibrahim, Tarikh-i Kashmir, Srinagar, 1957.

36   Chapter 3 Sufism: Cementing Bonds betwee....

[21]Baba Dawood Khaki, Rishi Nama, Per. ms, R & P Deptt., Srinagar, ff. 60-85 ab.

[22]Tarikh-i Sayyid Ali, ff. 31ab, 39-40ab.

[23]Mohammad Ishaq Khan, Sufis of Kashmir, Srinagar, India: Gulshan Books, 2011.

[24]Charles Tolman, Psychology, Society and Subjectivity: An Introduction to German Psychological Critique (London: Routledge, 1995), pp. 56-60; Mushtaq A. Kaw, "Popular Islam in Chinese Central Asia", Central Asiatic Journal, Vol. 50 (2), 2006, pp. 246-63.

[25]Mushtaq A. Kaw, "Popular Islam in Chinese Central Asia", Central Asiatic Journal, Vol. 50 (2), 2006, pp. 246-63.

[26]Anthony D. Smith, "Structure and Persistence of ethnie", in Guibernau and John Rex, (eds.)The Ethnicity Reader: Nationalism, Multiculturalism and Migration,Oxford: Malden, 1997, p. 32.

[27]MushtaqA.Kaw, "Turkey's Relations with Central Asian Republics," Journal of Central Asian Studies, Vol. XVIII (1), Srinagar: Central Asian Studies, University of Kashmir, Srinagar, 2009.

[28]Alexander Bennigsen& Marie Broxup, The Islamic Threat to the Soviet State, New York, 1983, p. 109.

[29]DilipHiro, Between Marx and Muhammad: The Changing Face of Central Asia, London: Harper Collins, 1994, pp. 25, 32.

[30]MushtaqA.Kaw, "Central Asian Contribution to Kashmir's Tradition of Religio-Cultural Pluralism," Central Asiatic Journal , Vol. 52 (2), autumn 2010, pp. 237-55.

[31]See for details, I. A. Karimov, Uzbekistan along the Road of the Deepening Economical Reforms, Tashkent Uzbekistan, 1995.

[32]N.N.Vohra (ed.) Culture, Society and Politics in Central Asia, Delhi, India International Centre,1999, p. 227.

[33]Maria Elisabeth Louw, Everyday Islam in Post-Soviet Central Asia, USA: Routledge, 2007.

[34]Mushtaq A. Kaw, "Samarqand and Bukhara: the Tale of two cities," Greater Kashmir, November 4, 2009, Oped Page.

[35]Wahhabism defines a school of thought espoused by Muhammad Abd al Wahhab of Arabia in the 18th century (1703-1792) and was initially meant for Arab Peninsula. Besides other things, it recognised no human interpretation (ijtihad) orchange in the Prophetic Islam as per the changing circumstances: ChristophSchuck, "A Conceptual Framework of Sunni Islam," Politics, religion & Ideology, Vol. 14 (4), 2013, p. 497, http:////dx.doi.org/10.1080/215676 89.2013.829042; see also, Talimiz Ahmad, The Islamist Challenge in West Asia: Doctrinal and Political Competitions After the Arab Spring, New Delhi: Pentagon Press, 2013.

[36]Salafism explains a thought of the 2nd half of the 19th century with IbnTaimiyya as its strong exponent. It advocates a return to Islam to the ancestral tradition (salaf in Arabic). Salafism is exactly congruent with Wahhabism except in terms of space and time: Schuck, "A Conceptual Framework of Sunni Islam," op.cit, p. 497.

Sufism in India and Central Asia 37

[37]For details see, Al-Zawahiri, "Bitter Harvest: Sixty Years of the Muslim Brotherhood," in Gilles Kepel and Jean–Pierre Milelli (eds.), Al Qaeda in Its Own Words, Cambridge, MA: Belknap, reprint 2008, pp, 306-10.

[38]Sebastien Peyrouse, "The Rise of Political Islam in Soviet Central Asia," Current Trends in Islamic Ideology, Vol. 5, May 23, 2007, p.1.

[39]Olivier Roy, Globalised Islam: The Search for a New Ummah, New York: Columbia University Press, 2004, pp.78, 85.

[40]Olivier Roy, The Failure of Political Islam, Cambridge, Mass.: Harvard University Press, 1994, pp. 214-15.

[41]"Republic of Uzbekistan: Crackdowns in the Farghona Valley, Arbitrary Arrests and Religious Discrimination," Report May 1998, Human Rights Watch, Vol. 10, No. 4 (D).

Michael R. Feener, op.cit, pp. 152-54.

[43]International Crisis Group, "Repression and Regression in Turkmenistan: A New International Strategy," Asia Report No. 85, Brussels 2004.

[44]ushtaqA.Kaw, "Rethinking Islam in Contemporary Central Asia," In Central Asia Today: Countries, Neighbors, and the Region (eds.) SunatulloJonboboev, MirzokhidRakhimov and ReimundSeidelmann, Germany: CUVILLIER VERLAG Gottingen, 2014, pp. 393-418.

[45]AbulFazl (Ain-i Akbari) and Jahangir's (Tuzuk-i Jahangiri)accounts contain a detailed accounts of the Rishi cult in Kashmir. The modern historians of Kashmir also mention Rishis in diverse respects: A. Q. Rafiqi, Sufism in Kashmir, Varanasi: Bharatiya Publishing House, and Ishaq Khan, Kashmir'sTransition to Islam, New Delhi, 1994.

[46]JayalalKoul, LalDed (New Delhi, 1973), pp. 129-30; Shashibhushan Dasgupta, Obscure Religious Cults (Calcutta, 1976), pp. 65-70;Islam in Kashmir (Fourteenth to Sixteenth Century), p. 91.

[47]Mohammad Ishaq Khan, Sufis of Kashmir, Srinagar, India: Gulshan Books, 2011, pp. 21-22.

CHAPTER 4

The Role of Sufis in Diplomatic Relations Between The Khanate of Khoqand and India

Sherzodhon Mahmudov

Some scholars have traced the earliest diplomatic relations between the Khoqand Khanate and India to 1825, but the archival documents and manuscripts reveal important information about diplomatic relations which was actually established much earlier. While there were several key factors that contributed to the development of these relations, the primary concern of the rulers of Khoqand was to establish a close relationship with India that could be used to their advantage within the Central Asian region.

However, despite the historical importance of these diplomatic relations, the relations of the Khanate with India (especially with the Maharajah of Jammu and Kashmir), and the role of religious leaders (ulemas) as ambassadors have remained poorly studied. In many sources, it belonged to the 19th century and it was established that the Khoqand Khanate actively pursued diplomatic relations with India. Historical compositions, official correspondences and archival documents written in the 19th century show that leaders of Sufi orders took an active part in the establishment of these relationships. Sufi leaders got more effective results in their ambassadorial activities than merchants and statesmen. Written sources also contain information about embassy missions led by Sufi leaders.

Miyan Khalil Sakhibzada was a descendant of one of leader of the Naqshbandiyya-Mujaddidiyya Sufi order – Imam Rabbani Akhmad al-Sirkhindi. This person was a leader of the Naqshbandiyya-Mujaddidiyya Sufi order and had a lot of murids (followers) not only in India and Central Asia, but also in Russia. This information was also corroborated by the "India Office Letters" stored in the British library. Miyan Khalil Sakhibzade arrived from India to Khoqand in 1826 by the invitation of the ruler Muhammad Ali-Khan (1822-1841). Analysis of his spiritual and political activity in Central Asia gives us information about his role in diplomatic relations.

Also religious leaders (ulemas) such as Tash Khodja sudur and Khodja Bek led an embassy mission sent to India by the Khoqand Khanate. Written sources and archival documents dedicated the history of the Khoqand Khanate and contain information about their activities as ambassadors. This paper aims to study these issues and to analyze the dynamics of the embassy missions between the Khoqand Khanate and India.

It is true that in Central Asia, it was formed and developed several states and faced the crisis with the influence of some factors. However, countries obliged to governing the existed political, socio-economic life and used several means of statehood to implement their duties proficiently. Particularly, they tried to solve some problems appeared in political, socio-economic life through establishing international relations. One of these states was the Khanate of Khoqand which formed in Central Asia in 1709. In the beginning, its territory consisted of only the Fergana valley. Later, some territories of modern Kirghizstan, Tajikistan and Kazakhstan were united under the Khanate.

Each country used the talented and capable statesmen, merchants and religious leaders in the establishment of own diplomatic relations. In partly, rulers of the Khanate of Khoqand tried to hold diplomatic relations with neighbouring countries for developing political, military, trade-economic and cultural spheres.

It was fixed in written sources that the Khanate conducted diplomatic relations with China concerning Eastern Turkestan in the 18th century. Since the 19th century Khoqand started to adjust diplomatic relations with other countries also. Certainly, these processes were promoted by some reasons. The First, in this time elements of the statehood has been rather generated in the Khanate, and the state strengthened own political and economic status, recognized by other countries. Second, Tashkent borrowing strategic and special place in the trade of Central Asia as it has been joined to the Khanate, and the third the Russian empire threatened to the sovereignty of the state.

Despite the fact that the history of diplomatic relations between the Khanate of Khoqand and India was poorly studied, researchers are based only studied trade and cultural relations between two countries and on the analyse

Sufism in India and Central Asia

41

data of the National archive of India and the Ottoman archive. Also, it was not enlightened in those works that main factors and results of the establishment of diplomatic relations, the role of personalities such as Sufis, religious leaders and others took part in embassy missions.

Scholars who studied the history of the Khanate paid more attention to its foreign relations. They especially investigated the relationship of the Khanate with the Russian Empire, Ottoman Empire, China, Eastern Turkistan, the Emirate of Bukhara and the Khanate of Khiva. However, Khanate relations with the India begun and developed in the first half of the 19th century was left out of the sight of scholars.t

Historical compositions, official correspondences and archival documents which were written in the 19th century showed that the religious leaders actively took part in the establishment of these relations. Sufi leaders got more results in their ambassadorial activities than merchants and statesmen. Historical compositions also contains information about that religious leaders led an embassy missions. Religious leaders studied in madrasahs and had perfect knowledge and skills. Also the tolerance of Hanafi trend and its strong influence on the ethics of religious leaders have led to positive results in their activities.

Reflexion of relationships between the Khoqand Khanate and India in legends.

It is known that the rulers of the Khoqand Khanate tied their genealogy with Zahiriddin Mukhammad Babur through the legend of "Golden Cradle" ("Oltin Beshik"). The question of legitimating the authority of the Khoqand Khanate learned by Uzbek and foreign historians like Miyon Bukruk Solikhov, A. Qayumov, T. Beisembiyev, Kh. Bobobekov, A. Erkinov, S. Levi and others. Some of them suggested that rulers of Khoqand, in fact, were descendants of Babur. And others concluded that it was a fiction invented to justify the right of rulers to the political authority. According to the legend of the "Golden Cradle" when Babur came to India in 1512 and was became a father of a son. To protect his son from the dangers of the road, he left him in banks of Nayman-say (little river in the Fergana valley) which flowed from the south side of Khoqand. Representatives of Uzbek tribes found that the baby was wrapped in gold and precious things. They seized and divided the found things among themselves. As a result, the tribe of Ming got this baby and called him as Oltin Beshik-Khan.

After that Babur created his own Empire in India sent his ambassadors to Khoqand in order to bring his son. But the tribe of Ming which brought up the child sent their representative to Babur asking about that when Altin Beshik-Khan grows up to make him their ruler. Certainly, this story connected with the genealogy of rulers (Khans) of Khoqand took an important place in the ideology of the Khanate which was formed in the 18th century and shows that the dynasty of Ming tried to tie their first state relationships with India.

Citizens of the Khoqand Khanate and India

Ways of Hajj Pilgrimage had significance in the lives of Muslim people and political processes determined directions of the road. A part of Khoqand citizens went to pilgrimage to Mecca through territories of India in the 18th-19th centuries. It is known that there were three directions of the way of the Pilgrimage from Central Asia to Mecca: the first through India, the second through Iran and the third through territories of the Ottoman Empire. Data of archival documents show us the three ways, the way through the Ottoman Empire was often used by citizens of Khoqand. But Hajj pilgrimage travellers written by pilgrims about their pilgrimage stories give us information about some of citizens of the Khoqand who went to Mecca through India. In the 18th – 19th centuries the way through Iran did not use at all by reasons of religious conflicts between Sunni and Shiah confessions.

The Hajj pilgrimage way took an important place in the integration of various cultures. Here we could give us an example of the Naqshbandia-mujaddidia Sufi order to Central Asia especially to the Khoqand Khanate came from India. Relationships between Indian and Central Asian Sufi orders learned by scholars like Stephen Dale, Alam Payind, Jo-Ann Gross, Scott Levi, T. Beisembiev. In the beginning, they studied an extension of the Naqshbandia-mujaddidia Sufi order in India in their works and then they analyzed the spread of the order in the territories of Central Asia from India at the second

Sufism in India and Central Asia 43

half of the 17th – 18th centuries. Here, it emphasized that the Naqshbandia-mujaddidia order spread in the Bukharan Khanate from India as a result of activities of famous Sufi leader MusaKhan Dakhbedi. Musa Khan Dakhbedi went to the pilgrimage to Mecca through India, and in Kashmir he met Miyan Abid who was descendants of famous Sufi leader Akhmad Sirkhindi. Musa Khan Dakhbedi became his murid (follower) and after returning to Bukhara founded here a branch of the Naqshbandia-mujaddidia order. But there are not special works which studied the spread of the Naqshbadia-mujaddidia order from India to Central Asia. In our article dedicated to the role of Sufi leaders in diplomatic relations within the framework of the topic which is try to tell something about the extension of Naqshbadia-mujaddidia order in the Khoqand Khanate from India.

The first cultural interrelations between the Khoqand Khanate and India connected with first processes of the extension of the Naqshbandia-mujaddidia Sufi order in Fergana valley, in part with the activity of the traveller from Margilan Sayyid Abdullah Khan Tura. The Japanese scholar Yayoi Kawahara wrote that Abdullah Khan Tura went from Kashgar to India in order to get an education from Miyan Abid. Then Abdullah-Khan with the recommendation of Miyan Abid came back to Margilan and lived there. As a result of lack of written information related the activity of Abdulla Khan Tura Yayoi Kawahara in her article called oral data about him as a legendary. But Abdullah Khan Tura brought from India the unique copy of the Holy Quran and this copy now is stored by his descendants. Yayoi Kavahara learnt the unique copy of the Holy Quran and suggested that indeed, it made in India. She did not ignore the story of bringing of the Holy Quran to Khoqand, visit of Abdullah Khan to India and becoming a follower of the leader of naqshbandia-mujaddidia Sufi order sheikh Miyan Abid.

The widespread of the Naqshbandia-mujaddidia Sufi's order in Khoqand was connected with the activity and life of Miyan Khalil Sakhibzada Ishan in Khoqand. Also, Miyan Khalil Sakhibzada took an important place in establishment of diplomatic relations between the Khoqand Khanate and India. First interrelations between two countries began in 1825 with initiative of the ruler of Khoqand Mukhammad Ali-Khan. According to the local historical sources of Khoqand Mukhammad Ali-Khan sent special embassy to India and through it asked Miyan Khalil Sakhibzada to come and live in Khoqand. But the sources did not indicate the date of sending of ambassadors. However, it is known that Miyan Khalil Sakhibzada came to Khoqand in 1826.

The role of Miyan Khalil Sakhibzada in relationships between the Khoqand Khanate and India.

Little diplomatic ties were established between the Khoqand Khanate and India, thereby only the work of Mukhammad Anwar Khan contains brief informations about them. (Since the work of Mukhammad Anwar Khan was not dedicated to Khoqand-Indian relations, and it highlights relationships between Central Asia, Russia and England). In diplomatic relations of Khoqand Khanate took an important place the ambassadorial activity of Muhammad Khalil Sakhibzada, who was from descendants of one of the leaders of the naqshbandia-mujaddidia Sufi order – Imam Rabbani Akhmad al-Sirkhindi. In the sources, it contains information in the history of Khoqand Khanate that his name is fixed as Sakhibzade Khazrat, Khazrati Sakhib, Khazrati Ishan Sakhibzada, Miyan Khalil Sakhibzada and etc. In the archival documents the full name of this person was Muhammad Khalil Sakhibzada, and the people called descendants of Miyan Khalil Sakhibzada and Imam Rabbani as Miyans.

Miyan Khalil Sakhibzada Ishan arrived at Khoqand in 1826 by the invitation of its ruler Muhammad Ali-Khan. In the written historical sources there are different data on his native place. In one copy of the manuscript of the composition of "Tarikhi Shakhrukhi" (the History of Shahrukh) of Niyaz Muhammad Khuqandi it was fixed that he came to Khoqand from Bukhara, and in other copy it was written that he came from Peshawar. Also Pulatjon Qayumi in own composition of "Khoqand tarihi va uning adabiyoti" (History of Khoqand and its literature) wrote that this person came to the Khanate from Delhi. But it should not be confused him with the person, who was famous with the name of Sakhibzada kalon, who came into Bukhara and was a pir (patron, spiritual guide) of Amir Khaidar. The name of Sakhibzada Hazrat was Miyan Fazl Akhmad Sakhibzada and both of these two persons were representatives of one dynasty.

Sufism in India and Central Asia

There is some information about Miyan Khalil Sakhibzada below. He was born in 1785 and died in Khoqand in 1869. This person was a patron of the Naqshbadia-mujaddidia Sufi order in the Khoqand Khanate and had a lot of murids (followers) not only in Central Asia, but also in Russia . Moreover, Miyan Khalil Sakhibzada got a title of naqib in the Khoqand Khanate and played a certain role in the state administrative system.

What was a reason for the invitation clerics and leaders of the Sufi orders by Khoqand rulers to own country or the country which has not such people? It is impossible to assume that this kind of persons did not live in Khoqand. Of course, in Khoqand lived own domestic Sufi scholars. But Khoqand rulers (Khans) more trusted to ancestors of Imam Rabbani in foreign affairs, rather than local leaders of Sufi movements. Below we offer assumptions on this issue.

Descendants of famous Khodja Akhrar and Makhdumi A'zam who lived in Khoqand Khanate before coming in Muhammad Khalil Sakhibzada, occupied various administrative posts in the Khanate. In part, Ma'sum Khan Tura who was a grandson of Ortiq Khodja from descendants of Makhdumi A'zam and Jahangir Khan Tura who was from descendants of Khodja Khidoyatulloh (Afaq Khodja) lived also in Khoqand. But Khoqand rulers Umar-Khan and Muhammad Ali-Khan tried to control all the activity of Jahangir Khan Tura. Main reasons for this kept normal relations with China. This factor was fixed in written sources. Khoqand Khans got the right for privileges for free trade and levying of custom duties on behalf of themselves on the territory of Eastern Turkestan and giving thanks to the tight control of the descendants of Afaq Khodja and not giving them permission to leave the territory of Khoqand. If we pay our attention to other another side of the problem Bukharian ruler Amir Khaidar (1800-1826) was a murid (follower, adherent) of Miyan Akhmad Sakhib (Sakhibzade Kalon) who was from descendants of Imam Rabbani. It is known that interrelations between Khoqand Khanate and Bukhara emirate were not good. Khoqand ruler Muhammad Ali-Khan though being a murid (follower) of descendants of Imam Rabbani and involving them into social-political life tried to not complicate interrelations with Bukhara emirate. Also Central

Asian Sufi branches' (tariqat) leaders honoured descendants of Imam Rabbani. Bukharian sheikh Khusain, when he was informed on that Muhammad Khalil Sakhibzada that ordered to his followers that Azim Khodja Ishan and Jalaliddin Khodja, who finished their study in Bukhara and were returned to local place to not entering Khoqand as a sign of respect for the sheikh. Azim Khodja Ishan and Jaloliddin Khodja were sheikhs (leader, schoolers) of the Nashqbandia Sufi order. Moreover, it is fixed in written sources that Azim Khodja Ishan took an important place in social-political processes in the Khanate in 1840-1842.

Miyan Khalil Sakhibzada was one of the persons, who took an important place in the social-political life of the Khanate and below we can try to analyze his ambassadorial mission. Written historical sources on the history of Khoqand contain data about his activity. The first embassy mission of this person was to the Russian empire begun in August of 1841. Khoqand ruler (Khan) Muhammad Ali-Khan (1822-1841) appointed him as an ambassador for a reason. Firstly, Muhammad Ali-Khan respected him as a person, secondly the name of the leader of the Naqshbandia-mujaddidia Sufi branch Imam Rabbani Akhmad Sirkhindi was famous in all part of Central Asia, including Muslim regions of the Russian Empire and Ottoman Empire. In part Muhammad Yunusjan shigovul who took a position in administrative system in that time wrote in his work "Tarikhi Aliquli Amir-i lashkar" that "this person has a lot of followers (murids), pupils and friends among noghays and are under Russian ruling and others people". These data fixed also in "India office letters" stored in the British library. In part, it is written in them that this person has a lot of followers among Kypchak, Kazakh and Kyrgyz tribes.

New Step of Khoqand-Indian Relations

We met certain difficulties in the investigation of the topic due to the fact that Khoqand-Indian relations hardly had been studied. K. Warikoo wrote that the first embassy mission from Khoqand to India sent in 1837. But he did not describe the aim of this diplomatic mission and did not give information about ambassadors. But by us, we were discovered archival documents in the

Ottoman archives in Istanbul, which contains important data about relationships of the Khoqand Khanate with India. Khoqand ambassador Mukhammad Zakhid Khodja was sent to Istanbul in 1837. The descendants of Juybar Sufi leaders (sheikhs) presented to the Ottoman sultan Makhmud II (1808-1839) the letter of Khoqand ruler which contained information about Khoqand-Indian relations. Mukhammad Zakhid Khodja told about that, military specialists came from India to Khoqand a year before and conducted military exercises with Khoqand soldiers using modern methods. So, it can be assumed according to Ottoman documents military specialist came from India to Khoqand in 1836 and before it perhaps in 1835-1836 Khoqand sent the diplomatic mission for this purpose. Since the Khoqand Khanate to improve its military system tried to establish diplomatic relations with the Ottoman Empire and India, which is confirmed by documents stored in "the Ottoman archive" and "National archive of India."

Also Ottoman sultan Makhmud II (1808-1839) asked Mukhammad Zakhid Khodja about that with which countries the Khoqand Khanate established friendly relations. The Ottoman sultan offered the ambassador of Khoqand to strengthen diplomatic ties with India, and through it with Great Britain. Despite the fact that this diplomatic mission was established between the Ottoman Empire and the Khoqand Khanate, raised Khoqand-Indian relations to a new step and the activity of Muhammad Zakhid Khodja Ishan, who was the representative of the dynasty of Juybarid Sufi leaders (sheikhs), took an importance in the development of relationships.

In 1854 the Khoqand ruler Khudayar-Khan (1845-1858) sent to India next embassy mission and written sources of Khoqand did not enlightened it. However, documents stored in Indian National archive contain full information about this diplomatic mission. The documents which are kept in Indian archive with the name of the chief of this embassy missions were given in two variants: in some documents were written as Shahzada sultan and in others as Shahzada Sultan Mukhammad-Khan. But we could not find a person with the name of Shahzada Sultan among representatives of the ruling dynasty in Khoqand. There is a possibility to assume that the name was changed for security

48 Chapter 4 The Role of Sufis in Diplomatic...

purposes. It should be emphasized that names of some rulers of Khoqand were differential in written sources and in their seals. In part, the name of Sherali-Khan (1842-1845) was written on his seal as Sher Mukhammad Ali-Khan. Also the name of Miyan Khalil Sakhibzada was written in the form of Mukhammad Khalil Ishan naqib in the letter sent to the Russian Emperor. These things show that the official names of the famous person and their names spread among the people were different. The funds of the National Archives of India have also kept the English translation of the letter of Khoqand ruler. The letter shows us the main purpose of the Khoqand Khanate from sending this embassy mission. The Khoqand Khanate asked India to send specialist which can work with chemical substances and metals for increasing its military power.

In 1864 from the Khoqand Khanate to India went two consecutive embassy missions: the first embassy led by Mulla Khodja Bek udaychi came to Lahore and the second led by Tash Khodja sudur went to Kashmir. The sources related to the history of Khoqand gave little information about this embassy missions in part of only the work in "The history of Alimquli Amir-i lashkar" of Mukhammad Yunusjan Shigovul briefly described it. Also archival documents contained data on the activity of Mulla Khodja Bek as an ambassador, but embassy mission of Tash Khodja sudur is not described in details. In general both of Tash Khodja sudur and Mulla Khodja Bek were influential religious leaders in the Khoqand Khanate. Processes of their destination as on ambassadors can help us to clarify some facts. Mukhammad Yunusjan Shigavul which we have mentioned above took a post of shigavul in 1863-1865. Shigavuls were responsible for nomination of the candidates for leading embassy missions to the ruler (Khan) and for acceptance and safety of foreign ambassadors in the Khoqand Khanate. According to his composition "The history of Aliquli Amir-i lashkar" (Tarikhi Aliquli Amir-i lashkar) the candidacy of influential Sufi and religious leaders of Khoqand and Tashkent was nominated by Mukhammad Yunusjan for general (mingbashi) of Khoqand Aliquli Amir-i lashkar in 1863-1865. In part, Mukhammad Yunusjan emphasized that the Sufi leaders performed their mission more successfully in compare with other ambassadors and gave examples of supporting his position.

Sufism in India and Central Asia

As the Sufi leaders, they were respected not only by the common people, as well as by government officials, which could lead their ambassadorial missions to successful outcomes. Here as an example he told about the diplomatic activity of Miyan Khalil Sakhibzada. Thereafter on behalf of the ruler (Khan) of Khoqand Sultan Sayyid-Khan chief vizier Aliquli Amir-i lashkar sent Tash Khodja sudur to Kashmir in 1864 and Mulla Khodja Bek to Lahore. Main purpose of the Khoqand government from this embassy mission was to find allies in its struggle against the annexation of its territories by the Russian empire. In this response, the embassy mission led by Gulam Rabbani sent from Peshawar to Khoqand in 1865. These were the hard time for Khoqand, since the Russian Empire began military campaigns in the northern territories of the Khanate (Tashkent and southern Kazakhstan). According to the archival documents of the British library Miyan Khalil Sakhibzada gave information about that Gulam Rabbani lived in Bukhara. In our opinion by reason of the beginning of annexation of the Khoqand Khanate by the Russian Empire Miyan Khalil Sakhibzada Ishan wanted to send the ambassador Gulam Rabbani to Bukhara to keep him from falling under the influence of the Russian Empire or to ensure his safety. But some documents gave us information about that Gulam Rabbani in 1867 was in Khoqand.

In its turn, some ambassadors sent to Khoqand by India a represent five to the Naqshbandia order. In part, the ambassador Khodja Akhmed shaikh was from very influential leaders of the Naqshbandia Sufi order. He came with special diplomatic mission into the Khoqand Khanate from India, on behalf of British administration in India. We could not find documents which contain data about the life and activity of Khodja Akhmed sheikh. Thereby we continue our researches concerning with the activity of Khodja Akhmed sheikh and hope in the future we can find new facts about him.

Conclusion

Analysis of the data of written sources shows that ambassadors sent for diplomatic missions specially selected and had noble origins. In letters, they were written their statuses and titles in the Khanate also that fixed as sayyids. Thereby ambassadors, who were selected from representatives of religious leaders, were highly respected by the population and rulers of every country. In addition, we can say that Sufi leaders appointed as ambassadors took special place in the Islamic world and Khoqand rulers (Khans) tried through them to solve regional problems in foreign affairs.

The purposes of sending of embassy missions from the Khoqand Khanate to other countries were differential. In partly, it was sending diplomatic missions to India and to the Ottoman Empire Khoqand rulers (Khans) attempted and to rely on its spiritual aid and strengthen the military power. It was so diplomatic missions to Russian Empires which were connected with trade relations of the Khanate. Activities of Sufi leaders as ambassadors took an importance in the development of these relations.

References

[1]Culture, 1500-1800. New Delhi: Oxford university press. 2007.; Jo-Ann Gross. The Naqshbandia Connection: From Central Asia to India and back (16th-19th Centuries) // India and Central Asia: commerce and culture, 1500-1800. New Delhi: Oxford university press. 2007. pp.232-260; Temur Beisembiev. Fargana's Contacts with India in the Eighteenth and Nineteenth Centuries (According to the Khokand Chronicles) // India and Central Asia: commerce and culture, 1500-1800. New Delhi: Oxford university press. 2007. pp. 260-271.

[2]Miyon Buzruk Solihov. O`rta Osiyo O`zbek adabiyoti tarihiga umumiy qarash, 1-qism.-Tashkent, 1930.; Aziz Qayumov. Qo`qon adabiy muhiti. Toshkent. 1961.; Timur Beisembiev, 'Legenda o proiskhozhdenii kokandskikh khanov kak istochnik po istorii ideologii v Srednei Azii: po materialam sochinenii kokandskoi istoriografii,' in Kazakhstan, Sredniaia i Tsentralnaia Aziia v XVI–XVIII vv., Alma-Ata, 1983, pp. 94–105. Haidarbek Bobobekov, Qoqon Tarikhi, Tashkent, 1996.; Aftandil Erkonov, 'Imitation of Timurids and Pseudo-Legitimation: On the Origins of a Manuscript Anthology of Poems Dedicated to the Kokand Ruler Muhammad Ali Khan (1822-1842),' Graduate School Asia and Africa in World Reference Systems, Martin-Luther-University, Halle-Wittenberg, Online Working Paper No. 5; idem, "Oltin Beshik" afsonasi va Daqoiqiy Samarqandiyning "Bakhtiyornoma" asari, // Jahon Adabiyoti, 4,2014, Tashkent. pp.181-188.; Scott C. Levi, 'The Ferghana Valley at the Crossroads of World History: the Rise of Khoqand, 1709–1822, Journal of Global History, 2, 2 (2007), pp. 213–32.; idem, The Legend of the Golden Cradle: Babur's Legacy and Political Legitimacy in the Khanate of Khoqand // History of Central Asia in Modern Medieval Studies, Tashkent, 2013, pp. 102-117.

[3]Yayoi Kawahara. Margelanskiye "Tura" v Kokandskom Khanstve // Ajames. Annals of Japan Association for Middle East Studies. –Tokyo, 2005. No. 20 – 2. – P. 269-294.; idem. "Sviatye semeistva" Margelana v Kokandskom Khanstve v XIX v. Mir Islama/ Pax

Islamica, 1(4) 2010. pp. 121-139 (in Russian).; idem. Private Archives on a Makhdumzada Family in Marghilan. NIHU Program Islamic Area Studies, Central Eurasian Research Series №7. Tokyo. 2012.

[4]Stephen F. Dale and Alam Payind.The Ahrari Waqf in Kabul in the year 1546 and the Mugul Naqshbandiyyah. // India and Central Asia: commerce and culture, 1500-1800. New Delhi: Oxford university press. 2007; Jo-Ann Gross. The Naqshbandia Connection: From Central Asia to India and back (16th-19th Centuries) // India and Central Asia: commerce and culture, 1500-1800. New Delhi: Oxford University Press. 2007. pp. 232-260; Scott Levi. Idia, Russia and the eighteenth-century transformation of the Central Asian caravan trade // JESHO 42.4 1999 pp. 519-548; Scott Levi. Indian merchants in Central Asia // India and Central Asia: commerce and culture, 1500-1800. New Delhi: Oxford University Press. 2007.; Temur Beisembiev. Fargana's Contacts with India in the eighteenth and nineteenth Centuries (According to the Khokand Chronicles) // India and Central Asia: commerce and culture, 1500-1800. New Delhi: Oxford university press. 2007. pp. 260-271.

[5]Yayoi Kawahara. Margelanskiye "Tura" v Kokandskom Khanstve // Ajames. Annals of Japan Association for Middle East Studies. –Tokyo, 2005. No. 20 – 2. – P. 269-294; idem. idem. Private Archives on a Makhdumzada Family in Marghilan. NIHU Program Islamic Area Studies, Central Eurasian Research Series №7. Tokyo. 2012.

[6]Yayoi Kawahara. "Sviatye semeistva" Margelana v Kokandskom Khanstve v XIX v. Mir Islama/ Pax Islamica, 1(4) 2010. pp. 121-139 (in Russian).

[7]Yayoi Kawahara. "Sviatye semeistva" Margelana v Kokandskom Khanstve v XIX v.

[8]Mohammad Anwar Khan. England, Russia and Central Asia (A Study in diplomacy) 1857-1878. Peshawar. 1963.

[9]Central State Archive of Uzbekistan. C.S.A.Uz. F. I-715. Op.1. d.3.

[10]Mulla Niyaz Mukhammad Khoqandiy. Tarikhi Shohrukhiy. "Tarikhi Shokhruhi". manuscript C 468. Sanct-Peterburg branch of Institute of Oriental studies of Russian Academy of Sciences. f.146 б.

[11]Temur Beisembiev. "Tar'rikhi Shakhruhi" - kak istoricheskiy istochnik. Alma-Ata. 1987. P.105. (In Russian Language).

[12]Otabek Juraboev. Irfon she`riyatining sulolaviy namoyondalari // Sharq yulduzi. Tashkent. 2-2009.P. 165. (In Uzbek Language).

[13]Muhammad Yunusjan Shigovul Toyyib. "Tarikhi Aliquli Amir-i lashkar". manuscript №12136 Institute of Oriental Studies of the Uzbekistan Academy of Sciences f. 64 b.

[14]A title of naqib of Miyan Khalil Sakhibzade confirmed in letter written to Russian emperor by Khoqand ruler. The title of naqib was religious and given to descendants of Prophet Muhammad in Khoqand Khanate. It is written in sources that the age of nominate was not important in the giving of this title. In part, in 1818 this title was given to the author of the composition "Muntakhab at-tawarith" Muhammad Khakim khan tura and this procedure meant that the presentatove of ruling dynasty tried to connect own genealogy with sayyids (prophet's descendants).

[15]Khoqand ruler (khan) Umar-khan took also a position of shaikhul-islam.

[16]Afaq Khwoja was a great-grandson of the famous Naqshbandi Sufi teacher, Jalaliddin Ahmad al-Kasani (1461–1542) (also known as Makhdūm-i`Azam, "the Great Master"), and was revered as a Sufi teacher in his own right. He was born in 1626 year in Kumul.

[17]Muhammad Nasriddin al-Khanafi al-Khasani al-Bukhari. Tukhfat az-zairin. Edited by Kh.Turaev. // IFEAC № 2. 2003. – P.17. (In Russian Language)

[18]Both of these two persons are from irfani poets. Uzbek young scientist O.Djurabaev published many articles about activity of them. And this information is taken from "Khoqand tarikhi va uning adabiyoti" ("History of Khoqand and its literature") of Pulatjon Qayumi. See about it in: Juraboev O. Irfon she'riyatining sulolaviy namoyondalari // Sharq yulduzi. Tashkent, 2-2009. P. 164-171.

[19]Muhammad Yunusjan Shigovul Toyyib. "Tarikhi Aliquli Amir-i lashkar". manuscript №12136. Institute of Oriental Studies of the Uzbekistan Academy of Sciences f. 64 б.

[20]India Office. OMF. L/P&S/5/259. P. 194.

[21]Archive of Prime Ministry of Turkey (=APMT), HAT. 781/36565 A.

[22]Account of the Khanate of Kokand. Foreign S.C. (24th November, 1854, 1-25) (National Archives of India).

[23]Foreign S.C. (24th November, 1854, 1-25) (National Archives of India)

[24]Foreign S.C. (24th November, 1854, 1-25) (National Archives of India)

[25]Foreign S.C.(24th November, 1854, 1-25) (National Archives of India)

[26]Muhammad Yunusjan Shigovul Toyyib. "Tarikhi Aliquli Amir-i lashkar". manuscript №12136. Institute of Oriental Studies of the Uzbekistan Academy of Sciences f. 66 a.

[27]Muhammad Yunusjan Shigovul Toyyib. "Tarikhi Aliquli Amir-i lashkar". manuscript №12136. Institute of Oriental Studies of the Uzbekistan Academy of Sciences f. 64 a.

[28]Sodhi Hukm Sing. A History of Khokand. Lahore, 1878. P. 2.; India Office Records. L/P&S/5/260. P. 2-3.

[29]India Office Records. L/P&S/5/260. P. 2-3.

CHAPTER 5

Sheikh Badruddin Samarqandi: Founder of the Firdausi Silsilah in India

Nishat Manzar

One of the offshoots of the famous Kubraviya branch of Suhrwardi *silsilah*[1] is Firdausi *silsilah* which was introduced in India by an eminent person of his time Sheikh Badruddin Samarqandi (d. c.1298- 99 CE).[2] He was a disciple of Sheikh SaifuddinBakharzi[3] (d. 1260 CE), the latter being the spiritual successor of Sheikh Najmuddin Kubra of Khwarizm. Saifuddin Bakharzi was sent to Bukhara by his master and he stayed there till the end of his life. Sheikh Bakharzi directed Badruddin Samarqandi towards Hindustan where he made Delhi his abode. Since Sheikh Saifuddin Bakharzi died in 1260, his disciple Sheikh Badruddin Samarqandi would have arrived in Delhi sometime before it.[4] Hence, his sojourn in Delhi was a long one. There is some confusion about the place of his burial. Sheikh Nasiruddin Chiragh Dehalvi and Sheikh Abdul Haq Muhaddis Dehalvi, two eminent Sufis and scholars of fourteenth and sixteenth- seventeenth century respectively, refer the locality as Singola/Singhola[5]. Whereas he is actually buried along the eastern wall of Firoz Shah Kotla in Delhi, that was then called as Indrapat village (Indraprastha of antiquity). Hence, his being buried in Singola does not seem correct as it would have been very difficult for someone to attend frequently the *samā'* at the *jamā'tkhānah* of Sheikh Nizamuddin coming all the way from such a far off place. Badruddin Samarqandi was a friend of such an illustrious mystic of his time Sheikh Nizamuddin Auliya of Chishti*silsilah* (d. 1325 CE) and due to his fondness for *samā'* the former used to regularly visit his *jamā'tkhānah* in Ghayaspur to listen to it, Ghayaspur being in proximity of Indrapat.[6] There is referenceto the *urs* (death anniversary) ceremony of Sheikh Saifuddin Bakharzi also, that it was celebrated by both – Badruddin Samarqandi and Nizamuddin Auliya alike, and *langar* (food distributed as an act of charity) was distributed both from Chishtiya and Firdausiya hospices on the occasion.[7]

54 Chapter 5 Sheikh Badruddin Samarqandi: Founder of the....

It is quite surprising that there is little information about Sheikh Badruddin Samarqandi in contemporary and semi-contemporary sources, despite the fact that he was a friend of the most eminent figure of his time Sheikh Nizamuddin Auliya and founder of a new tradition of mysticism, in the Subcontinent, *i.e.* Firdausi. Modern scholars dismiss him in a few sentences. They rather, speak more about his predecessor and successors than him. None of them specifically speaks about the period of his arrival in India and most of them missed on the year of his death too. They fail to spot the place where his *khānqāh* (hospice) was located, although references of the village Indrapat/Indraprasth frequently occur in our medieval sources. There is hardly any reference to his ideology or teachings. SaiyidAthar Abbas Rizvi only credits him with founding his *silsilah* in India; his arrival in Delhi after KhwajaQutbuddinBakhtiyar Kaki had migrated here; his friendship with Sheikh Nizamuddin Auliya and fondness for *samā'*; and his death that occurred sometime during the period of Alauddin Khalji. Another modern scholar Khaliq Ahmad Nizami, who wrote extensively in the history of mysticism in India, does not credit him with anything worth noting, and have to say only that Firdausi order (and Shattari order too) 'did not make any important contribution during the period under review', *i.e.* thirteenth century.[8] They all, however, are unanimous in acknowledging the contribution of one of his successors to the Firdausi tradition, Sheikh Sharafuddin Ahmad YahyaManeri (1263- 1381) who settled in the region of Bihar and lived to a ripe old age.[9]

Fortunately, a successor of Sheikh SharafuddinYahya Maneri, Shah Shu'aib Firdausi in his *Manāqib-ulAsfiya,* which is one of the earliest accounts of the Firdausi Sufis in India, sheds some light on the life of Badruddin Samarqandi. Shah Shu'aib compiled the account in c. 1424-25. Here he came out with valuable information about Sheikh Badruddin Samarqandi and introduces, to some extent, the reader to the ideology of the saint also.

It naturally arouses curiosity in the mind of a reader/researcher – why such a treatment was meted out to a person who was so close to the Chishti saint Sheikh Nizamuddin Auliya, the most renowned figure of the thirteenth-fourteenth century Delhi. His contribution as the founder of the Firdausi tradition of mysticism also has not been duly recognised. Answers have to be sorted through from the contemporary and semi-cotemporary sources, both historical and hagiographical. Some important hagiographical works which speak about him, though briefly, are *Siyar-ul Auliya* by Saiyid Mohammad Mubarak Kirmani (popularly known as Amir Khurd),[10]*Khair-ulMajālis* by Hamid Qalandar[11]*Jawāmi-ul Kilim* by Saiyid Mohammad Akbar Husaini,[12] *Akhbār-ulAkhyār* by Sheikh Abdul Haq Muhaddis Dehalvi, *Kalimāt-us Sādiqain* of Sadiq Hamadani Dehalvi,[13] etc. Among the accounts of historical important are *Tarikh-i Firoz Shahi* (c. 1400 CE) by Shams Siraj Afif and Āin-i Akbari (1595 CE) of Allami Abul Fazl. This paper aims at exploring the possible reasons behind the paucity of information about him. At the same time, a discussion on his beliefs and ideology would be made, which would also help us understand why he was ignored by all, but few.

The most significant question to be addressed here is, why Sheikh Badruddin Samarqandi was not given due space in the contemporary chronicles. One of the possible reasons could be that in the thirteenth and the fourteenth century in Delhi and some cities in north India (like Nagor, Ajodhan, Hansi and Ajmer, etc.), Chishtis had firmly established themselves and had been, almost, ruling over the hearts of people. They were respected by the majority, including rulers and the nobles, and had created a niche for themselves in the contemporary society. At the same time, major contribution in the form of collections of biographies and discourses of the eminent mystics, especially of Chishti tradition has been made by the Chishtis itself. It is surprising, and disappointing at the same time, that none of the disciples of the Firdausi saint Sheikh Badruddin compiled any work on his life, neither in his lifetime nor after. Hence, whatever is preserved in the thirteenth century for posterity is contained in the Chishti sources only. Much later, in the fourteenth and the fifteenth century, Firdausi Sufis repeated almost the same that had been recorded earlier, with certain exceptions. The first representation of Badruddin Samarqandi can be seen in *Khair-ul Majālis* (c. 1357 CE) where the narrator speaks of his relationship with Sheikh Nizamuddin Auliya, but in brief. He is also talked about in relation to one of his successors in Delhi namely Sheikh

Ruknuddin Firdausi. Sheikh Ruknuddin had settled in Kilokhari (a new township in Delhi) developed by Kaiqubad along the river Yamuna, which was close to the village Ghayāspur where Sheikh Nizamuddin resided. They did not share amicable relations. Disciples of Chishtisufis accused him of confronting with Sheikh Nizamuddin and that his sons ridiculed the great Chishti Sheikh. When two of the sons of Sheikh Ruknuddin drowned in Yamuna, Sheikh Nizamuddin's followers recounted it as a curse uttered indirectly from the mouth of Sheikh Nizamuddin.[14] While the author of *Khair-ulMajālis* identifies the sufi as Sheikh Imaduddin, in *Manāqib-ul Asfiya*[15] and *Akhbār-ulAkhyār* he is mentioned as Sheikh Ruknuddin. A modern scholar says that Sheikh Imaduddin was the successor of Sheikh Ruknuddin, while author of *Manāqib-ul Asfiya* refers to Sheikh Ruknuddin as the son of Imaduddin.[16]

These incidents of so called enmity between Sheikh Nizamuddin and Sheikh Ruknuddin or Imaduddin Firdausi, suggest that, it did affect the writings of those who wrote in the fourteenth century and others who followed them. However, it is very surprising that Sheikh Nizamuddin Auliya, though continuously in touch with him, does not invoke the memory of his intimate friend Sheikh Badruddin Samarqandi, not even once, in his conversations entitled as *Fawāid-ulFuād*, which were recorded by one of his disciples Amir HasanSijzi. It makes the silence more evocative when Sheikh Nizamuddin relates some of the stories[17] of the master of Sheikh Badruddin, namely Saifuddin Bakharzi who lived in Bukhara. Whereas, he recalls many incidents about his other immediate contemporaries, like Nur Turk and Minhaj-us Siraj, etc., but does not say anything about Sheikh Badruddin. Sheikh Nasiruddin Chiragh Dehalvi, a successor of Sheikh Nizamuddin, however, discusses Sheikh Badruddin, but only once, which is in connection of his talk about the *langars*[18] organised in Delhi by the mystics during the lifetime of his master. That in those days prices were very low and mystics distributed food among fellow friends and poor on a large scale.[19] Here Sheikh Nasiruddin acknowledges Sheikh Badruddin Samarqandi who lived a life of poverty, and that people like him were not found in the town anymore. He also elaborates that Sheikh Badruddin lived in Sinkola and used to visit Sheikh Nizamuddin frequently. His fondness for *sama'* is also evoked in the discussion that took place in the same meeting with the disciples and friends.[20] Spiritual master of Sheikh Badruddin (Sheikh Saifuddin Bakharzi) rather appears a favourite of all, including Sheikh Nasiruddin, and he shared a peculiar story about Sheikh Bakharzi that has not been narrated elsewhere. That in Bukhara people used to celebrate four Eids in a year- one of them being the *urs* ceremony of Sheikh Bakharzi. Two Eids were similar to those Muslims celebrate in general, *i.e.*, *Eid-ulFitr* and *Eid-ulAzha*. The remaining fourth one was celebrated in Bukhara sometime in the month of Shā'bān. In *Khair-ul Majālis*, there is additional information on the villages assigned for the upkeep of the mausoleum (*rauza*) of Sheikh Bakharzi, that revenue of thirty villages. Each village (*deh*) yielding an income of forty thousand *dirhams*, was allotted for the upkeep of the *rauza*[21] However, he avoids saying anything about Bakharzi's immediate successor in India.

Another semi-contemporary source that sheds some light on the life of the founder of the Firdausi order is *Siyar-ul Auliya*, which contains the biographical sketches of the eminent Sufis. Although it does not offer us anything remarkable on the life of the person under discussion but it is astonishing on the same account that the author even does not include Sheikh Badruddin among the friends of Sheikh Nizamuddin. He speaks of at least thirty seven sufis and scholars of Sheikh Nizamuddin, who were either friends or the disciples of the Sheikh, except Sheikh Badruddin, although both the Sheikhs shared cordial relations throughout.[22] His account of Sheikh Badruddin is found elsewhere in the pages of his collection of *tazkirāhs*, when he cites the occurrences related to his participation in *samā'* along with his friend Sheikh Nizamuddin Auliya. Somehow, the information is very brief and does not help much in understanding the personality traits of Sheikh Badruddin in the contemporary scenario. Anyhow, he has, but few, words of admiration for him and calls him as a *darvesh* and *buzurg* and that he was the spiritual successor of Sheikh Saifuddin Bakharzi.[23] Sixteenth- Seventeenth century mystic and scholar Sheikh Abdul Haq Muhadddis Dehalvi has also not been able to provide satisfactory information about the early Firdausi Sufis in India.[24] Similar is

58 Chapter 5 Sheikh Badruddin Samarqandi: Founder of the....

the case with the author of *Kalimāt-us Sādiqain*, who recorded the account of mystics buried in Delhi roughly up to 1614.

One of the important works of historical importance compiled in the end of the fourteenth century is *Tārikh-i Firoz Shāhi* (c. 1400 C.E.) by Shams Siraj Afif. Detailing the events related to the construction of the city of Firozabad in Delhi by Firoz Shah (1351-1388), he informs that the Sultan selected the location of the village Kavin along the bank of the Yamuna for building the imperial palace and houses of nobles in its vicinity. For the purpose, he acquired the land of the eighteen villages located nearby. Two things are worth notice in the list. While two *sarāis* named after the two eminent mystics of the recent past, *sarāi* of Malik YarParran and *sarāi* of Sheikh Abu Bakr Tusi (by coincidence a friend of Sheikh Nizamuddin Auliya) are categorically mentioned, there is no reference to the Sufi who lies buried at the very place where the eastern wall of the fort, now known as Firoz Shah Kotla, along the river Yamuna was raised. His grave looks over the most central part of the fortress where the Jāmi' Mosque and the plinth having over it Aśokan Pillar is situated. Information contained in the two medieval sources say that he was buried in Sinkola/Singola, but Afif does not include any such locality in the list of eighteen villages encircled to build the fortress.[25] Why Afif failed to notice the presence of the grave of Sheikh Badruddin Samarqandi so close in the vicinity of the Fort, is beyond comprehension.

Nothing could be more intriguing than the silence maintained by the sufis of Firdausi order in this context. The most renowned person in the Firdausiya tradition and a prolific writer at the same time, fourteenth century saint Sheikh Sharfuddin Yahya of Maner (in modern Bihar) stands out in the galaxy of medieval Indian sufis. He wrote series of letters[26] (hundred to be specific) to one of his disciples Qazi Shamsuddin of Chausa to instruct him in the path of mysticism. In his advice and solutions to the problems sent to him by his disciple Qazi Shamsuddin, he quotes examples to support his views from the life of Prophet, Pious Caliphs, sufis, mendicants and various other persons. To our surprise, there is no citation from the life of Sheikh Badruddin Samarqandi, notwithstanding that he had introduced his own tradition in India.

Although, author of *Akhbār-ulAkhyār* Sheikh Abdul Haq Muhaddis Dehalvi specifically cites *Malfuzāt* of Sheikh Sharfuddin Yahya Maneri as the source of his information on Badruddin Samarqandi, unfortunately this information is wrong. Here he declares that Sheikh Najmuddin Kubra was the spiritual guide of Sheikh Badruddin Samarqandi (whereas Sheikh Kubra was the teacher of Sheikh Saifuddin Bakharzi, the latter being the teacher of Sheikh Badruddin). Problem aggravates when the biographer refers to *Siyar-ul Auliya* in the same passage (where he acknowledges correctly) that Sheikh Badruddin was an adherent of Sheikh Bakharzi.[27] It suggests that either Sheikh Abdul Haq mistakenly quoted the *Malfuzāt* of Sheikh Sharfuddin, or he himself was not sure of the spiritual lineage of Sheikh Badruddin. It is regrettable that the dates of his birth and death also appear incorrect.[28]

Among the works of the sixteenth century *Akbar Nāmah* and Āin-i Akbari have no parallel in the genre of official histories. AbulFazl in his *Āin* includes the biographical sketches of Sufis and scholars also. However, case of Sheikh Badruddin had not been dealt with separately. He rather clubs information on Sheikh Badruddin Samarqandi with one of his disciples Sheikh Najibuddin. Interestingly, he is the first author who suffixes the word 'Firdausi' with Sheikh Badruddin's name.[29] It clearly implies that memory of the Sheikh had faded by the sixteenth century where even great scholars like Sheikh Abdul Haq or AbulFazl could not recall properly or find accurate information on the life of Sheikh Badruddin. Somehow, Sadiq Hamadani, author of *Kalimāt-us Sādiqain*, still brief, but has more accurate information about the spiritual lineage of Sheikh Badruddin. He concedes that he had been a disciple of Sheikh Saifuddin Bakharzi, had come to settle in Delhi from Bukhara, and was friends with Sheikh Nizamuddin Auliya. About his burial place, it simply situates among the graves of the mystics of 'Old Delhi' (*Dehli-i kuhna*). He also has words of appreciation for him that he was a great man of his time, good natured and extremely good looking at the same time. SadiqHamadani also emphasises the repeated fact that he used to listen to *samā'* in the company of Sheikh Nizamuddin. Of these scholars, none exactly records anything remarkable on the philosophy or teachings of the Sheikh. The irony is that a sign board

60 Chapter 5 Sheikh Badruddin Samarqandi: Founder of the....

put inside the *dargāh* (resting place) complex of Sheikh Badruddin, refuses to acknowledge the sufi as a Firdausi either. Here his name carries the suffix 'Chishti' along with his name Sheikh Badruddin. Another sign board put nearby diverts his spiritual lineage towards Khwaja Muinuddin Chishti and his name has been placed above Sheikh Nizamuddin in the same tradition.[30]

One can concentrate on two issues about the life of Sheikh Badruddin and the introduction of his tradition in India- one, lack of information about his life; and two, the absence of information on his philosophy and teachings in the contemporary texts. It is well known that immediate successors of Sheikh Badruddin were not on good terms with his friend Sheikh Nizamuddin Auliya who survived the former for almost a quarter of a century. Whether it was either the sons of Sheikh Ruknuddin or Sheikh Imaduddin Firdausi is not confirm,[31] but in Chishti sources, they have been projected as the main culprits. They openly criticised the great Chishti Sufi and explicitly commented upon his accomplishments. Chishti literature of the period indirectly approves the calamity that befell on these young men when they drowned in the Yamuna. While some of the medieval texts advocate that Sheikh Nizamuddin was never into a habit of cursing, Sheikh Abdul Haq clearly declares that there existed no amity between Sheikh Nizamuddin and Sheikh Ruknuddin Firdausi. This incident (of drowning the sons of Sheikh Ruknudddin or Sheikh Imaduddin, in the Yamuna River in Kilokhari, Delhi) has been commonly shared by all with certain variations. This incident, perhaps, offended all those in the Chishti tradition. Hence, they avoided anything related to the Firdausi sufis, although Sheikh Badruddin had nothing to do with it as this incident that occurred much after his death.

On the second issue-why the sources are completely silent on his teachings or philosophy, the plausible reason could be that he did not share anything in this matter with the Chishtis or others. In Delhi where Chishtis were contributing profusely to the hagiographical literature,.[32] Unfortunately, Firdausi Sufis failed to contribute anything about their own order worth recalling. Firdausi should not have expected much (or anything) from the Chishtis, as in *Khair-ul Majālis* the author once declared that 'one who is not the friend of our *pīr* (spiritual master), is not a friend of ours either.'[33]

Sufism in India and Central Asia

In this state of general apathy, a descendent of Sheikh Sharfuddin Yahya of Maner, called Shah Shu'aib Firdausi comes to our rescue. He compiled a valuable account on the life of Firdausi sufis sometime in the fourteenth-fifteenth century.[34] Brief account of Sheikh Badruddin Samarqandi in his Manāqib-*ul Asfiya* indicates that he too had to struggle with the meager information on the life of the founder of the Firdausi order in India. Not going much into the details on his early life, the author concentrates more on the reasons of his being not so popular in the contemporary society and after. That the times when Sheikh Badruddin resided in Delhi, people of Hindustan considered someone 'sheikh' (or a sufi of great repute) only when one was found seemingly endued with miraculous powers, or someone who could assure his followers of having experienced a 'vision'. Those who failed in such ventures were not considered worth quoting. That once he came to meet his favourite disciple in Delhi Sheikh Qutbuddin Bakhtiyar Kaki and cautioned him not to perform miracles as it could invite the fury of his opponents, especially *ulama* (scholars) in imperial service.[35] The story of Sheikh-ul Islam's[36] complaint against Sheikh Qutbuddin is suggestive in a way, as the author Shah Shu'aib directs his criticism towards those Sufis and the disciples who gave unnecessary importance to the performance of miraculous acts. Such expectations from the Sufis hampered the growth of the Firdausi order in its early days in Delhi in the thirteenth and early fourteenth century. Shah Shu'aib tries to convince that it should not cast any doubt in the minds of people about the status of Sheikh Badruddin Samarqandi in the contemporary society, especially among the contemporary mystics. To him, the Sheikh believed in complete surrender to the will of Allah. Also, in the eyes of Sheikh Badruddin keeping one's faith intact and holding back powers that enable a person to perform miracles, were the signs of greatness. People anticipated miracles from him is also confirmed from an event recorded in *Jawāmi-ul-Kilim* (conversations of Chishti sufi Sheikh Gesu-Daraz[37] about Sheikh Badruddin Samarqandi.[38] Once a group of people approached him to pray for rain as that year they were facing immense hardships due to acute draught in Delhi and areas in its vicinity. But the Sheikh refused to oblige and expressed his inability

Chapter 5 Sheikh Badruddin Samarqandi: Founder of the....

in doing so. A well-wisher suggested him to seek help of a hermaphrodite Khwaja Rahat living a life of a mystic in seclusion inside the Siri Gate. He accompanied him on a particular day, though reluctantly. Finally, it rained in Delhi, not due to the usual prayers performed by Sheikh Badruddin- prayers that are to be performed on such occasions by the Muslims, or according to the practices prescribed in his own tradition, but only when he invoked the mercy of Allah as per the instructions of Khwaja Rahat. A very different and only event of its kind, recorded in *Kalimāt-us Sādiqain*, establishes the truth that he enjoyed close relations with nizamuddin Auliya. It Nevertheless it points out towards the stature of the man in the eyes of his contemporaries or sufis of the younger generation, like Amir Khurd, that it was not so high. The visit of Sheikh Badruddin with Sheikh Nizamuddin to enquire about the well- being of Amir Khurd and Amir Khurd posing a question before Sheikh Badruddin, specifies that he could not impress Amir Khurd.[39] This incident recorded by the author is wrong in itself, as Amir Khurd perhaps was not born when Sheikh Badruddin died, or would have been very young to involved in ascetic practices and conversation with mystics is much senior to him.[40]

Regarding Sheikh Ruknuddin Firdausi, Shah Shu'aib criticises the followers of Sheikh Nizamuddin that they always wished for the misfortunes happen to Sheikh Ruknuddin Firdausi and whenever some tragedy occurred, they would immediately associate it with the curse their Sheikh had used against Sheikh Ruknuddin. Shah Shu'aib speculates that some kind of debate must have been taken place between them, which might have turned the relations between the two sour. To Shah Shu'aib, however, Sheikh Ruknuddin Firdausi always remained indifferent to such developments and would remain absorbed in contemplation without responding to such acts of enmity and resentment.[41] He rather reconciles with the thought that those who face malevolence, get reward in this world and hereafter as well. Shah Shu'aib confirms that Sheikh Ruknuddin was really very popular for his piety and devotion in his life-time itself. Although, Sheikh Badruddin Samarqandi was not responsible for the tensions between Firdausi and Chishti Sufis which,

Sufism in India and Central Asia

perhaps, was a later development, but his image did suffer on this account when people did not record his contribution either, which could be of the benefit for the readers in posterity to understand the early history of Firdausis in India. Author of *Manāqib-ulAsfiya* identifies him as the extinguisher of *bid'at* (innovation), a *muhaqqiq* (researcher/ or one who strives to seek the path of God) and a great scholar who was well versed in all the branches of knowledge. To him the true form of *karāmat* (miracle) was to remain abide by the law of Allah. In case someone claims to have possessed the ability to display miracles, it is better to hold it back. He always inspired his disciples to seek knowledge, especially knowledge of faith. In his view, God grants someone the ability to perform miracles just to strengthen his place in the mystic path; otherwise one endued with the blessings of manifestation is in itself a sign of graciousness of him. Most important point about the mystic philosophy of Sheikh Badruddin Samarqandi is that he was the follower of the path of *shattār*, which was different than the path which followed by the mystics usually to attain Union with God.[42] This path was to be traversed rapidly and one could cross the stages in the way Union with God swiftly. At the same time, it was the most difficult option too. Their motto was- 'annihilate yourself before you actually experience death'. It was the path of *majzūbān-i Haq* (completely absorbed in His thought). In this tradition, sufis were expected to avoid performing *karāmāt* (miracles). Manifestation- *Kashf-i yaqīn,* was considered a blessing (*nemat*) by the great Sheikh. Author of *Manāqib-ulAsfiya* asserts that the path followed by Sheikh Badruddin Samarqandi was different and superior to others. While his contemporaries followed the path of *riyāzat-o mujāhida*, Sheikh Badruddin preferred that path (*ravish*) of *muhibbān-i Haq* (friends of Truth/Allah). Here he imitated the way of the master of his master Sheikh Najmuddin Kubra, who did not believe in traversing gradually 'various stages' to reach the goal, *i.e.* Union with God. *Shattāris* would invest all their energies in achieving this goal rapidly employing all their physical and spiritual energies; hence people like him were called *shattār*. Contemporary texts do suggest that path followed by Sheikh Badruddin was not common among other mystics of his time. Perhaps he had nothing to share with fellow sufis of the time except his interest in *samā'*. Nevertheless, though in brief, authors during the Sultanate period and

64 Chapter 5 Sheikh Badruddin Samarqandi: Founder of the....

after who prepared biographical accounts and put together conversations of their masters and renowned Sufis, vouch for his piety.

In this way, we come to a conclusion that Sheikh Badruddin did not have much to share in terms of orientation with his contemporaries, especially the Chishtis. Although a friend of Sheikh Nizamuddin Auliya and having fondness for *samā'*, avoided performing miracles. Unfortunately, none of his contemporaries bothered to write much about him. Whatever was written about him after his death is not enough to draw a satisfactory picture of his contribution towards the society and mystic tradition. People who followed his path also failed to recall his memory, except a few like Shah Shu'aib Firdausi. The greatest Sufi of Firdausi tradition in India, Sheikh SharfuddinYahya of Maner does not recall even a single event from his life while instructing one of his disciples Qazi Shamsuddin of Chausa in his letters.[43] His words quoted from his own conversations *Malfuzāt-i Sheikh Sharfuddin* in a sixteenth century text *Akhbār-ul Akhyār* appears to be incorrect. Nature of information about the early Firdausi Sufis suggests the kind of tensions that prevailed among the mystics of different orders, restricting them to write about 'others' who do not share amicable relations with them, especially their spiritual masters.

References

[1]Suhrwardi *silsilah* was founded by Sheikh Shihabuddin Suhrwardi (1145-1234/35). He was initiated into the mystic tradition by his uncle Sheikh Abu'n- NajibSuhrwardi (1097-1168). The most notable of his disciples was AbulJannab Ahmad bin Umar al Khwaqi, popularly known as Sheikh Najmuddin Kubra of Khwarizm (1145/46-1221). His followers started identifying themselves after him, and they came to be known as Kubraviyyasufis. Many prominent names are attached to this order. Sheikh Najmuddin Kubra's disciples took his tradition to almost all the (eastern) parts of the Islamicate. In India Firdausiya branch became popular in north India, while Kashmir became the stronghold of the Hamadaniya branch. Other offshoots are known as – Baghdadi / Nuriya, Khurasani / Rukniya, Ightishashiya and Nurbakhshiya. S. A. A. Rizvi, *History of Sufism in India*, 2 volumes, Delhi, 1978. Vol.I, pp. 86-93.

[2]Year of his death is not particularly mentioned in the contemporary sources. Modern works generally mention the year of his passing away in 1298/99. Mohammad Asim Al-Qadri Sambhali, *Rahnumā-i Mazārat-i Dehli*, Delhi, 2007, p.230. The year of his death has been established on the basis of the inscription placed above the grave which says that he attained *visāl* (Union with God) in 698 AH / 1299 CE. Also, Md. Talha, *Bihar ke Firdausi Silsileka Brihadltihas- 14th to 17th Century* (Hindi), unpublished thesis submitted to Jamia Millia

Islamia, New Delhi, 2011. Pp. 28- 30; Sadia Dehalvi, *Sufi Courtyard: Dargahs of Delhi*, 2012. Medievalsufi texts refer to the event sometime during the reign of Alauddin Khalji as there is a reference of him in *Khair-ul Majālis* that Sheikh Badruddin used to organise grand *langars* frequently along with Sheikh Nizamuddin. Since the prices were very low due to Sultan's policies, it was possible to do so for the sufis by spending only a small amount. Khaliq Ahmad Nizami, *Khair-ul Majālis (ed.)*, A.M.U., Aligarh., 1959. p. 185, 55th Majlis.

[3]Bakharz, also known as Guwakharz, is situated in modern Afghanistan, south of the town of Jam on Hari Rud near Herat. There is a popular story about Sheikh Bakharzi's becoming *a* sufi and a disciple of Sheikh Najmuddin Kubra. That he was a *wa'iz* and used to give sermons. He was quite averse to sufis and their way of life. In his sermons he would speak against them. In one of his meetings, Sheikh Kubra also came to listen to him. On seeing him, Sheikh Bakharzi could not contain himself and targeted him directly. When the sermon was over, Sheikh Kubra got up and while leaving turned back and asked why 'that' (Sheikh Bakharzi) sufi has not come yet. Sheikh Bakharzi rushed towards him; fell on his feetand followed him up to his house. Thus, he immediately became a follower. Sheikh Kubra ordered him to go to settle in Bukhara, where he died and was buried. *Khair-ul Majālis*, pp. 180-181, 53rd Majlis. Sheikh Bakharzi is also said to have converted the Mongol ruler Kharbanda to Islam. He rather converted after he dreamt of the Sheikh Bakharzi who appeared to him dressed up in a particular fashion. The *hikāyat* (fable, narrative) contained in *Khair-ul Majālis* says that his queens, family and all those in the imperial service also embraced Islam, and that he went to see the Sheikh when he heard that he is still alive in Bukhara. He was named as Khuda Banda by the Sheikh. Historically, it does not seem correct as Sheikh Saifuddin Bakharzi died in 1260 and Khuda Banda Aljaitu ruled between 1280-1316. On the other hand, SaiyidAthar Abbas Rizvi, on the authority of Minhaj-us Siraj informs that Sheikh Bakharzi is said to have converted Mongol Khan Berke (1257-1267) to Islam, but has his own reservation about it. He does not credit the Sheikh for the conversion of Berke. *History of Sufism in India*, vol. I, p. 227. Unfortunately, Rizvi confuses Kharbanda/Khudabanda Aljaituwith Berke. He treats the two as one, as he quotes from *Khair-ul Majālis* also. Somehow, Rizvi failed to identify the two Mongol rulers. While Berke was the son of the Jochi, eldest son of Chingiz Khan and brother of Batu Khan of Blue Horde who ruled over the territories lying north of Aral and Caspian Sea, Khudabanda was the great grandson of Hulegu (Halaku) and ruled over Khurasan with his capital at Sultaniyah.

[4]S. A. A. Rizvi, vol. I, p. 227. Some modern works put the event during the last years of Iltutmish's reign, *i.e.* 1234-1236. Malik Mohamed, *Foundation of Composite Culture in India*, 2007. p. 219.

[5]*Khair-ul Majālis,* p. 185, 55[th]Majlis.Singola/Singhola is a locality (rather an urban village) in the northern most part of Delhi adjoining the modern state of Haryana. Distance between the actual burial place of Sheikh Badruddin Samarqandi near Firoz Shah Kotla, and Singola/Singhola village is around 30 km.

[6]Ghayaspur is now known after the name of the great sufi as Nizamuddin. There is a distance of four- five kilometres between the *khānqahs* (hospices) of Badruddin Samarqandi and Nizamuddin Auliya.

7*Khair-ulMajālis,* p. 185, 55[th]Majlis. By this time, however, the word Firdausiya was not applied to the tradition of Sheikh Badruddin Samarqandi. It was a later development when his successors, especially after Khwaja Ruknuddin, became popular as *Pīran-i Firdaus*. *Manāqib-ul Asfiya*, ed. & tr. M. A. Arshad, Bihar Sharif, Nalanda, 2001. Also, S. A. A. Rizvi, Vol. I, p. 227.Author of a biography of Sheikh Sharfuddin Yahya Maneri compiled in the early years of the twentieth century has his own explanation about the suffix Firdausiya, but without any clue to his source of information. To him, it was Ziauddin Abu Najib Suhrwardi who took the hand of his disciple Sheikh Najmuddin Kubra in his own hands after seven days of his initiation and said that your are from the *Mashāikhān-i Firdaus* (should be *Mashāikh-i Firdaus,* mystics of Heaven). And that, from that day he came to be called as Firdausi. Zamiruddin Ahmad, *Makhdum Sharfuddin Yahya Ahmad Maneri*, 1901. P. 112. It, however, does not appear correct as Sheikh Najmuddin Kubra was the disciple of Sheikh ShihabuddinSuhrwardi, and the latter was the disciple of Ziauddin Abu NajibSuharwardi. Sheikh Kubra does not seem to have ever used the suffix for him.

8Khaliq Ahmad Nizami, *Some Aspects of Religion and Politics in India During the Thirteenth Century*, Delhi, 1961. P. 59. SaiyidAthar Abbas Rizvi is also equally brief about him, indicating the Sheikh Badruddin did not occupy a significant place in the life of people of Delhi.

9Sheikh Badruddin Samarqandi was succeeded by two of his *khalifāhs*- Sheikh Ruknuddin Firdausi and Sheikh Najibuddin. Sheikh Sharfuddin was the disciple of Sheikh Najibuddin.

10He was a disciple of Sheikh NizamuddinA uliya and compiled the *tazkirāhs* comprising the biographical sketches of eminent sufis. The exact year of the compilation is not known. Scholars believe that it was some time in the late 1350s or early years of 1360s that biographical account was prepared when the author was around fifty years old.

11Discourses of Sheikh Nasiruddin Chiragh Dehalvi.

12Discourses of Saiyid Mohammad Gesudraz.

13he work was compiled by Sadiq Hamadani sometime in 1614 CE in Delhi. It contains around 120 biographies of mystics of different orders buried in Delhi over a period of time. It also includes account of some of the Sultans and kings whose resting place is in Delhi. Text was published by SalimAkhtar from Lahore.

14It is said that sons of Sheikh Ruknuddin used to criticise Sheikh Nizamuddin Auliya. One day some of the followers of Sheikh Nizamuddin went to attend a function at the *khānqāh* of Sheikh AbuBakrHaidariTusi (d.1325, now popularly known as MatkaPir in Delhi). Here Sheikh Ruknuddin's sons (mistakenly mentioned as Imaduddin's sons) were also present who used foul language against Sheikh Nizamuddin. They immediately reported the matter to the Sheikh Nizamuddin, who in response to the report just narrated a story about a *darvesh* visiting his own master Sheikh Fariduddin. During the course of narrating the story when he came to the point that the *darvesh* drowned in a pond because he had annoyed Sheikh Farid for making undue demands, at the same moment news came that sons of Sheikh Ruknuddin/Imaduddintoo drowned while taking a bath near Kilokhari. *Khair-ulMajālis*, 60[th]Majlis, pp. 237- 239. In *Khair-ulMajālis* the name of the sufi whose sons drowned, is Ruknuddin which seems correct because it is he who lived in Kilokhari.

Sufism in India and Central Asia 67

[15]In *Manāqib-ulAsfiya*, however, it is not clearly mentioned that Sheikh Ruknuddin lost his sons. Shah Shu'aib only gives the impression that Sheikh Nizamuddin's followers made Sheikh Ruknuddin the subject of condemnation and that whenever any calamity befell the latter, they would associate it with the curse put on them by Sheikh Nizamuddin.

[16]S. A. A. Rizvi, *History of Sufism in India*, Vol. I. pp.227- 228. Unfortunately some basic details even about the immediate successors of Sheikh Badruddin Samarqandi are not found in place. Near contemporary sources fail to record the names of spiritual successors in a satisfactory manner and create a kind of confusion in the mind of a reader.

[17]There are seven incidents related to the life of Sheikh Saifuddin Bakharzi spoken of in *Fawāid-ulFuād*. Khwaja Hasan Sani Nizami (text edited and annotated), *Fawāid-ul-Fuād*, Urdu Academy, Delhi, 1990. pp. 58.222-223, 375, 419, 428, 433.

[18]Food distributed as an act of charity. It was a common practice among all the mystics in the where they prepared food out of the charities received and distributed it without any discrimination.

[19]This was the period of Sultan Alauddin Khalji (1295-1316) who had controlled the prices of all kinds of commodities and food grains. Of these the biggest *langars* were arranged by RamzanQalandar and Malik YarParran. *Khair-ulMajālis*, 55[th]Majlis, p. 185.

[20]Sheikh Nasiruddin also narrated the tradition, usually quoted by others too, of celebration of theurs (death ceremony) of Sheikh Bakharzi by both- Sheikh Badruddin and Sheikh Nizamuddin.*Khair-ulMajālis*, 53[rd]Majlis, pp. 181- 182.

[21]93[rd]Majlis, p. 266.

[22]Saiyid Mohammad Mubarak Kirmani/Amir Khurd, *Siyar-ulAuliya*, tr. Abdul Latif, 1999, Delhi. Pp. 300-328.

[23]*Siyar-ul Auliya*, p. 545. A popular event of the life of Sheikh Badruddin is reported here. That once performing *raqs* (spiritual dance in a state of ecstasy), he put his turban on the musical instrument called *chang*.

[24]*Akhbār-ulAkhyār*, tr. Mohammad Fazil, Delhi, 1994.P. 250.

[25]Shams SirajAfif, *Tārikh-i FirozShāhi*, text published from Bibliotheca Indica, Calcutta, 1890.P. 135. In the list of villages where Firozabad was founded, names are included of QasbahIndrabhat, Sarāi Sheikh Malik YārParrān, Sarāi Sheikh AbubakrTusi, village of Kāvin, Katihwāra, Lahrāvat, Andhāvali, SarāiMalika, area around the tomb of Sultan Razia, Bahari, Mehraula and Sultānpur.

[26]These letters are published as *Maktubāt-i Sadi*.

[27]*Akhbār-ulAkhyār*, p. 250.

[28]Sheikh Abdul Haq provides the dates of his birth and death as 613- 698 A. H. The date of birth corresponds to c. 1252 CE. While his spiritual guide Sheikh SaifuddinBakharzi died in 1260 CE, it is beyond comprehension that Sheikh Badruddin was sent to Delhi at such a tender age before he was eight years old.

[29]The next sentence in the text of AbulFazl is a bit confusing. Whether he is speaking of Sheikh Badruddin or his *khalifa* Sheikh Najibuddin is not clear, as he says that 'some

68   Chapter 5 Sheikh Badruddin Samarqandi: Founder of the....

say that he and ShaykhImaduddinTusi were the disciples and vice-regents of Shaykh Ruknuddin'. In either case, the information is wrong. Sheikh Ruknuddin and Sheikh Najibuddin were the spiritual successors of Sheikh Badruddin Samarqandi. *Āin-i Akbari*, vol. III, pp. 407-408.

[30]Present care taker of the *dargāh* (shrine) is Pir-Saiyid Mohammad Iqbal 'Chishti' Samarqandi who claims to be the *sajjādahnashīn* of the grave of 'Hazrat SaiyidBadruddin Chishti Samarqandi'. Similar treatment has been meted out to his successor Sheikh Imaduddin whose *dargāh* is located in the vicinity of tomb of Sheikh Nizamuddin, facing Lal Bahaudur Shastri Road, New Delhi. In the last few years his identity has been changed from a Firdausi sufi to a Chishti. In response to an enquiry by a researcher, the explanation came from the caretakers that people generally go to the grave of Sheikh Nizamuddin avoiding Sheikh Imaduddin. To attract visitors they have put up a signboard declaring his last name as 'Chishti'. No need to say that some monetary benefits can be accrued by declaring him to be a Chishti.

[31]Author of *Khair-ulMajālis* says that it were the sons of Sheikh Imaduddin Firdausi who openly condemned Sheikh Nizamuddin Auliya. The way they have been identified is also worth noting. Author of the said work does not record their names, but simply calls them as *pisrān-i Imād* ('sons of Imad') without showing any reverence to the Firdausi sufi, a practice not usual among the scholars of the time. pp. 202-203.

[32]Like *Fawāid-ulFuād, Khair-ulMajālis*and *Siyar-ulAuliya*.

[33]*Khair-ulMajālis,* 6th Majlis, pp. 28-29. It was uttered in response to an anecdote narrated by Sheikh Nasiruddin Chiragh Dehalvi. That a blind pupil of a pious scholar would not take the shorter route to his teacher's lessons because an enemy of the teacher lived in that particular lane who would often speak fowl about the teacher. Hamid Qalandar approved the act of the blind student and dedication of the blind pupil despite his physical condition, and justified the act with the words quoted above.

[34]His life span appears to be a long one as his date of birth and death is mentioned between 1289-1421CE.

[35]It is reported that when Sheikh Moinuddin reached Delhi he first went to meet the Sheikh-ul Islam Najmuddin Sughra who was the chief *sadr* of Delhi. Seeing him, Sheikh-ul Islam turned his face and after much persuasion indulged in conversation and immediately complained against Sheikh Qutbuddin, indirectly making him responsible for decline in his own (Sheikh-ul Islam's) popularity among the masses.

[36]Sheikh-ul Islam was the honorific title of the head of the department of *Sadārat* under the Sultans of Delhi. This particular Sheikh-ul Islam was in the service of Sultan Iltutmish (1210- 1236).

[37]He was the spiritual successor of Sheikh Nasiruddin Chiragh Dehalvi.

[38]Saiyid Mohammad Akbar Husaini, tr. Moinuddin Dardai, Delhi, 2000. pp. 408-410.

[39]*Kalimāt-us Sādiqain*, p. 100. The anecdote recorded here itself is very strange. That once Sheikh NizamudddinAuliya along with Sheikh Badruddin went to see Amir Khurd on getting to know that he was immersed in contemplation almost sitting unconscious of his

Sufism in India and Central Asia

whereabouts. As he was in this state for a while, on reaching near him Sheikh Badruddin picked conversation by saying to draw or divert his attention. That he had been from many places and happened to see such and such people. Sheikh Nizamuddin asked him to be brief. In the meantime, Amir Khurd raised his head and asked - 'O Badruddin, you claim to have seen many people in different places, did anybody also see you?' It sums up Sheikh Badruddin's image in the eyes of the students of his friend Sheikh Nizamuddin that Amir Khurd was hardly impressed with what Sheikh Badruddin claimed to have experienced during his journeys. However, it also suggests that perhaps Sheikh Badruddin was trying to speak of the relative position (*maqāmāt*) of the gnostics he had met during his journeys, but Amir Khurd questioned the very status of the Sheikh in the eyes of those whom he met while visiting those towns.

[40]*Siyar-ulAuliya* was compiled sometime in late 1350s or early 1360s by Amir Khurd when he was fifty years old. Sheikh Badruddin died perhaps in c. 1299 CE, or during the reign of Alauddin Khalji in the early years of the fourteenth century. It seems impossible for someone not even born yet or very young, to have gone into a state of contemplation and pose serious questions before Sheikh Badruddin in the presence of his *pīr*.

[41]*anāqib-ulAsfiya*, pp. 251-252

[42]It was the tradition of their predecessors, especially Sheikh Najmuddin Kubra who defined three ways to God – that of *arbāb*, *abrār* and *shattār*. While the first two demanded the seeker of path to be particular about the tenets of the religion and ascetic way of life, those who opted for the manners of *shattārs* were supposed to begin from the stage where others ended their spiritual journey. They were entitled for a cloak specific for mystics- *khirqa*, only when they attained perfection, not in the beginning like others. *Manāqib-ulAsfiya*, pp. 246-249.

[43]These letters are now known as *Maktūbāt-i Sadi*.

CHAPTER 6

Sufism and Sufi Shrines in Jammu Hills

Jigar Mohammed

Sufism entered India in the 12th century as a new socio-religious trend. The arrival of Sufism in India was welcomed by the indigenous population. With in short period it spread in different parts of India. From Punjab to Rajputana, from Jammu and Kashmir to Kerala Sufism was influenced the opinion and life of the people. Though on the eve of the entrance of Sufism population of the Muslims in most parts of India was virtually negligible, Sufis hardly faced any local resistance or obstruction in terms of their settlement. It is true that the Sufism emerged in Islamic land. But it received better social response in India and adjusted with its indigenous cultural trends in a very diligent manner. Sufism became a source of regional identity in India from 13th century onwards. It is important to mention that in modern and contemporary India the sufi shrines of the different regions represent the regional identity very effectively. The Sufi shrines of Ajodhan, Sirhind, Ajmer, Gulbarga and Delhi are still working as confluence of the different regional identities through the religious tourism. From 13th to 18th century Sufism participated in the making of the regional identities as the source of unity in differences. Some of the Sufis such as Hamiduddin Nagoriand Shaikh Nasiruddin Chiragh Dehlavi suffixed the nomenclature of their own locality with their original names. It is well established that several Sufis contributed to the flourishment of vernacular language as a medium of inter-faith dialogue and communication between them and common people. Richard Maxwell Eaton has shown that the Sufis of Bijapur contributed hugely for the promotion of vernacular idiom and Dakhni language.

Sufis' short poems and folk poetry became popular literature of the Bijapur. Highlighting the importance of folk poetry of the Sufis of Bijapur Richard Maxwell Eaton writes, "The bulk of the folk poetry written by the Sufis was sung by village women as they did various household chores.

The most common types included the *chakki-nama*, so called because it was sung while grinding food grains at the grindstone or chakki and the charkha-nama, sung while spinning thread at the spinning wheel or charkha. Other types of such folk poetry included the lori-nama, or lullaby, the shadi-nama of wedding song, the suhagan-nama or married woman's song, and the suhaila or eulogistic song."[1] For Eaton, the popularity of the Sufis' folk literature continues till modern period. He writes, "Sufi folk literature can be found to day in both written and oral traditions. Despite the intrusion of modern media in the villages, folk poetry relating to household chores is still sung."[2]. Khaliq Ahmad Nizami also finds Sufis's Khanqahs as sources of the growth of the common medium of communication among the persons of different linguistic background. According to him, "The eagerness of the Muslim mystics to establish closer relations with the Hindus and understand their religious life and thought facilitated the evolution of a common medium for the exchange of ideas. Since the earliest known sentences of the Hindi language are found the mystic records, the fact that the birth place of the Urdu language was the Khanqah of the medieval Sufis, can hardly be doubted."[3] In Kashmir the Shaikh Nuruddin or Nand Rishi, one of the most popular Sufis of Kashmir composed his poetry in Kashmiri language, which could be easily understood by the common people of Kashmir. Though the use of Kashmiri language in his poetry Shaikh Nuruddin Rishi strengthened the concept of the Kashmiri identity. He started the process of the vernacularization of the Kashmiri culture. According to Chitralekha Zutshi, "Nooruddin was able to create a framework for a regional culture though his use of the Kashmiri language to propagate a devotional religion, which was, significantly, outside the purview of the state."[4] Besides the use of vernacular language, the Sufis of India respected the other regional cultural values in terms of food, clothes, houses and means of livelihood. Most of the Sufis lived in a very simple house, ate simple food, used very simple dress and propagated the non-violence. Sufis like Shaikh Hamiduddin Nagauri propagated vegetarianism. Similarly, in Kashmir, Nuruddin Rishi propagated the concept of non-violence. It is important to mention that majority of the population belonged to peasant and artisanal social groups. When they found Sufis respecting their sentiments through their life styles, the common people of India found it very convenient to take inspiration from the Sufism for the completion of their socio-economic duties. Their regional life styles were very much encouraged when Sufis also lived accordingly. Virtually Sufis extended legitimacy to the regional identities.

Several modern historians have studied the Sufism of India. But most of them have studied the teachings and practices of the Sufis prescribed by their silsilas (orders). Khaliq Ahmad Nizami and S.A.A. Rizvi present monumental works on Sufism dealing with the Sufis, their orders, philosophy and activities. Sufism at regional level has received little attention of the historians. Richard Maxwell Eaton's *Sufis of Bijapur* and A.Q. Rafiqi's *Sufism of Kashmir* are detailed study of Sufism at regional level. But these studies deals with the Sufis about whom huge *malfuzat* literature are available. Hardly any attempt has been made by the modern historians to study the Sufis and their shrines existing in the hills where socioeconomic life was slower than plain areas. Moreover, Malfuzat literatures are also virtually non-existing. It is necessary to mention that in the hills Sufis worked more vigorously than other areas because of topographical, demographical and economic factors. The present paper concentrates on the Sufism in the Jammu hills.

Almost all leading Sufi Silsilas, coming to India, made the Punjab region as their halting place. The Chishti, Suhrawardi, Qadri and Naqshbandi Silsila scame to Punjab first, afterwards they travelled to the different parts of India. From Usman Hujwiri to BaqiBillah all the Sufis irrespective of their *Silsilas* found favourable atmosphere in the Punjab for the performance of their Sufistic activities. Therefore, they made different parts of the Punjab as the centres of their Silsilas. Once they succeeded in inviting the people to their centres and conveyed their Sufistic thoughts, they became confident that their philosophy and teachings had scope in the region in terms of social development.

Jammu region was closely associated with the Punjab in terms of its boundary, culture and climate. Therefore, it drew the attention of the Sufis for the spread of their philosophies and teachings. It is important to mention that during the medieval period twenty two principalities existed in the modern Jammu region. Hutchison and Vogel put all these principalities under the

Punjab hill states.[5] The Mughal sources such as the *Ain-i-Akbari* and *Kulasat-ut-Tawarikh* also show the most of the states of the Jammu hills were either parts of the Suba of Lahore or Subaof Multan.[6] Moreover, under Maharaja Ranjit Singh almost each part of the modern Jammu and Kashmir states were part of the Lahore Darbar. The socio-economic and geographical affiliation of Jammu region to the Punjab led to cultural exchange between these regions. Different routes from Punjab to Kashmir passed through the Jammu region. The most parts of the Jammu region were hilly terrain and its population belonged to the Hindu community. Fredrick Drew, who came to Jammu and Kashmir state in the 19th century during the reign of Maharaja Ranbir Singh (1857-85) and travelled in the different parts of the state, found Jammu as the most powerful state and other hill states were largely feudatories of Jammu.[7] The Sufi settlements of the different parts of the India sub-continent show that Sufis never treated places and people in preferential order in terms of making the centres of their activities. They settled in all those areas where they could perform their activities and spread their teachings. They made no distinction between hills and plains, between desert and fertile and between urban and rural areas in terms of carrying Sufism. For them, each place and social group had potentialities of betterment. Therefore, the topography of the Jammu region did not become the source of discouragement of the Sufis in terms of their settlement. It was an established practice that the Sufis sent their disciples to the different regions for the propagation of the Sufism. Consequently, the different areas of the Jammu hills witnessed the arrival of the Sufis during the medieval period and this process continued till the nineteenth century.

Like Punjab, Sufism entered Kashmir during the fourteenth century. Sayyid Sharfuddin, popularly known as Bulbul Shah, came to Kashmir in the early 14th century. At the time of his arrival Kashmir was ruled by the Damra dynasty and Suhadeva (1301-20) was the contemporary ruler. Sayyid Sharfuddin was a Suhrawardisufi and came to Kashmir from Turkistan. The Kubrawiya Silsila was introduced in Kashmir by Mir Sayyid Ali Hamdani, popularly known as Shah-i-Hamadan, during the second half of the 14th century. Sayyid Hilal, a Naqshbandi Sufi, came to Kashmir and settled there

Sufism in India and Central Asia 75

in the beginning of the 15th century. Similarly, Shaikh Niamatullah Qadri also visited Kashmir for short period. His disciple ShaikhMirak Mir settled in Kashmir and introduced the Qadri Silsila there. More importantly, in Kashmir an indigenous Sufi silsila, known as Rishi Silsila emerged during the 15th century. Since the Jammu hill states were the border states of Kashmir seems that the Sufism of Kashmir influenced the social life of the Jammu region.[8] Thus two border regions of Jammu *i.e.* Punjab and Kashmir had various centres of Sufism and the Sufis of these regions had started the processes of expanding the areas of their activities. Jammu being situated in between Kashmir and Punjab attracted the attention of the Sufis to make its different areas as the centres of their activities. It is important to mention that Sufis of the various silsilahs generally travelled to the different places for social interaction and propagating the philosophy and teachings of their own silsilahs. Khwaja Moinuddin Chishti, the founder of Chishti silsilah, visited Samarqand Bokhara, Harvan (in Naishapur), Baghdad, Tabriz, Aush, Ispahan, Sabzwar, Mihan, Khirqan, Astarabad, Balkh and Ghazni before his arrival in Lahore. After a short stay in Lahore he went to Ajmer.[9] Similarly, other Sufis believed in travelling in various areas for achieving and imparting knowledge. The practice of travelling in distant areas brought Sufis to the Jammu hills.

The modern Jammu region is divided into the districts such as Jammu, Kathua, Udhampur, Doda, Punch and Rajouri, Samba, Riasi, Kishtwar and Ramban consist of several sufi shrines. As far as the sources of the history of the Sufis and their shrines in the Jammu hills are concerned, most of the shrines have no contemporary record. It is either the present Sajjadanashin or oral traditions which speak the history of these shrines. A large number of legends are associated with the arrival, settlements and the activities of the Sufis of Jammu and these are narrated by both controllers and the followers of the shrines. It is very interesting to mention that the Sufis and their shrines have been made parts of the local culture by the oral traditions and these legends, folk lores and tales are preserved in the local languages and dialects such as Dogri, Kishtwari, Bhadrawahi, Gojriand Pahari etc. Some nineteenth century sources such as the Gulabnama of Diwan Kirpa Ram, Rajdarshani of

Ganeshdas Badehra and some travel accounts also contain some information regarding the role of the Sufis and their shrines in the socio-economic life of the Jammu hills.

However, it is confirmed that like other parts of the Punjab and Kashmir the Sufis of the different orders settled in the Jammu hills. The Sufis such as Pir Roshan Shah Wali, Pir Lakhdatta, Baba Budhan Shah, Pir Mitha, Pir Zahiri Wali Shah, Pir Shahan Shah Wali, Pir Muhabbat Ali Shah, Baba Sher Khan Pathan, also known as Sanjha Pir, Faqir Baba Faiz Bakhsh Shah Bukhari, Qutub Zaman Hazrat Baba Jiwan Shah, Panch Pir, Rah Baba and Baba Barkat Ali Shah etc came to Jammu and settled in the different areas such Jammu proper, Satwari, Akhnur, Kunjwani and Rihari. ShaikhFarid-ud-din Qadri, Hazrat Muhammad Asrar-ud-din, Hazrat Muahmmad Akhyar-ud-din, Shaikh Zain Alla Din, Baba Latif-ud-din Rishi and Zain-ud-din Rishi settled in Kishtwar.[10] Baba Pir Shah Tode settled at Kathua district of Jammu and Kashmir state. Mustafa or Nua Baba, Pir Baba Karam Shah, Hazrat Nadir Ali Shah Baghdadi, PirWali Shah settled in the different parts of modern Udhampur district. Pir Sayyid Ghulam Shah Badshah settled at Shahdara Sharif of the modern Rajouri district.[11] Similarly, Baba SainLal Din settled in Rajouri. Hazrat Nadir Ali Shah Baghdadi settled at Ram Nagar of Udhampur district. PirLakhdatta founded his residence at Banni (in Tahsil Basoli, district Kathua). Allapir settled at Punch. Hazrat Kasim Shah and Hazrat Haji Muhammad Akram settled at Dera Mehta in Doda district and Doda proper respectively. Panch Pir settled at Jammu, Basoli, Rajouri, Purmandal and Ramnagar. Hazrat Shaikh Abdul QadirJilani settled in Punch.[12] several other shrines of the sufi saints exist in Punch, Rajouri, Doda, Udhampur and Jammu districts.

The philosophical backgrounds, in terms of the Silsilah, of the most of the Sufis of Jammu hills are not known. Since the information regarding the life and works of these Sufis are based on hagiographical traditions, the present *Sajjadanashin* or *GaddiNashins* (controllers of the Sufi shrines) narrate the miracles, social activities and the social support of the Sufis. But there were Sufis whose identity in terms of *Silsilah* is well established. In Kishtwar majority of the Sufis belonged to either Qadiri Silsilah or Rishi order. Hazrat

Shaikh Zain-ud-din and Hazrat Baba Latif-ud-din belonged to the Rishi Silsilah, originated in Kashmir.[13] Sayyid Farid-ud-din, Israr-ud-din, Shah Abdal, Sayyid Bahauddin Samani, Darwish Muhammad and Yar Muhammad of Kishtwar belonged to the Qadiri Silsilah.[14] It is important to mention that the genealogical history, philosophy, activities and social contacts of the Qadiri Sufis are recorded in a Malfuz manuscript, entitled Rauzat-ul-Arifin, written by Hafiz Zia-ud-din Hafiz Nasruddin of Kishtwar. Baba Jiwan Shah of Jiwan Shah Muhalla, district Jammu belonged to the Chishti Silsilah. He is known to be from the family of ShaikhFarid-ud-din Ganj-i-Shakar of Ajodhan.

From their regional background point of view the Sufis of Jammu hills can be divided into four categories:

Sufis coming from Punjab and making their setttlement in Jammu,

Sufis coming from Kashmir,

Sufis coming from foreign lands and

Indigenous Sufis of Jammu hills.

The hagiographical traditions showed that majority of Sufis of Jammu hills came from Punjab. Pir Lakhdatta, Baba Buddhan Ali Shah, Baba Jiwan Shah of Akhnur, Baba Rah, Baba Jiwan Shah of Jiwan Shah Muhallah, Pir Baba Tode Shah, PirWali Shah, Mustafa Baba or Nau Baba, SainLal, Pir GhulamBadshah came to Jammu from the different parts of Punjab. Some of the Sufis either came from Kashmir or initiated into Sufism by the Sufis of Kashmir in Jammu hills, particularly in Kishtwar, Doda, Badhrawah, Punch and Rajouri. According to the oral tradition such types of the Sufis were initiated into the Sufism either by Mir Sayyid Ali Hamadani or ShaikhNur-ud-din Rishi. HazratMiskin Shah Kishtwari, Hazrat Sayyid Abu Sikandar Ali, Zain-ud-din Rishi and Latif-ud-din etc. were the products of Kashmir Sufism and came to the different areas of the modern Doda district. The arrival of some Sufis in the Jammu hills is associated with some foreign countries also. PirRoshan Ali or Nau Gaza Pir, Hazrat Shah Muhammad Ghazi, PirMitha, Faqir Baba FaizBukhari, Baba Barkat Ali, Hazarat Nazar Ali Shah etc. came from Mecca, Baghdad, Iran, Arab and Kazakistan. Some of the natives of Jammu hills also got initiated into the Sufism. Hazrat Shawan Sarkoti, Pir Muhabbat Ali, Pir Wali Shah and Baba SainLal Din belonged to the Jammu hills.[15]

Even there were some indigenous Sufis who first accepted Islam and then got initiated into the Sufism. Majority of such types of the Sufis belonged to the Rishi order of Kishtwar.[16] The geographical background of the Sufis of Jammu hills shows that the Jammu hills had potentialities of the social discourses among the Sufis and common people of heterogeneous character. It also shows that Jammu hill states were well connected with different parts of India and foreign countries in terms of propagation of the Sufism. Jammu hills not only welcomed the arrival of Sufism, but more importantly also acted as the meeting places of various thoughts through Sufism.

The emergence of the Sufism in the Jammu hills can be traced from the 13th century. The process of the coming of the Sufis to the Jammu region and their settlement continued till early 20th century. It is believed that Pir Roshan Wali Shah was the earliest Sufi who came to Jammu from Macca in the first half of the 13th century (1242). According to the hagiographical traditions, majority of the medieval Sufis came to Jammu from 15th to 19th century. Pir Lakhdata, Pir Buddhan Ali Shah, Hazrat Zain-ud-din Rishi, Baba Latif-ud-din Rishi, PirMitha, Pir Zahir Wali Shah, Sanjha Pir or Sher Khan Shah Pathan and Baba Karam Shah belonged to the 15th century. A large number of the Sufis came from Punjab during the late 18th century and 19th century. The Sufis like Baba Jiwan Shah, Baba Rah, Qutub Zaman Hazrat Jiwan Shah, Mustafa or Nau Gaza Baba etc. came to Jammu from the Punjab during the 19th century. It is important to mention that the Sufis who came from Punjab either during the 18th century or 19th century, it was the period of the political crisis. For example during the period of Ahmad Shah Abdali's invasion Punjab faced law and order problem and political instability became the dominant trend of the region. Whereas, Jammu region was remained a peaceful region. According to Ganesh Das Badhera, the author of Rajdarshani, Ranjit Dev(1733-83), the king of Jammu state, had enforced law and order very effectively and Jammu was called Dar-ul-Aman(Abode of Peace) during his period.[17] It seems that Sufis found congenial atmosphere in the Jammu region for the propagation of their philosophy and serving the people. Similarly, majority of the 19th century Sufis of Jammu came from Punjab after the death of Maharaja Ranjit Singh *i.e.* 1839. It is an established fact that after the death of the Maharaja Ranjit Singh political chaos and law and order problems cropped up on large scale due to the occurrence of the struggle for throne among the successors of the Maharaja. Whereas in Jammu hills, Maharaja Gulab Singh (1846-57) established security very effectively. Consequently, again several Sufis of the Punjab understood the Jammu hills more suitable than Punjab for their mystic activities. They came and settled in the Jammu. Thus the growth of the Sufism in the Jammu hills was also associated with the political stability of the areas concerned. It is important to mention that the Sufis of Punjab were the followers and propagators of the non-violence.

The Sufis of the Jammu were addressed with the different terms. These terms varied from period to period. The most popular term used for the Jammu hills Sufis was the Pir. The Pirterm was or is used mostly for the Sufis of the period from 13th to the 17th century. Pir Roshan Ali Shah, Pir Mitha, Pir Lakhdata, Pir ZahirWali Shah, Pir Shahan Shah Wali were the famous Sufis of the Jammu hills for whom the term Pir is used from medieval period onwards. The Shah term was also very much used for the Sufis. Bargad Ali Shah, Pir Ali Shah, Fazal Shah, Mangal Shah, PirBukhar Shah, Pir Sufi Shah, Qasim Shah and Khaki Shah and Sayyid Shah GhulamBadshah were the prominent Sufis who were addressed with the term Shah. The term Sayeen was used by some of the famous sufi saints of the Jammu hills. The terms Shaikh, Sayyid, Baba and Qalandar were also used for the Sufis of Jammu hills. It has already been mentioned that some of the Sufis of Kishtwar used the Rishi term as symbol of their identity in terms of their order. However, the terms Pir, Shah, Sayeen, Shaikh, Sayyid, Baba and Qalandar etc. were not used to show the identity in terms of Silsila. These were used for the Sufis in general term.

From the 13th century onwards Sufism became one of the popular philosophies in the Jammu hills and the activities of the Sufis received tremendous social support. The Sufis performed different types of the activities. Most of the Sufis of the Jammu hills performed miracles (*Kashfwa Karamat*).

80 Chapter 6 Sufism and Sufi Shrines in Jammu Hills

Some of the miracles of Pir Roshan Ali Shah are mentioned by the Rajdarshani. It is said that the king of Jammu was so much impressed from the miracles of Pir Roshan Shah Wali that he came to meet the sufi. The king is known as Raja Sarab-li-Dhar. The later was so much influenced with the miracles of the Pir that he requested the Pir to settle in Jammu. The Pir accepted the offer of the king and settled down at Jammu. The king provided all types of facilities to the Pir. Another miracle, narrated by Rajdarshani is associated with the death of Pir Roshan Shah Wali. Ganeshdas Badehra, the author of Rajdharshani, found the shrine and Khanqah of Pir Roshan Wali to be very popular and thriving during the 19th century. But the countries of the Punjab and Hindustan would be trampled under hoofs of the seeds of the Musalman. "So I a feeble ant, has been deputed by the Holy and popular Rasul to guard Jammu." He uttered such words, took off his skull from his head like turban, walked headless for some steps and going near the Gumat gate, sat inside and gave up the ghost. They buried him there as per his will. His Khanqah exists to this day and enjoy the same reverence."[18] About the Pir Mitha it is famous that once he tied his horse nearby his hut and went out of his home. After some time the horse felt thirstiness, there was nobody to provide water to the horse. But suddenly a fountain was raised and two trees sprang up. The horse drank the water and ate the leaves of the trees and met his both thirstiness and hunger. Several such types of miracles are associated with the almost all the Sufis of the Jammu hills. But these miracles had great significance in terms of the popularity of the Sufis. A large number of the persons became the followers of the Sufis. Several persons became the disciples (Murids) of the Sufis.

The Sufis of Jammu also worked for the spread of the philosophy of Unity of Being(*Wahadat-ul-wujud*). They popularized the concept of living together and inclusiveness. They concentrated only on those social activities which were meant for the welfare of the people. It is known that the Sufis not only organized discourses among the persons of different religious background, but they also organized *langar* (free kitchen). Some of the Sufis are also known to have contact with Sikh Guru Nanak. They not only derived legitimacy from the Sufism, but, more importantly, they also sought legitimacy from Guru Nanak. It

Sufism in India and Central Asia 81

is said that Pir-Mitha came to Jammu from Multan. But when he was at Multan, Guru Nanak came to Multan along with his disciple Mardana. Pir Lakhdatta met the Guru. He was very much impressed from the personality of the Guru. He presented some grains for the Guru so that he could cook and eat it. Though the Guru accepted the offering of the Pir, he did not eat it himself and gave it to Mardana. The Pir understood that the Guru did not eat grains. Therefore, he offered some milk to him. Again the Guru gave it to Mardana. The Pir was very much surprised and understood that since the Guru was a non-Muslim, he did not accept anything from the hands of a Muslim. The Guru understood the suspicion of the Pir. He called him and taught him the spirituality. Afterwards, the Pir concentrated only on the social services. Similar association between Baba Buddhan Shah and Guru Nanak is said to have existed. Friendship between Buddhan Shah and Guru Nanak is attested by both the sufi tradition of Jammu and Sikh traditions of both Punjab and Jammu. According to one oral tradition, both Baba Buddhan Shah and Guru Nanak liked the company of each other. Therefore, they met frequently. Whenever, Guru Nanak met Baba Buddhan Shah the latter offered milk to him and both of them exchanged their views with each other pertaining to social and spiritual aspects. The Baba also went Anand Sahib and met Guru Nanak and stayed there for some time. Thus, the Sufis of Jammu hills respected the sentiment of others and established that every opinion deserved to get the attention of people. They became bridge among the persons of different religions and other social background. Their Khanqah and shrines acted as the meeting places of the different religions. In the words of MriduRai, they became instrumental in establishing the concept that "regions pray together and stay together."

The Sufis of the Jammu hills also worked to maintain ecological balance. They taught the people that tree plantation was the pious work. Many of the Sufis participated in the plantation of trees. Similarly, they also founded the water sources, particularly the baolis. The trees planted by the Sufis and the water sources founded by them had medicinal values. The leaves and fruits of these trees and water of the sources cured certain diseases. Pir Lakhadata is famous for the plantation of such trees and foundation of water resources. It is also said that Shah Ghulam Shah Badshah of Rajouri planted a tree which became everlasting tree, known as Sadabahar. It is still surviving. It produces a type of fruit throughout the year. It is prohibited to pluck the fruit. Only those can be used which comes down the tree naturally. It is known that whosoever gets the fruit and eats it, his or her prayer is granted. The uniqueness of this fruit is that it never perishes. It is also known that the use of the leaves of this tree is also very useful in getting a child.[19] Since both the trees and water were sources of the livelihood of the hill people, the Sufis participation in these works made them sacred works and discouraged the cutting of the trees and pollution of water. It is important to mention in both Islam and Hinduism, tree plantation of trees is treated a pious work.

The social services of the Sufis were very much appreciated and supported by the people of the Jammu hills. The extent of the people's affiliation with the Sufis can be estimated from the fact that the shrines of these Sufis are well protected by the people generation after generation. Still a large number of people visit these shrines on every Thursday and offer sweets and flowers. The Sajjadanashin or Gaddi Nashin organised and continue to organize annual *Urs*[20] in the memory of buried Sufis. It may be mentioned that not only the common people of Jammu hills work together in terms of protecting the shrines and propagation of the teachings of the Sufis, but the Maharajas of Jammu from Maharaja Gulab Singh onwards worked for the preservation of these shrines. It is known that Gulab Singh, as a jagirdar of Maharaja Ranjit Singh, requested the Maharaja for the grant of land to the shrine of Shah Ghulam Badshah, situated in Rajouri district. Maharaja accepted the request and granted land for the expenses of the shrine.[21] Similarly, Maharaja Gulab Singh granted fifty Kanal lands to the shrine of PirWali Shah at Katra in Udhampur district.[22] Both Maharaja Ranbir Singh (1857-85) and Maharaja Pratap Singh extended financial support and renovated a number of the Sufi shrines of Jammu hills. More importantly, Jai Singh, the king of Kishtwar, accepted Islam under the influence of Sayyid Farid-ud-din Qadiri during the 17th century and received the title of Bakhtiyar Khan.[23] Baba Jiwan Shah was very much respected by the Maharaja Pratap Singh (1885-1925) and his brother Amar Singh. It is known that Maharaja Pratap Singh extended financial support to Baba Jiwan Shah both in cash (wazifa) and kind to meet the expenses of his mystic activities. The Maharaja loved to meet the Baba. Therefore, he frequently invited the Baba to his palace. Maharaja is said to have presented a hukkaand a dhoosa to the Baba during his visit to the palace.[24]

The location of the Sufi shrines is also the symbol of the identity of the area concerned. Even some of the localities of the Jammu hills are known in the name of the sufi of the area. The localities such as Pir Mitha, Lakhdata Bazar and Jiwan Shan are some instances in this regards. Thus, the Sufis of Jammu hills not only brought the people together during medieval period, but their shrines inspire the people to work together in contemporary period. Even some of the shrines are maintained by the Sikhs and Hindus. The Sufis contributed to making the Jammu region as the meeting place of the different opinions, religious trends and people of different classes. Pluralism was both propagated and practiced by them. They received tremendous social support in the intensification of the concepts of peace and non-violence. They also initiated the process of the dialogue between indigenous and non-indigenous culture and established that association. Both of them were a long lasting source of social security and economic progress of the region. The existence of the sufi shrines almost in all localities of Jammu region in contemporary period, irrespective of topography and nature of population, is a certificate of the everlasting influence of their philosophy and practice on social life of Jammu region.

References

[1]Richard Maxwell Eaton, *Sufis of Bijapur*, (1300-1700), Princeton University Press, Princeton, New Jersy, 1978, p. 157.

[2]Richard Maxwell Eaton, *Sufis of Bijapur*, p. 158.

[3]Khaliq Ahmad Nizami, *Some Aspects of Religion and Politics in India during the thirteenth Century*, Idarah-i-Adabiyat, Delhi, 1974, p. 264.

[4]Chitralekha Zutshi, *Language of Belonging, Islam, Regional Identity, and the Making of Kashmir*, Permanent Black, Delhi, 2003, p. 23.

[5]J. Hutchison and J.P. Vogel, *History of Punjab Hill States*, Low Price Publications, Delhi 1993, pp. 514-729.

[6]Abul Fazl, *Ain-i-Akbari, Vol.II*, Eng. Tr. by Jarret, Corrected and further annotated by Sir J.N.Sarkar, Low Price Publication Delhi, 1994, pp. 324–25.

84 Chapter 6 Sufism and Sufi Shrines in Jammu Hills

[7]Frederick Drew, *The Jammu and kashmir Territories, A Geographical Account*, Jay Kay Book House, Jammu, 1999, pp. 9–10.

[8]A. Q .Rafiqi, *Sufism in Kashmir*, Crown Publisher, Srinagar, 2003, pp. 19, 35–154.

[9]Khaliq Ahmad Nizami, *Some Aspects of Religion and Politics*, pp. 183–84.

[10]Shiv Nirmohi, *DuggarKeDarvesh*(Hindi), Udhampur, 2005, pp. 44–146.

[11]ShivjiDhar, *Tarikh-i-Kishtwar*(Persian), Jammu, 1962, pp. 36–37.

[12]Rafiqi, *Sufism,* p. 191.

[13]Mirza Zafarullah Khan, *Tazkirah-i-Bemisal, Rajgan-i-Rajour*(Urdu), Jallandhar, p. 137.

[14]Shiv Nirmohi, *Duggarke Darvesh*, p. 154.

[15]Rafiqi, *Sufism*, p. 191.

(Both Sayyid Ali Hamadani and Nuruddin Rishi enjoyed huge social support in Kashmir. Sayyid Ali Hamadani belonged to Hamadan of Persia and came to Kashmir during second half of the 14th century. He introduced Kubraviya*silsila*Kashmir. But Nuruddin Rishi was an indigenous Sufi of Kashmir. He introduced Rishi order in Kashmir. Nuruddin Rishi was very popular among both the Muslims and Hindus. The latter called him Nand Rishi).

[16]Molvi Hashmatullah Lakhnavi, *Mukhtasar Tarikh-i-Jammu waKashmir* (Urdu), Jammu, 1992, p. 166. G.M.D.Sufi, *Kashir,Vol.I,* Delhi, 1974, pp. 66, 115–16.

[17]Shiv Nirmohi, *Duggarke Darvesh*, pp. 44–163 (ZohraKhatoon, Muslim Saints and their Shrines, p. 29).

[18]Ganeshdas Badehra, *Rajadarshani*, Eng. Tr. by S.D.S. Charak, Annotated by Anita K. Billawaria, Jay Kay Book House, Jammu, 1991, p. 74.

[19]Sadullah Sad Faridabadi, *Shah Farid-ud-din Baghdadi* (Urdu), Doda, 2000, pp. 94-96.

[20]Urs is the death anniversary of a Sufi saint in South Asia.

[21]Shiv Nirmohi, *DuggarKeDarvesh,* pp. 44–163.

[22]Mridu Rai, *Islam, Rights and History of Kashmir, Muslim Subjects*, Delhi, 2004, pp. 76-77.

[23]KhushDilMaini, *Ziarat-I-Sayyid Baba Ghulam Shah Badshah, Shahdara Sharif*(Urdu), Jammu, 2000, pp. 3–4.

[24]ZohraKhatoon, *Muslim Saints and their Shrines*, Jay Kay Book House, Jammu, 1990, pp. 42–43.

CHAPTER 7

Kalimat al-Sadiqin: A Sufi Biographical Account

Gulfishan Khan

The chapter seeks to highlight an important but hitherto largely unstudied sufi *tazkira* or the biographical dictionary entitled *Kalimat al-Sadiqin* compiled by Muhammad Sadiq Kashmiri Hamadani, in 1023A.D. /1614 A.D. The work is a *tazkira* of the Sufi-saints mostly buried in Delhi up to the year 1023/1614. It is a memoir of the saints as well as of the city. Of late, *tazkira* writing has been acknowledged as "one of the most powerful process of cultural production at any point in the history of Islamicate South Asia."[1] Like poetry, *Tazkira* too, as a literary genre usually contains biographical accounts of poets, scholars, scientists and men of learning. It was considered an effective means to transmit the extraordinary achievements to the posterity. The author was a pupil of well-known mystic figure Abul Muayyid Razi al-Din Uwaisi Naqshbandi Khwaja Baqi Billah (1563-1603), popularly known as Khwaja Baqibillah and Shaikh Abdul Haq Muhaddith Dehlawi (1551-1642), the traditionist and historiographer of Mughal India. The author was an Indo-Persian elite who lived in Delhi during the late sixteenth and early seventeenth century. The main emphasis of the author is on the geographical location which has been termed as the Muslim sacred space.

The dictionary underscores the urban connected Sufi masters especially the location in the present case was the Sultanate capital of Delhi. It devotes satisfactory details to the lives of Qutub al-Din Bakhtiyar Kaki and Nizam al-Din Awliya as the foremost Indian saints in the Tughlaq capital. The dictionary is compiled strictly in chronological order and the author begins with the biography of Chishti saints, the pan-Indian Sufi order and ends with an account of contemporary Naqshbandi saints.[2] However, it was precisely the period when many eminent mystics belonging to the Naqshbandi order migrated to India from Central Asia. Naqshbandi silsila born of twelfth century *tariqa-i-Khwajgan* path or order of the masters, founded in Bukhara by

Bahauddin Naqshband (d.1389), the patron-saint of Bukhara, spread in India following the arrival of Khwaja Baqi Billah, the spiritual teacher of the author whom he lovingly called "Hazrat-i-Ishan." Therefore, five of the sufis Khwaja Baqi Billah and his successors described in the biographical dictionary had Naqshbandi affiliations as Delhi during the period became centre of mystic activities of this important Central Asian order (*silsila*). Nonetheless Chishti and Suhrawardy saints predominating. It is a saints hagiographical dictionary intended for the edification of all those who either pursued the Path or admire those who do it. Therefore, it's also included sufi affiliated saintly figures such as Sufi-poet Amir Khusrau and the renowned historian Zia a-Din Barani.

Portraying the City of the Saints: Delhi

One of the most distinctive features of the *Kalimat* is the depiction of the Delhi as a Muslim sacred space and the simultaneous reiteration of the historicity of the heritage city. The author sought to emphasise that the city had been the principal centre of power, culture and learning. Delhi was central in the vision of the author due to the mystical notion of territorial *wilayat* of a Shaikh's spiritual authority also and in the mystical world-view Delhi always consisted a separate *wilayat*. However, the author unfailingly pointed it out that the historic city was also important as many influential potentates, powerful kings, high-ranking nobles, learned savants also lived and died in the city. More significantly, the city was their final resting place also. Many renowned personalities such as the eminent scholars, revered saints, famous philosophers, famous kings, illustrious nobles are lying buried in the city. "Know, may God support you with the light of gnosis, that Delhi is a very large and noble city and that many of saints of the nation (*ummat*) have said things about it to describing the qualities (*tausif*) like, "One in a thousand and very few out of the multitude recognise its greatness." Thus, whoever has the least understanding and the slightest knowledge will surely recognise as after the two holy cities of Mecca and Medina (*Harmayn-sharifain*), if there is any nobility to be found in a place or greatness in a land, it is this noble land which is distinguished completely over the rest of the cities and is exceptional. And therefore, it is said by the common folk that Delhi is a little Mecca and even the elite have no doubt of its greatness.

Sufism in India and Central Asia

Everyone asserts its exaltedness, whether due to the fact that the great ones of the religion, the learned (*ulama*) among the people of certainty, the great Sheikhs, the reputable wise men, the powerful rulers, and the exalted nobles have filled this city and have been buried here, or due to its fine buildings, delightful gardens and pleasant localities it is the capital of India. Delhi had also been the seat of many of the powerful kings. The city had been a favourite abode of many of the chosen ones of God and near ones of kings and therefore each of its localities is full of divine blessings. It has such sacred monuments as the Qadamgah of his holiness, the refuge of the prophecy, Prophet Muhammad, peace be upon him, Hauz Shamsi, Masjid-i-Idgah, Masjid-i-Khwaja Muin uddin and Khanqah of Hazrat Sultan al-Mashaikh (King of the mystics) and the city of Firuzabad, are some of the most blessed famous sites of the city.[3]

According to some esteemed personages, since of the people of mystical intuition elaborately said that, "All of Delhi is declared to be a mosque," this entire city is distinguished from other places by its greatness and nobility. Entire Delhi is as sacred as a mosque. The city occupies unique position amongst the cities of India. He wrote that the verses of Khwaja Khusru beautifully illustrate the grandeur and magnificence of the city. Sadiq recited the long narrative poem entitled *Qiran al-Sadayn* (The Conjunction of the two auspicious planets) of Amir Khusrau composed in 1289, and dedicated to Sultan Kay Qubad (r.1287-90).[4] In this poem the poet asked God to protect Delhi from calamities and misfortunes. He lavishly praised the newly constructed congregational mosque (*Masjid-i-Jami*) and public water tanks (*Hawz*) concluding his description with the flourishing state of the capital Delhi *Hazrat-i-Dehli*.

"In summary, these verses of Khwaja Khusrau inform us of the greatness of this city and certain of its sites".

Noble Delhi, shelter of religion and treasure,

It is the Garden of Eden, may it last forever.

A veritable earthly Paradise in all its qualities

May Allah protect it from calamities.

If it but heard the tale of this garden,

Mecca would make pilgrimage to Hindustan. [5]

Sources of Information

The other remarkable feature of *tazkira* is use of Indian sources especially the *malfuz* literature produced in India. Inspiration is drawn from *malfuz* and historical works produced on Indian soil and not from Persian models. It is also not a *tariqa* based *tazkira* rather the saints and their teachings and the impact of teachings on society is important. Among the major sources of information employed by the author are *Akhbar al-Akhyar* (Tales of the Great Ones) of Shaykh Abd al-Haq Muhaddith Dehlawi (d.1642) written during the third phase of the Akbar's period, 999/1591. It seems *Akhbar al-Akhyar* had gained considerable popularity among the learned sufi circles as early as the first quarter of the seventeenth century. Moreover, Sadiq was a pupil of the learned author. He corresponded and exchanged ideas with him on many academic issues such as the critical study of *Hadith* literature. Therefore, it is not unlikely that he would have been in possession of a personal copy of this important work which he used as a work of reference to construct his own biographical account. Evidently, another Sufi-tazkira *Safinat al Awliya* (Ship of the saints) completed in 1640 of the Sufi prince Dara Shikoh (d. 1659) is also modelled on *Akhbar al-Akhyar*. Like *Akhbar al-Akhyar* it also describes only the Indian saints. But *Kalimat al-Sadiqin* lacks the freshness of the *tazkira* of Abd-al-Qadir Badauni and the comprehensiveness of Abd al-Haq. Nonetheless, it remains important for its emphasis on geographical location rather than the silsilas. One of the distinctive features of biographical accounts of the Sufi-Shaykhs embodied in *tazkira* is emphasis on noble ancestry, biological and spiritual both and pursuit of learning.

Fawa'idu'l-F'uad (Morals for the heart) of Amir Najmu'd-Din Hasan Sijzi, (b.652/1254), the Badaun born distinguished poet-disciple of the ShaikhNizam al-Din Auliya constituted another major source of information. *Siyar al-Arifin* (Lives of the Gnostics) of Suhrawardy adept Shaykh Jamali (d. 1536) is the other hagiographical account cited by the author. Some standard historical works are also mentioned such as *Tabaqat-i-Nasiri* and *Tarikh-i-Firuzshahi*. The well-known fourteenth century Sufi text *Siyar al-Awliya fi Muhabbat al-Haq Jalla wa ala* known as *Siyar al-Awliya* the earliest biographical account

Sufism in India and Central Asia

of Chishti-Sufi saints written by Sayyid Muhammad bin Muhammad Alawi Kirmani (d.770/1368-9) better known as Amir Khurd, a young intellectual disciple of Shaikh Nizam al-Din Awliya is most frequently quoted. It was compiled during the reign of Firoz Shah Tughlaq, and constituted a major source of information mainly for the Chishti saints of the first cycle.[6] It concentrates on the first cycle of the Indian Chishtiyya (twelfth to fourteenth century. The author provided the most satisfactory account of the three representative Chishti saints Khwaja Bakhtiyar Kaki, Nizam al-din Awliya, and Nasir al-Din Chiragh-i-Dehli, while the historical narrative is largely taken from the *Tarikh-i-Firuzshahi* of Zia al-din Barani. *Siyar al Awliya* (Lives of the Saints) a fundamental Chishti hagiography authored by Mir Khurd Kirmani 30 years the saint's death remained the most cited work in the text under study especially for the reconstruction of the biographical accounts of the standard bearer of the Chishti spirituality.

One of the most interesting features of the *Kalimat* is inclusion of the biographical accounts of rulers. Amongst the rulers the author provided almost contemporary biographies of Emperor Akbar and his son and successor Nur al-Din Jahangir. Both the rulers are mentioned with their full imperial titles "Jalal al-Din Muhammad Akbar badshah son of Muhammad Nasiruddin Muhammad Humayun Padshah Jannat Ashyani, who is nested in the garden of Paradise." The kingship acquired fresh lustre with his accession to throne. He acquired Delhi by defeating Hemu, the most dangerous rival, whose forces were routed at Panipat in 1556. He assumed the title of Ghazi. Sadiq noted Mughal imperial expansion under Akbar as the most remarkable achievement of the emperor. Sadiq felt obligation towards emperor who made Delhi part of his empire by defeating Hemu. He ruled for more than 52 years with grace and authority.[7] Emperor Jahangir is remembered and mentioned as a pious king. On the death of Akbar in 1013 (AH)/1605, Jahangir ascended the throne under the title of Abul Muzaffar Nuruddin Jahangir Padshah Ghazi. He is portrayed as a sensible ruler, kind hearted and generous, who hated oppression and had passion for justice. His reign brought peace and prosperity to people and on political side there was stability and strength. The emperor is profusely praised for his generosity under the *shaikhs*, *ulama*, and scholars plied their vocation peacefully. The emperor's benevolence towards them was ever augmenting. [8]

The Saints

The first mystic described in the *Kalimat* is Khwaja Bakhtiyar Kaki (d. 1235) the eminent disciple and Khalifa of Muin al-Din Chishti, the founder figure of Chishti silsila in India, settled in Delhi during the reign of Iltutmish the first ruler of Indo-Muslim state (1206-1210), builder of Qutub Minar. He is described as one of the most distinguished sufi in the Chishtia order, and the chief of Chishti saints in Delhi. The description is largely derived from *Siyar al-Awliya*. "He was one of the exalted saints. He was among the greatest of the saints and the most illustrious of the pure in heart. He found great favour with God. He was specially distinguished by his ability to renounce the renunciation of the world (*tarkwatajrid*). He was content in abject poverty." On the authority of *Akbar al-akhyar* he wrote: "He completely immersed himself in remembering God. When anyone came to pay a call to him, it would be sometime before he came back to himself. Only then he would give his full attention to the visitor. Whether they discussed his own affairs or those of his visitor, after some time he would say "Excuse me" and would return to his concentration on God. Even if one of his children happened to die, he would not be aware of what had happened till some time later." [9]

Further it is noted as part of the biography of the Sahikh that he was the principle spiritual successor of Khwaja Muin al-Din Sijzi. His father's name was Shaikh Kamal al-Din Ahmad Musa. He lost his father when he was only two and half years old. *Dalil al-Arifin* (Conversations of Muinuddin Chishti (d. 1236) whose compilation is attributed to Khwaja Bakhtiyar Kaki) is quoted as the source to describe his life prior to his arrival in India. It describes his spiritual teachers and long journeys undertaken with his preceptor in pursuit of learning and spiritual quest in major centres of Islamic learning and culture in Central Asia, Iran, and the Middle East. It is specifically noted that it was at Baghdad that Qutb al-Din joined his Chishti order and later followed his Shaykh to India.While *Siyar al-Awliya* is quoted his relation with other

Sufism in India and Central Asia

prominent contemporary sufis. Another work called *Silsilat al zahab* of Shaykh Muhammad Nur Bakhsh is also mentioned. Many anecdotes are cited on the authority of *Akhbar al-Akhyar*. While his nine aphorism are derived from *Fawaid as-salikin* (Conversations of Bakhtiyar Kaki), compiled by his disciple Farid al- Din Ganj-Shakar (d.1265).

Further, the author describes the well-known death events of Chishti Sufi masters Qutub al-Din Kaki, the pre-death ecstasy experienced by Khwaja Bakhtiyar Kaki, and of Nizam al-Din. The demise of Hazrat Qutub al-Din Kaki was an event of great significance to the Sufis. The episode is taken from *Siyar al-Awliya*. It is narrated that the Khawaja graced with his presence the Mehfil-i-Samaa at the Khanqah of Shaikh Ali Sijzi, a fellow disciple of Khwaja. When the Qawwal was recited the following verse of Ahmad-i-Jam (Ahmad of Jam, Persian Sufi, in the Seljuk period, a contemporary of Ghazali, nicknamed Zinda pil, Elephent Colossus b. 44/1049-50/536/1141. Ahmad's works were available in the library of Firuz Shah.)

"The martyrs of the dagger of tasleem (surrender to Allah's will) Each moment get a new life form the Unseen World."

Those slain by submission's dagger,

Each moment find new life from beyond'

(Ahmad-i-Jam d.536/1141)

This line so moved Khwaja that he was rushed home in state of trance. For four days and four nights he remained in ecstasy (in a state of *alam-i-tahayyur*). Regaining consciousness, the Khawaja desired the verse to be repeated each time he regained consciousness which always occurred at the time of obligatory prayers. He then lapsed back into an ecstatic state. On the fifth night, 14 Rabiul Awwal 633 A.H. (27th Novemeber 1235 A.D.) he departed to his heavenly abode. He lies buried in Mehroli (near the Qutub Minar), a suburb of present day in Delhi. Khwaja died on 14 Rabi I 633A.H. in the same year that Sultan Shamsuddin Iltitmish who was a contemporary and also a devotee of Khwaja, died on 14 Shaban. May God illuminate his grave! Shaikh Ali Sijzi, a disciple of Muin al-Din Chishti a contemporary of Sultan Iltutmish, is also derived from *Dalil al-Arifin*.[10] Khwaja Tatmaji, a son of Khwaja Qutub al-din is the other saint described who lies buried next to his father. He was a contemporary of Sultan Raziya who despite being a woman is said have possessed all the qualities of a king.[11]

Similarly, the event of the death of Shaykh Nizam al-Din Awliya (1243-3 April 1325) especially the emotional reaction of his learned and devoted disciple and friend, is recorded in the biography of Amir Khusrau. It is narrated that when Nizam al-din Awliya breathed his last, Khusrau was away in Bengal on Mohammad Tughlaq's royal mission. When he heard the news, he rushed back to Delhi. He wore black dress of mourning and went to visit his mentors' grave and behaved like a madnan due to utter grief which he felt on the passing away of his beloved teacher-friend. After this, it is said, Khusrau's condition started deteriorating and six months later he died. Sultan Ghiyasuddin Tughlaq also died after nine months. He is also buried near the grave of Shaikh.[12] This incident is remembered as the highest point in Khusrau's relationship with Nizam al-din. But the popular verse, "The beloved sleep on her couch with her face covered with her curled lock; Oh Khusrau, Return to your own home for the entire world is covered by night." is not mentioned.

Sadiq provided a detailed narrative of the life, thought and activities of Sultan al-Mashikh King of the saints, Shaikh Nizam al-Din Awliya (640-1/1243-4/725/3 April 1325), the foremost Indian saint of his generation in the Tughlaq capital. The author has freely drawn on the Chishti sources for the ideological profile of Shaykh as pointed out earlier.

"His full name was Muhammad bin Ahmad bin Ali Bukhari. He was called Sultan of the Shaykhs or king of the mystic (*shaikhs*) and Nizam al-Din Awliya. He was one of the dearly beloved of the house of God. The country of Hindustan due to the effects of his blessings has become a garden. His illumined tomb is the centre of pilgrimage of the sons of Adam until today. He was a contemporary of Sultan Alauddin whose reign experienced prosperity due to the prayers of Shaikh. Shaikh's barakat were the true cause of the glory of his reign."

On the authority of *Fuwad al-Fuad* and *Akhbar al-Akhyar* under the subtitle "Description of the death of Sultan al-Mashaikh may his grave be hallowed (*quddusu sirru-hu*), he wrote, "For forty days before his death Nizam al-Din ate nothing. As the end approached, he said, "The time of prayer has come. Have I said my prayers? If they replied," You have said them, he would reply, "Then I must say them again." He would perform every prayer twice and add, "I am going I am going." He instructed his servant Iqbal: "If anything of any sort remains in this house, it will have to be accounted for on the Day of judgment. You must distribute everything, except the minimum that is necessary for the daily subsistence of the dervishes. "But then he corrected himself: These are the effects of a dead man, why should they be preserved.? Give it all away and sweep the room clean "As soon as they cleared the storerooms, a host of people gathered and snatched the up and the goods. Then the servants pleaded we are poor men After you have gone, what will become of us." "The charity that will arrive on my tomb (rauzat) will suffice for you." "Who," they asked, "will be able to divide it among us?" "That men who is willing to relinquish his own portion," was the Shaikh's reply.[13] Thereafter, he bestowed his successorship (*khilafat*) and spiritual care of Delhi (wilayat-i-Dihli) upon Nasir al-Din Mahmud. He died at sunrise on Wednesday the 8th of Rabi al-akhir 725/AH.[14]

Shaykh Nasir al-Din Mahmud Chiragh-i-Dehli was the principal Khalifa of Hazrat Nizam al-Din Awliya. Indeed Shaykh Nasir al-Din Mahmud (d. 1356) is described as the foremost and most distinguished of the successors of Shaikh Nizam al-Din Awliya. He was known for knowledge, intellect and passion. He was heir to the spiritual mastery and knowledge of the mysteries possessed by his illustrious guide. After the death of Shaykh Nizam al-Din Awliya it was to him that the spiritual care of Delhi (*wilayat-i-Dehli*) passed. He was distinguished by his perfect loyalty to his Shaykh as well as his life of poverty, patience, forbearance and surrender to the will of God. His master advised him, "You ought to remain among the people, take upon yourself the burden of their hardships and calamities, and give them in return as much as you can provide."[15]

The author noted that Nizam al-Din Awliya was mentor and patron saint of the famed Amir Khusrau (1254-1325), the versatile and witty poet of India, lovingly styled as "God's Turk," by his mentor. Further the historian nonpareil Ziauddin Barani, (1285-1357) and Hasan Sijzi Dehlawi, the distinguished lay-disciples are also included in the dictionary of saints. Badaun-bornpoet and a sensitive lyricist Hasan Sijzi Dehlawi (d. 1328) who recorded the oral discourses of his beloved master, the well-known Fuwaid al Fuad thus not only preserved his chaste words for the future generations, but also initiated a distinct Indian literary genre called malfuz literature also finds but not a separate biography. Implicit in the biographies of these disciples was the idea that they acted as source of inspiration and as the embodiment of piety, learning and hope. Similarly, the renowned chronicler of Delhi Sultanat, Ziauddin Barani also found a place more as a lay disciple of Nizam al-Din Awliya than a scholar and historian. However, his works such as the history of Delhi Sultanat entitled Tarikh-i-Firuzshahi, Masir-i-Sadat, Inayatnama-i-Ilahi, Salat-i-kabir, Sana-i-Muhammadi and Hasratnama are also mentioned. The celebrated historian is described as an entertaining conversationalist and having been a friend of the poets Khusrau and Amir Hasan. He died in 758/1353 was buried near the grave of Nizam al-Din at Ghiyaspur.[16] Nafahat a-uns (Breezez of Intimacy) of Jami completed in 147, is quoted in his account of Khusrau and his relations with Hasan and Barani.[17]

Indo-Persian Sufi-poet and hagiographer Hamid bin Fazlullah popularly known as Shaikh Jamali (d. 1536) is also described in the most fulsome terms. He is said to have travelled extensively through out the Islamic world from Central Asia to the Maghrib and from Anatolia to Yamen and meet a number of prominent Sufis incuding Jami Maulana Nuruddin Abdur Rahman Jami (1414-92) the Persian poet, polymath, and Sufi a culminating figure in the elaboration of Perso-Islamic culture with whom he had interesting discussions in Herat. He associated himself intimately with Delhi Sultans. His relations with Sikandar Lodi were especially cordial on him death he wrote in a masnawi. After the overthrow of the Lodis by the Mughals he developed friendly relations with Humayun often accompanied later on military expeditions.

Sufism in India and Central Asia

He compiled a lengthy diwan and a mystical masnawi *Miraat al-Mani* and *Siyar al-Arifin* a *tazkira* of the Indian saints of Suhrawardiya and Chishti orders, a classic of hagiography which is also utilised by the author. He was a disciple of Samauddin Suhrawardy saint for whom he constructed a tomb. Shaikh Jamali died in the year 942AH/1536-7 and lay buried in the tomb which he constructed during his life time.[18]

The Naqshbandisilsila is the last of the *silsilas* described by the author. Among the prominent Shaykhs Sadiq provide a current biography of this mentor based upon his personal experiences and observations. Besides he also quoted the *Malfuzat*, letters and correspondences of the author to which it seems that he was privileged to have direct access. Sadiq paid rich emotional tribute to his murshid, mental and moral preceptor whom he reverentially called Hazrat-i-Ishan. Born in Kabul on 16 December 1563 he arrived in India from Kabul and made Delhi the centre of his spiritual activities which is also his final abode. He was a spiritual disciple of Maulana Khwajgi Amkangi (d.1600) (of Amkina near Samarqand) from whom he learnt the mystical practices of meditation *muraqaba* and collection *zikr*. Thereafter, he received his early education from Sadiq Halwai and in his company he went to Samarqand to pursue further studies. It was there where he cultivated a taste for *tasawwuf* and gave up his formal religious studies in favour of mystical quest. His mystical ideas were imbued with deep humanitarian spirit and compassion to the people of God. He endeavoured to sooth the hearts of those in distress. His influence soon spread far and wide. He advocated strict adherence to Shariate the practices of the Prophet (Sunnat) and denounced *bidat* or innovation in religious sphere. He practiced and also preached fidelity to *sharia* in political, social spheres as well as in the devotional life. He is lying buried near the Qadamgah of the Prophet Muhammad, Refuge of the Prophethood.[19] The author also produced fifty-five discourses of the saint.[20]

The biographical accounts of some of the prominent saints and disciples of Baqi Billah were show the popularity of the Naqshbandi silsila who worked for its spread in India as well as in other countries. He sought to highlight their role in strengthening and propagating the teachings of the order in India and abroad in the Islamic lands in the seventeenth century. Small townships like Sambhal, Jhinjhana, Saharanpur and Sirhind also came under the influence of the order. Sadiq provided biographical accounts of the four major khalifas: Taj al-Din (d.1642), Shaykh Khwaja Husamuddin (d.1633), Shaikh Ahmad Sirhindi Faruqui (1624), one of the major successor of Baqi Billah. (KS pp. 187-192) and Shaikh Ilahdad (1640) were some of his prominent successors.

Another distinguished khalifa of the Shaikh was Shaykh al-Arifin Mian Shaykh who belonged to the township of Sambhal and had the privilege to perform the Haj.[21] Through the efforts of Shaikh Taj the silsila spread far and wide including Makkah, Medina, Hejaz and Yemen. Another disciple and successor of Baqi Billah was Janab Mian Shaikh Ilahdad who is said to have remained occupied in the khanqah's people's services and he was the travellers who came and stayed in the hospice. He practised non-existence (*nisti*) and annihilation (*fana*). He was known for living in ecstasy and rapture.[22]

The other eminent disciple Khwaja Husamuddin Ahmad's activities were mainly concentrated in the twin capital cities Agra and Delhi. However, the case of Husamuddin Ahmad is also unique as having served the Mughal emperors later he gave it up to pursue the life of a mystic. He was born in 1569 at Qunduz in Badakhshan and came to India with his father in 1575. Born and brought up in Badakhshan he possessed a natural inclination for Hindustan. His ancestors had been associated with the Timurids and therefore they were received with open arms by Akbar. His father Qazi Nizam Badakhshi arrived in India and joined the court where he gradually rose to the high status of a noble (*amir*) and was honoured with the title of Qazi Khan and later in lieu of his outstanding military services rendered to the Mughal empire was granted the title of Ghazi Khan. Scion of a gentry's family Husamuddin began his life in the service of state as a high ranking imperial officer (*mansabdar*) gave up professional life in preference for saintly life when he was in the prime of his youth. He sought spiritual discipleship of Khwaja Baqi Billah. From Khwaja he learnt the path of a wayfarer (*suluk* and *tariq*) silent recollection or recollection in the heart (*zikr khafi*) and permission to enroll disciples.

Sufism in India and Central Asia

He led an extremely pious life and is said to have recited the complete text of the Holy Quran within two days. He remained occupied in dissemination of word of God among the seekers of truth.[23] He was an excellent poet and wrote verses. He was endowed with all the desirable human qualities. He sought to emphasis virtues such as patience and reliance upon God. When he died at Akbarabad in 1633 his body was brought to Delhi and buried in the tomb of Khwaja Baqi in Qadam Sharif. Sadiq Hamadani also composed a chronogram on his death. He described Husamuddin a fellow-mystic and close associate as one of the saintly figure whose existence was manifestation of divine mercy on earth. After the premature death of Baqi he took the responsibility and raised the children. He remarked that the popularity of the noble order called Naqshbandiya Ahrariya is due to the sincere efforts of him.[24]

The ideas of Shaikh Ahmad Sirhindi a pupil of Khwaja Baqi Billah chosen one of the *tariqa* and considered an embodiment of divine mystery had far reaching influences. He is described as a pivotal charismatic figure that developed new spiritual practices and redefined the identity of Sufi. Sirhindi also founded a new branch the Mujaddidi of the order. As a result some of the major sufistic influences emanated from the Indian soil. The doctrine of *Wahdat al-shuhud* the oneness of the sight [of God] the shadow of God cannot, come under any circumstances. It was to be identical to God which was propounded by Shaikh Ahmad in three volumes of his letters known as *Maktubat-i-Rabbani*. He rejected Ibn al-Arabi's doctrine of *Wahdat al wujud* unity of existence, divine unity is not *Wahdat al-wujud* as he [God] is not one with anything. He is the-Supreme and All Holy-and the world is the world.' This version of *tariqa* called Mujaddadiya from *mujaddid* or renovator a name by which Ahmad Sirhindi became commonly known was adopted by all Naqshbandi groups throughout the Muslim world. Sufism underwent a great doctrinal change which had major social and political consequences in Central Asia at the end of the seventeenth century when Central Asian Sheikhs became aware of it. Sadiq Hamadani the fellow disciple noted: Before his death my spiritual preceptor, my exalted. Khwaja Baqi Billah was inclined towards the ideas of Shikh Alauddaula Simnami (1261-1336) [a passionate exponent of *Wahdat us shuhud* (unity of

98   Chapter 7 Kalimat al-Sadiqin: A Sufi Biographical Account

perception)] and he began to criticize the ideas of Muhiuddin Ibn al-Arabi (d.1240) under the influence of his own major disciple Shaikh Ahmad Sirhindi Faruqi.[25] Sadiq Hamadani observed that Shaikh Ahmad laid great stress on the order's duty to remain faithful to the commandments of Quran. He made Sufism subservient to Sharia. He preached fidelity to Sharia in the political and social spheres as well as devotional life. He advocated rejection of all forms of innovation in Islam and declared that Islam represented absolute perfection. He refused blind imitation and advocated restoration of Muslim law that is *sharia* based on a direct interpretation of the Holy *Quran* and *Hadith*. He was an embodiment of divine mysteries.

References

[1]Cf. Marcia K. Hermansen and Bruce B. Lawrence, "Indo-Persian Tazkiras as Memorative Communications," David Gilmartin, Bruce Lawrence, (eds.) *Beyond Turk and Hindu: Rethinking Religious identities in Islamicate South Asia*, India Research Press, 2002, p.150.

[2]Muhammad SadiqDehlawi Kashmiri Hamadani, *Kalimat al-Sadiqin*, ed., Muhammad SaleemAkhtar, Islamabad:Iran Pakistan Research Centre, 1988.

[3]Firuz Shah Tughlaq constructed the Sacred Enclosure of Qadam Sharif (1374) known as the Holy Footprint as a final resting place for his son Fateh Khan.

[4]*Kalimat*, pp. 4–5.

[5]Amir Khusrau, *Qiran al-Sadayn* (Lucknow: Newal Kishore, 1875) pp. 22–23.

[6]*Siyar al-Awliya fi Muhabbat al-Haq Jalla wa ala*" Muhibb-i-Hind Press, Delhi, 1889.

[7]*Kalimat*, pp. 139–40.

[8]*Kalimat*, pp. 157–8.

[9]*Kalimat*, p. 7.

[10]*Kalimat*, pp. 12–13.

[11]*Kalimat*, p. 14.

[12]Kalimat, pp. 81–86.

[13]*Kalimat*, pp. 44–45.

[14]Kalimat, pp. 44–5.

[15]Kalimat, pp. 55–63.

[16]Kalimat, pp. 87–89.

[17]*Kalimat*, pp.83, 87.

[18]*Kalimat*, pp. 122-3, The tombs of the poet and that of his teacher and mentor Shaikh

Samauddin and a mosque known as Jamali Kamali mosque built in red sandstone with marble embellishment that stands today in the heritage city, located in Archaeological Park in Mehrauli built by the saint himself and embellished with his own verses see, , *Monuments of Delhi Lasting Splendour of the Great Mughals and Others*, Compiled by Maulvi Zafar Hasan, ed. J.A. Page Vol. III, Mehrauli Zail, Aryan Books International, New Delhi, for a mosque of Maulana pp. 62, tomb of Maulana Jamali 91–94.

[19]For the description of the grave of Khwaja Baqi Billah see, *Monuments of Delhi Lasting Splendour of the Great Mughals and Others*, Compiled by Maulvi Zafar Hasan, ed. J.A.Page Vol. II, Delhi Zail, Aryan Books International, New Delhi, pp. 237–39.

[20]Kalimat pp. 161–182.

[21]Kalimat, pp. 192–3.

[22]Kalimat, pp.192–3.

[23]*Shah Jahan-Nama* (Book of Shahjahan)History 309, Library of Salar Jung Museum, Hyderabad (Andhra Pradesh).folios 918-9, Badshahnama, 333-4, Amal-i-Saleh Vol. 3, p. 364.

[24]Sadiq Hamadani Kashmiri Dehlawi, *Tabaqat-e-Shahjahani*, ed. Md. Ehteshamuddin, Institute of Persian Research, Aligarh Muslim University, Aligarh 2 Volumes, 2013, Vol. 2, pp 244-5, *Kalimat*, pp. 183–7.

[25]*Kalimat*, pp. 187–88.

CHAPTER 8

Central Asia to India: Immigration of Sufis and Urbanization in Medieval Rajasthan

Jibraeil

The study of Sufis and Sufism is attracting the attention of historians. No doubt their role in spreading the message of love and devotion made them popular among different strata of people. Consequently, large number of people started together in and around the seat of the saints. Many of the areas about Sufis have been studied by the scholars during the medieval society[1]. As a result an enormous corpus of literature has emerged on various aspects related to the Sufis and Sufism. One of the most significant areas where the Sufis contribution seems to be very effective was the inter-connections of their working centres and occurrence of the trade and commerce and its relations with Central Asia which directly or indirectly contributed to the urban settlement in and around India.

The throng of the people in large numbers at a place played a constructive role in the process of urbanization. At initial stage the preference of the saints was to stay in remote areas (*i.e.* Khwaja Hamiduddin Nagauri firstly settled down at Shiwal, a remote area of Nagaur which gradually developed into a *qasba*) but later on their popularity made these areas more populous and thus gradually developed into large townships and big urban centres. These large settlements attracted the attention of the traders and shop-keepers. Even the followers of the saints themselves adopted some small time trading activities for their livelihood, while Islam too accepted trade and commerce as a preferred profession. Sufi settlement gave it a further fillip[2]. Around which small trading activities were started and gradually big markets were developed as the number of devotees increased and the settlement was expanded.

Thus, the commercial enterprises, a prerequisite for sustaining any urban centre were embedded in the Sufi philosophy and catapulted the growth of urban centres. The regions where the Sufis established their *Khanqahs,* after their death (*wafaat*) their *mazaars* (mausoleum), attracted a large number of people to flock to the town and cities, thus giving rise to urban population.[3] To this activities, the centres transformed into prosperity and even today is advantageous for those people who are directly or indirectly involved in this activities. Through this study, our attempt is to highlight the contribution of Sufis in the making of the urban centres especially in Rajasthan during medieval period.

Apart from the residential houses for the laity, other constructions required by the growing population consisted of reservoirs, *bazaars,* mosques, *sarais,* building tanks, wells, hospitals, *madarsas, maktabs,* gardens, streets and other works of public utility.[4] Similarly, the communication system, both by road and if possible by the river, would have to be improved, linking the town with other major urban centres of the region.[5] The urban course of development was also affected by the extent to which the kings wish to invest in a particular town.[6]

The information about the Sufi saints and their activities in Rajasthan is available in abundance. They appeared in the region before coming of the Turks in India. They had started preaching activities on the western and northern outskirts of Rajasthan from the 8th century onwards. Among prominent Sufis who visited this desert region were Syed Roshan Ali, Syed Mohammad Tahir, Syed Anas Mashhadi and Hamiduddin Rehani in last decade of the eleventh century A.D.[7] they had visited Ajmer, Khatu, Didwana, and Nagaur respectively. Even after the conquest of India by the Turks, Sufism continued to flourish in the different centres of the country. [8] To better understanding paper is divided into three parts. First: Ajmer a great centre of Chishti Silsila; Second: Nagaur a centre of many Sufis and Third: Other centres of Sufis in Rajasthan (See Map-I).

Map-I: Plotted Sufi Centres of Medieval Rajasthan

Khwaja Moinuddin Chishti came to India from Chisht of Central Asia. He travelled in the last quarter of the twelfth century from Chisht to Ghazni then to Lahore and from this place to Multan then via near Patiala to Delhi and finally settled down at Ajmer[9]. His followers formed the popular Chishti[10] order. He commanded the respect of all the section of the society and continued to do even today. It is very significant that during the course of invasion of Turks and expansion of missionary activities, Muslim traders, craftsmen and soldiers also settled down in and around Ajmer, Nagaur etc. also encouraged of construction of mosques, tombs and involved in the religious fairs.[11] Firstly focused at Ajmer, is centrally situated in Rajasthan, was known by various names[12], founded at the foot of the hills on which stands the renowned fort now called Taragarh. In a final battle, Prithviraj-III defeated by Mohammad Ghori in 1192 A.D. and he took possession of Ajmer[13]. After a long time, Akbar obtained its possession and made it headquarter for his operations in Rajputana and Gujarat. Ajmer enjoyed considerable peace during the Mughal rulers[14].

104 Chapter 8 Central Asia to India: Immigration of Sufis....

Abul Fazl in his *Akbarnama*[15] records that Akbar visited Ajmer several times, and consequently the route of Agra to Ajmer developed. Large numbers of *sarais* were constructed for the benefit of traders. These *sarais* were furnished with lodging, wells and mosques with the *muezzins* and *imams*, separate boards for the Muslims and Hindus and fodder for their animals[16]. He walked from Agra to Ajmer, covering about 10 or 12 *Km* (25 to 30 miles) in a day and prayed for son[17]. A list of the emperors halting places[18] are mentioned below.[19] [See Map-II]

1. Mandhaker (Medhakar/Mindhakar)

2. Fatehpur

3. Passed Khanua, halted near Juna

4. Koraha

5. Basarwan (Bhasawar/Bhusawar)

6 Toda (Toda Bhim)

7. Kalawali (Karauli)

8. Kharandi

9. Disa (Dausa/Daosa)

10. Passed Hansmahal and encamped near Phulmahal

11. Sanganir (Sanganer)

12. Near Neota (Niota)

13. Jhak near Muizzabad (Mozabad/Muzamabad)

14. Sakhun (Sakoon)

15. Kajbul (Khajpur)

16. The Holy dwelling of the Khwaja in Ajmer.

Sufism in India and Central Asia

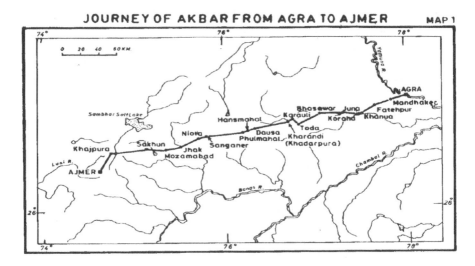

Map-II: Journey of Akbar from Agra to Ajmer

(Seat of Khwaja Moinuddin Chishti) based on *Akbarnama*[20]

Abul Fazl states about Mandhaker that the perfection and miracles of the Khwaja were often on the theme of discourses in the assemblies of his majesty. This suggests that the *dargah* of Khwaja Moinuddin Chishti had gained a significant position in the religious circles even before the advent of the Mughals. The popularity of the *dargah* reached to rural areas. While on a hunting expedition at Mindhaker (Medhakar) in January 1562, the young Emperor heard some minstrel singing about the glories and virtues of the great Khwaja of Ajmer. As Akbar was a seeker of divine truth, the impact of these songs made him ecstatic. In spite of the pleas of his followers against going to remote areas, where there is a danger from refractory elements, he did not give heed to their advice. He left Ajmer with a few attendants, sending message to Maham Anga, and other royal paraphernalia to join him by way of Mewat[21].

Akbar reached Ajmer and spent several days in devotion of God and good works. He distributed gifts among the attendants of the Shrine.[22] His Majesty (HM) also arranged for the management of the Shrine, and for the treatment of pilgrims and for the erection of mosques and *Khanqahs* in the territory[23]. In his third visit to Shrine, an order was issued for repairing and enlarging the fort of Ajmer. He also made suitable dwellings and gardens by the order of the nobles and officers[24]. Badaoni said that during the period of Akbar, on the Agra – Ajmer route a lofty college and high and spacious palaces were built on the road. His Majesty's extreme devotion induced him every year to go for a pilgrimage to that city and so he ordered a palace to be built at every stage between Agra and Ajmer and a pillar to be erected and a well sunk at every *kos,* which provided both shelter and water to the weary traveller.[25] Thus, the annual visit of Akbar to the Shrine, naturally enhanced its prestige and development of the Shrine. Abul Fazal also professes great regard and love for the Chishti saints[26]. Every winter in honour of Khwaja and Miran Sahib a fair (*urs*) was held, in present, held at Ajmer. It attracted thousands of pilgrims from all over India.[27] About festival; it is significant that the Hindu peasant festival was celebrated at *dargah* by the Muslims also. On the occasion of the *Holi,* the Hindus assembled at the main gate of *dargah,* reciting verses in praise of Khwaja Sahib, and rubbed *gulal* (red powder) at the steps of the gate. On the *Diwali* festival lamps were lighted at the *dargah* by Hindu devotees, [28] and the *dargah* was illuminated on this festival.[29] Supply of rose flowers and sandal, etc. by the Hindus must be taken note of.[30]

Akbar left Ajmer and started his journey towards Nagaur after wishing the *Dargah* of Khwaja Moinuddin Chishti on November 3, 1570 (Friday 4 *Jamadiul Aakhir,* H. 978)[31]. After the journey of 12 consecutive days finally Akbar reached at Nagaur on November 15, 1570 (Wednesday 15 *Jamadiul Aakhir* H. 978)[32] (See Map-III). He was welcomed at Nagaur by Khan-I Kalan Mir Mohammad who also organized a Lunch (*Bhoj*) in the respect of Akbar[33]. The Emperor was participated his *bhoj* and gifted him. Meanwhile, Emperor saw a *talab*. The people of the area had requested to emperor Akbar and said that the affluence and delight of the villages of Nagaur are depend, on these three *talabs* whereas one of them is Kayadaani presently called as Gilani or Ginani *talab*[34]. Akbar issued an order to clean and renovate all the water structures of the *qasba.* Later on, Ginani tank was reconstructed by Raja Rai Singh Rathore, elder son of Rao Amar Singh Rathore[35]. Second was Shamshi *talab* repaired by the order of Akbar [36]. Third was Shakkar *talab*, originally was known as Kukkur *talab* [37]. It has its own history which is explained in details by M.H. Siddiqui in his work on Nagaur[38]. We have surveyed this *talab* and the other monuments which are erected on the bank of this very large tank.

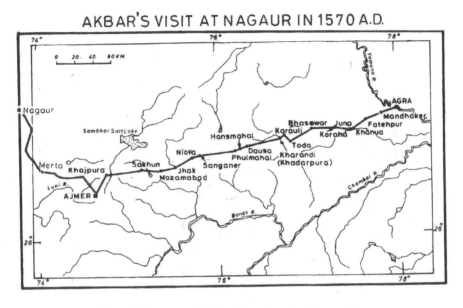

Map-III: Journey of Akbar from Agra to Nagaur via

Ajmer in AD 1570

The frequent visits of the rulers (especially Akbar) to Ajmer due to the Shrine of Khwaja Moinuddin Chishti benefited the people to settled around it. He initiated construction activities in *dargah* and outside it. Large numbers of buildings were constructed by his order. This created employment opportunities for the large number of city-dwellers. Artisans, masons, building workers, water-carriers and stone-cutters that got employment. Employment opportunities must have attracted large number of craftsman and skilled labours from outside Ajmer. This had enlarged the urban population of the city.

II Nagaur had been a well-known centre of Sufis and presently it is considered as the heritage town of India in general and Rajasthan in particular.[39] It is said that this *qasba* was reached at peak during the period of Shaikh Hamiduddin Nagauri (*Chishti Silsila*) and Qazi Hamiduddin Nagauri (*Suhrawardi Silsila*). After that, it was developed as the big mart town and junction of trade and commerce.[40]

Nagaur is the chief town of the same name in Jodhpur division of Rajasthan and lies in the latitude 27°12'N and longitude 73°44'E.[41] It was a place of great antiquity, [42] and being situated in the centre of Rajasthan; it shares its border with several other districts of the state. On the north, it is bounded by Bikaner and Churu, on the east, by Sikar and Jaipur, on the south, by Ajmer and Pali and on the west, by Jodhpur.[43] It is known in history as an important centre of Jainism[44] and Sufism[45]. After the defeat of Prithviraj-III in 1192 by Mohammad Ghori, it passed into the hands of Muslim rulers, who governed this place through a number of Turkish governors from 1195 AD. onwards[46]. According to Isami, Qazi Hamiduddin Nagori was appointed as *qazi* (Justice) of Nagaur, after the second battle of Tarain (1192). Nagaur was also a mint town under the Muslim Sultan of Delhi[47]. According to the different sources, minting of gold, [48] silver, and copper were much more familiar in the period of Sultan Shamsuddin Iltutmish[49], Ghiyasuddin Balban[50] and Mughal emperor Akbar[51]. Firoz Khan the son of Shams Khan Dandani, the founder of Khanzada Dynasty of Nagaur was also involved to mint the *tanka* coin at Nagaur in A.D. 1433.[52]

The above information shows the importance of Nagaur in Medieval Rajasthan. At the same time, the *qasba* was a prominent religious centre for the Jain while from very early times, even after the establishment of the Muslim rule, the activities of Jainism continued and constructed Jaina temples over there.[53] With the Muslim conquest of Nagaur, the influence of Islam is also noticed. The famous saints Rehani, Shaikh Hamiduddin Nagauri and Qazi Hamiduddin etc. resided at Nagaur and propagated the teachings of love and devotion[54]. Many people were attracted towards the faith and converted to Islam. Prominent among them was Rai Bisala, a feudatory of Prithviraj –III. After his conversion, he also built a mosque[55]. In the subsequent periods, several mosques were constructed.[56]

Nagaur was one of the important Sufi centres of Rajasthan and was well connected with other Sufi centres of Rajasthan like Ajmer, Ladnun etc. which provided opportunities directly or indirectly to the merchants or to those who were regularly visiting the Shrines. The expansion of routes in any region depends on numerous factors; particularly its geographical conditions favourable to traveling, the volume of trade, the nature of occupation of the bulk of the people and the attitude of the state.[57] Besides this, an important factor in the trade system is the travellers and the merchants, who played a vital role in the exploration of routes. They are the sort of people who made the world known by moving relentlessly from east to west and north to south[58] .With the coming of the Turks and Mughals and with the industrial and agricultural development, attention was given to Rajasthan traffic, in order to join new marts or to find new roads for marching armies etc[59]. Thus the town is a good marketing and trade centre for the adjoining rural population. Muslim families of the town were also known for their expert knowledge of dyeing and printing of *chundaris* and *saris*[60].

Its location on the Mughal highway and many favourable trade routes are proved for its growth in urban centre. A significant example is explored. A trader of Nagaur carried mustard (*sarso*) from Nagaur and sold it to Multan and further carried cotton from Multan which sold to Nagaur. The importance of that particular trader is also mentioned in the Persian sources that he was involved as a mediator for the correspondence between Shaikh Bahauddin Zakaria Suhrawardi of Multan and Shaikh Hamiduddin Chishti of Nagaur.[61] This information proves that Nagaur was connected with Multan by trade route. Besides this, many more routes were extremely important both concerning battles and trading point of views were also passing through Nagaur. A route from Delhi to Malwa was attached with Gwalior and Nagaur[62]. The important routes that passed through Nagaur can be shown below:

(A) External Trade Routes (Based on Epigraphic and Persian Sources):

Nagaur to Multan[63] : This route frequently used by a trader (See Map-IV).

Delhi to Malwa[64] : Gwalior and Nagaur attached with this route.

Agra to Nagaur[65] : Agra-Tonk-Toda[66]-Nagaur.

Mewat to Bikaner[67] : Mewat Region-Nagaur-Bikaner.

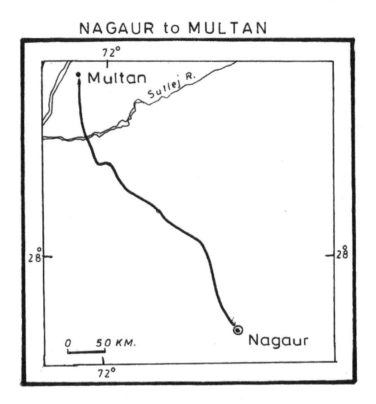

Map-IV: Nagaur to Multan

(B) External Trade Routes (Based on Persian, Rajasthani and other Sources):

Multan to Jodhpur[68]: Multan-Bahawalpur-Pugal-Bikaner-Nagaur-Jodhpur.

Jodhpur to Kashmir[69]: Jodhpur-Nagaur-Hardesar-Nohar-Sirsa-Bhatinda - Amritsar - Kashmir.

Bikaner to Deccan[70]: Bikaner - Nagaur-Merta-Bundi-Kota-Jhalara Patan- Ujjai-Deccan.

Delhi to Ahmadabad/Gujrat[71]: Delhi-Narayana-Narhad-Reni-Nagaur Ajmer-Ahmadabad/Gujrat

Agra to Ahmadabad/Gujarat[72]: Agra-Nagaur- Ahmadabad/Gujarat

Ajmer to Ahmadabad[73]: Nagaur was connected to this route.

Nagaur to Ayodhya[74]: Nagaur-Ajmer-Ayodhya.

Ajmer to Jodhpur[75]: Ajmer-Nagaur-Bikaner-Jodhpur.

(C) Internal Trade Routes (Based on Persian, Rajasthani and other Sources):

There were many internal trade routes which were connected to the important towns (Sufi centres) of Rajasthan with each other. These routes were highly beneficial to the traders, *banjaras*, and provided such type of other transport facilities, if needed. The important internal routes mentioned as below:

Nagaur to Pugal : Nagaur-Bikaner-Pugal[76]

Kota to Nagaur : Kota-Bundi-Deoli-Ajmer-Merta-Nagaur[77]

Bikaner to Jaipur : Bikaner-Nagaur-Rupnagar-Jaipur[78]

Bikaner to (Jodhpur) : Bikaner-Nagaur-Khiwasar-Jodhpur(Mandor)[79]

Bikaner to Pali : Bikaner-Nagaur-Jodhpur-Pali[80]

Bikaner to Udaipur: Bikaner-Nagaur-Pali-Desuri-Udaipur[81]

Rajgarh to Pali: Rajgarh-Churu-Nawalgarh-Didwana-Nagaur-Pali[82]

Jaisalmer to Jaipur: Jaisalmer-Pokaran-Phalodi-Nagaur-Rupnagar-Jaipur[83]

Jhunjhunu to Pali: Jhunjhunu-Fatehpur-Ladnun-Didwana-Nagaur-Pali[84]

Ajmer to Anupgarh: Ajmer-Merta-Nagaur-Bikaner-Mahajan-Anupgarh[85]

INTERNAL TRADE ROUTES
(MEDIEVAL RAJASTHAN)

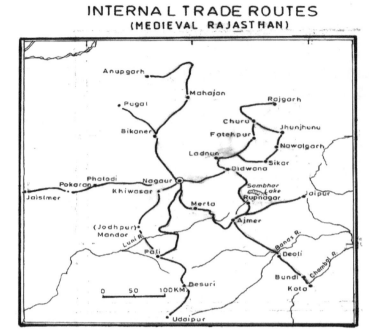

Map-V

The above trade routes were helpful in the growth of both internal and external trade of Nagaur and Ajmer during the medieval period. It was because of trade routes that the traders could frequently move with their goods, not only at the seats of Khwaja Hamiduddin Nagauri of Nagaur, Khwaja Moinuddin Chishti of Ajmer but other parts of Rajasthan as well as India.

Apart from this, following are the important Sufi saints who either visited are permanently settled at Nagaur and other centres of Rajasthan.[86]

Hamiduddin Rehani: His Shrine is situated near Bakhatsagar. He constructed a building which even today existed at Nohars of *Oswals* in Nagaur.

Qazi Hamiduddin Nagauri: He was the founder of Suhrawardi Silsila in the areas of Nagaur. He was an eminent scholar, appointed as *Qazi*, by Mohammad Ghori, was the first *Qazi* of Nagaur, continued on his post till the end of the reign of Iltutmish[87]. After the death of Iltutmish, *Qazi*, finally, shifted to the *Khanqah* of Khwaja Bakhtiyar Kaki in Delhi, died and buried

Sufism in India and Central Asia

here on November 1246 A.D.[88] Even today the existence of Suhrawardiya Silsila is present at *Mohalla* Suhrawardiya and at village Rohel Qaziyan near Nagaur.[89]

Sufi Shaikh Hamiduddin Nagauri (Siwal or Suwali): He was an eminent scholar and *murid* of Khwaja Moinuddin Chishti, appointed at Nagaur for the preaching of Chishtia Silsilah.[90] He passed almost the whole of his means of subsistence being a plot of land about the size required for pitching a tent. The Sheikh cultivated this himself, to appears to be a scientific and intensive way, and did not desire anything more than what the land produced.[91] He was very much involved for providing education to the persons residing in Nagaur and out of it. Sultan of Bengal, Ghiyasuddin (1367-1373) took education from him.[92] Thus the *murids* and the family member of Chishtia Sufi Hamiduddin Nagauri continued preaching of that Silsila at Nagaur and out of that place, during the period of Mughal's and even continued later.

Shaikh Fariduddin Nagauri: He was the grandson of Shaikh Hamiduddin Nagauri. Died in Delhi during the reign of Mohammad-bin-Tughlaq.[93]

Khwaja Hussain Nagauri: He was one of the descendants of Shaikh Hamiduddin Nagauri, visited the court of Sultan Ghiyasuddin (A.D. 1469-1500) of Malwa to see the hair of the Prophet. During his return journey, the Sultan offered a huge amount which the Shaikh reluctantly accepted but spent the whole amount in the construction of the mausoleum of Khwaja Moinuddin Chishti of Ajmer and Khwaja Hamiduddin Nagauri of Nagaur.

Shaikh Ahmad Khattu: In spite of Chishtia and Suhrawardiya, Maghribi Silsila was also established in a *pargana* Bara Khattu in Rajasthan. Its founder was Baba Shaikh Ishaq Maghribi, who was related to the African community and settled at Khattu.[94] He, as a boy received instructions from Baba Ishaq and lived there with him for a number of years. Baba Ishaq died and was buried in a grave which was dug during his illness under his own supervision.[95] Shaikh Ahmad set out on pilgrimage

114 Chapter 8 Central Asia to India: Immigration of Sufis....

to holy places in Arabia, Macca (for *Haj*) Iraq and Iran. He travelled to Arabia and stayed at Madina, after that returned to Delhi during the reign of Firoz Shah Tughlaq. From Delhi, he went to Khattu again and finally, he settled at Sarkhej in Gujarat on the request of Zafar Khan, the Sultan of Gujarat.[96] Here he died and was buried. His *Maqbara* there was constructed by Sultan of Gujarat.[97]

Other Centres of Sufis

Numbers of urban centres have been developed in Rajasthan during medieval times due to the settlement of Sufi saints who came to the different corners from the Central Asia or nearby areas. Some of them are being explained below:

Narhad Town: It was a flourishing town in the past is clear from the old remains of temples, images and other buildings.[98] In the 14th century it was mint town itself remained a place of pilgrimage in early and later medieval period. This place was ruled by the Pathan in the 14th and 15th centuries, a famous mosque was built during the reign of Pathans.[99] The Piraji of Narhad was the *Diwan* of Khwaja Moinuddin Chishti of Ajmer. During the rule of Pathan, water reservoirs particularly wells were constructed for the purpose of cultivation.[100]

Fatehpur Town: In this town there is a *dargah* of *Pir Haji* Nizamuddin Chishti (Nazmuddin),[101] where an annual *urs* fair is held.[102] Here, for commercial purpose, the famous *Churan Chatni,* Ayurvedic Medicines, *agarbatti, iter, zafran, panmasala* and candles were sold and also exported.[103]

Sikar Town: There is a *dargah* of *Hazrat* Shah Wali Mohammad Chishti, where an annual *urs* is held.[104]

Jhunjhunu Town: According to the sources, the family members of the Shaikh Kamaluddin dispersed and settled at different places considered as Jhunjhunu, Sikar and Fatehpur.[105] Shaikh Abdul Qadir was contemporary of Akbar who gifted a *mauza Bakara* at the distance of 3 *km* of southern of Jhunjhunu to Shaikh.[106] A *madarsha* was started in

Jhunjhunu town namely Qamrul Islam, after a well-known and greatly respected Muslim saints of the district, Hazrat Shah Oamruddin.[107]

Singhana Town: Shah Ghulam Imam Nickname Shaikh Manu, died in 1793, his *mazaar* is situated in the area of *qasba* Singhana.[108]

Pali Town: Shaikh Ghulam Moinuddin nickname Chandshah, his *mazaar* is situated in the area of Pali.[109]

Kapasan Town: Shaikh Abdurrazzak was born at a village of Gujarat and involved in devotion in the areas of Rajasthan and finally settled at a village Kapasan in Mewar now popularly known as Deewanashah. Earlier Kapasan was a small village but after his death, a shrine was constructed and now it is designed into a town.[110]

Galiakot: It is situated on the banks of the Mahi River and about 50 km south – east of Dungarpur town and is the important Bohra Muslim Pilgrimage centre of the region.[111] This town is famous for the tomb of the saint Syedi Fakhruddin, who spread the message of prophet of Islam in the medieval period. Each year, thousands of Daudi Bohra devotees and many more Muslims assemble come here from all over the country at the time of the annual *Urs*, which is held from 27th day of Muharram, the first month of *Hijri* calendar (Islamic Calendar) to pay homage to the saint.[112] Syedi Fakhruddin was a highly religious person with an ascetic temperament. He was known for his learning and saintliness[113].In the course of his wandering; he died at Galiakot village and was buried there. The village has since then become a place of pilgrimage for the Daudi Bohras.[114] The major work on the shrine started about 400 years ago, and the present shape to the dome was given in around A.D. 1954.[115] In the year of 1968, the shrine of Fakhruddin at Galiakot was visited by 12,000 devotees during the first week of the month of May, when the *Urs* was held.[116] Besides the Bohras, others are also visiting this centre. Due to the frequent visits of the Bohra Muslims from the every corner of Rajasthan as well as the outside of the State *i.e.* Gujarat and Surat.[117] Thus it took the designation of a town and developed as a trading centre which is connected by a trade route of Dungarpur to Banswara onwards.

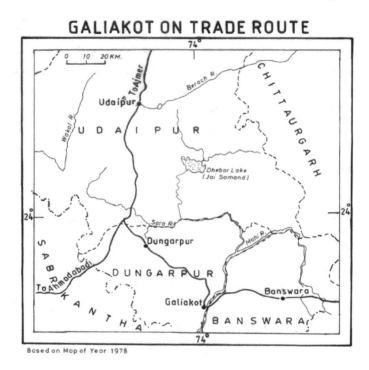

Map-VI

Above is a cursory survey of the Sufi activities in Rajasthan, in which we explored many urban centres where Sufi shrines are attracting the others every day in general and on the occasion of *urs* in particular. Through this survey we are in position to say that the teachings of the Sufi saints had a great impact on the people of different social strata irrespective of religion, caste and creed. Gathering of large number of people in and around the seat of the *dargah* gave boost up to the new settlement. Around which small trading activities were started and gradually big markets were developed as the number of devotees increased and the settlement was expanded. Even the Shrines flourished much when any king or reputed nobles were visiting the Shrines. In this regard Akbar's visit at Ajmer and Nagaur is the finest example. At the occasions of annual celebrations *(urs)* and the *muharram* large number of pilgrims from outside also gave impetus to the trading activities. The devotion of the Mughal rulers and local *zamindars* to the saint also played a significant role in the development of a place into urban centre. Their construction activities created employment opportunities for different kinds of people. Large number of skilled and unskilled workers gathered there and enlarged the population. Lastly these centres became the place of love and affection. Adoption of local customs and traditions by the saints also played an important role in promoting the concept of brotherhood, which also became an important factor for the expansion of the Sufi areas in the urban centres.

References

[1] Khaliq Ahmad Nizami, *Some Aspects of Religion and Politics in India during the Thirteenth Century,* Idara-i-Adabiyat-i-Delli, Second Edition, Delhi, 1974. Saiyid Athar Abbas Rizvi, *A History of Sufism in India,* Vol. I, Munshiram Manoharlal, New Delhi, 1978. Iqtidar Husain Siddiqui, *Mughal Relations with the Indian Ruling Elite*, Munshiram Manoharlal, New Delhi, 1983. Many more works by Historians of Aligarh School and others like Simon Digby, Refaqat Ali Khan, S.M. Azizuddin Husain, etc.

[2] Neeru Misra, *Sufism: The Social Bond in Medieval India* An Introductory Articles of Sufis and Sufism, edited by Neeru Misra, Manohar Publication, Delhi, 2004, p. 19. [The Prophet Hazrat Mohammad (PBUH) himself had interest in trade and before his mission, when he was at 12 gone to Syria for trade with his uncle. A trade and commerce has found wide recognition in Islamic and Sufi literature]. See Jibraeil, 'Nagaur: A Trading Junction in Medieval Rajasthan', published in a proceeding entitled *History of Marwar prior to Rao Jodha,* edited by Mahendra Singh Nagar, Published by Rajasthani Granthagar , Jodhpur, 2011, pp. 215-226. Another article of Jibraeil, 'Contribution of Sufis in the Growth of Urban Centres in Rajasthan during the Eighteenth Century', published in a proceeding entitled *Sufi Movement in Rajasthan,* edited by S.M. Azizuddin Husain, Published by Idarah-i-Adabiyat-i-Delli Delhi, 2007, pp. 62-75.

[3] M.A. Khan, 'Sufis and their Contribution in the process of Urbanization', an article in *Sufis,* edited by Neeru Misra, op. cit., p. 93.

[4] H.K. Naqvi, *Urbanization and Urban Centres under the Great Mughals,* IIOAS, Simla, 1972, pp. 5-8.

[5] Ibid.

[6] Ibid., p. 9. See Jibraeil, 'A Study of Towns Enroute from Agra to Ajmer Based on the *Akbarnama'*, in a Journal *Juni Khyat,* edited by B.L. Bhadani, Marubhumi Shodh Sansthan, Sridungargarh (Bikaner), 2011, pp. 85-95. Also see articles of Z.A. Khan, 'In Pursuit of Mughal Highways: A Study of Road Alignments Based on the Kos Pillars', published at the 45th Session of IHC, Annamalai, 1984, pp. 320-329.

[7] Khaleel Tanveer, 'Nagaur Ke Sufi Aur Unka Yogdan'(Hindi Article) in *Nagaur Ka Rajnitik Aur Sanskritik Vaibhav,* edited by D.B. Ksheersagar and Naval Krishan, Jodhpur, 1998, p. 75. [He cited *Ifazat-i- Hamdi* (Urdu), p. 7: But still needed verification of the dates].

[8]Neeru Misra, *Sufism: The Social Bond in Medieval India* An Introductory Article of Sufis and Sufism, op. cit., p. 17.

[9]Ibid., p. 15.

[10]Ibid., pp. 25-26. (It appears that the Chisht order derived its name from the Chishti town of Afghanistan which would have been the dwelling place of several Sufi saints of order).

[11]G.N. Sharma, *Rajasthan through the Ages,* Vol. -II, Rajasthan State Archives, Bikaner, 1990, pp. 337-38.

[12]K.C. Jain, *Ancient Cities and Towns of Rajasthan,* Delhi, 1972, p. 130.

[13]Ibid., p. 303.

[14]Ibid.

[15]Abul Fazal, *Akbarnama,* Translated into English by H. Beveridge, Vol.-II, rpt., Delhi, 1993, pp. 240-43.

[16]H.K. Naqvi, op. cit., p. 66.

[17]Ibid.

[18]Abul Fazal, *Akbarnama,* op. cit., pp. 510.

[19]Ajmer is 228 miles, west of Agra.

[20]Jibraeil, 'A Study of Towns Enroute from Agra to Ajmer Based on the *Akbarnama'*, op. cit., 2011, pp. 85-95.

[21]Abul Fazl, *Akbarnama,* Vol.-II, op. cit., p. 510. Also see attached Map-IV which is prepared as Journey of Akbar from Agra to Ajmer.

[22]Abul Fazl, *Akbarnama,* op. cit., p. 510.-11.

[23]Ibid.

[24]Ibid., pp. 516-17.

[25]Al-Badaoni, *Muntakhabut-Tawarikh,* Vol.-II, translated into English by W.H. Lowe, p. 176.

[26]Abul Fazal, *Ain-i-Akbari*, text-III, p. 202, English translation by Col. H.S. Jarrette, Vol.-II, Delhi, Edt. III, 1978. p. 388.

[27]G.N.Sharma, op. cit., p.338.

[28]S.L.H. Moini, 'The Hindu and the *Dargah* of Ajmer', An article in *Art and Culture,* edited by A.J. Qaisar and S.P. Verma, Jaipur, 1993, pp. 203-220. [In the function of *dargah* some of the post were enjoyed by Hindus like; *Peshkar* of *dargah,* many *Vakils, Mukhtars* and *Mutasaddis* of the *Diwan* and *Mutawalli* such as Asirdas, Bhim Singh, Lakhmi Narayan and Amrit Raj etc.]

[29]Ibid.

[30]Ibid., p. 220.

[31]M.H. Siddiqui, *Madhya Kaleen Nagaur Ka Itihas* (Book in Hindi), Jodhpur, 2001. pp. 83-84.

Sufism in India and Central Asia   119

[32]Ibid.

[33]Ibid.

[34]Other two *talabs* were Shams and Kukur (latter Shakkar) *talab*. The people of the area also explained to the emperor that many of the people migrated from their houses those were living near these *talabs* due to scarcity of water because almost all these tanks had been filled up by the sands.

[35]M.H. Siddiqui, *Madhya Kaleen Nagaur Ka Itihas*, op. cit., pp. 273-74.

[36]Ibid., p. 84.

[37]Ibid.

[38]Ibid.

[39]See the Survey Report of author's project entitled 'A Physical Survey of the Secular and Religious Buildings of *Qasba* Nagaur with Special Reference to Water Bodies during Medieval Period', submitted to the Mehrangarh Museum Trust, Jodhpur, in 2011.

[40]Jibraeil, 'Nagaur: A Trading Junction in Medieval Rajasthan', op. cit., pp. 215-226.

[41]*Rajasthan District Gazetteers*, Nagaur, edited by K.K. Sehgal, Jaipur, 1975, pp. 456-57.

[42]K.C. Jain, op. cit., p. 242 (Nagaur was known by various names such as Nagapura, Nagapattana, Ahipura, and Bhujangangagara).

[43]*Rajasthan District Gazetteers*, Nagaur, op. cit., p.1

[44]K.C. Jain, *Jaina Sources for the History of Nagaur*, published in *"Nagaur Ka Rajnitic Aur Sanskritic Vaibhav"*, op. cit., p. 128.

[45]Many Persian Source such as; *Sarur-us-Sudur*, *Ain-i-Akbari* etc. For details see M.H. Siddiqui, *Madhya Kaleen Nagaur Ka Itihas* (Book in Hindi), Jodhpur, 2001.

[46]K.C. Jain, *Ancient Cities and Towns of Rajasthan*, op. cit., p. 242.

[47]Ibid.

[48]Its weight was 70.6 *grain* (1 *grain*=0.0648 or 1.5 *Ratty*).

[49]Advard Thomas, "The Cronicals of the Pathan Kings of Delhi", p.78. A.B.M. Habibullah, *The Foundation of Muslim Rule in India*. 290 (Also see an article of M.H. Siddiqui, 'Madhyakaleen Nagaur ke Pramukh Shrot (A.D. 1260-1752)', pub. in *"Nagaur Ka Rajnitic Aur Sanskritic Vaibhav"*, op. cit., pp. 6-13.

[50]Shoshani Museum of Lahore still has some of the coins which were minted by Balban at Nagaur (M.A. Chuqtai, "Nagaur a Forgotten Kingdom", Bulletin of the Deccan College Research Institute, Poona, Part-2, No. 1-2, November, 1940 A.D.), p. 167.

[51]Abul Fazl, *Ain-i-Akbari*, Part-I, pp. 32-33.English translation by H. Blockman.(Nagaur was declared a *Sarkar* by Akbar, while total *Sarkars* were Seven under the *Suba* of Ajmer). The different types of copper coin of Akbar in Nagaur were minted such as; *dam adhela*-half of the *dam, pawala*-one fourth of the *dam* ,and *damadi* one eighth of the *dam*.

[52]Nizamuddin Ahmad, *Tabqat-i-Akbari*, pp. 201-202. Farishta, *Tarikh-i-Farishta*, p. 32.

120   Chapter 8 Central Asia to India: Immigration of Sufis....

[53]K.C. Jain, *Ancient Cities and Towns of Rajasthan*, op. cit., p. 247.

[54]Ibid., pp. 249-50.

[55]Our survey team could not find out the mosque of Rai Bisal while still we are trying to explore its location.

[56]K.C. Jain, *Ancient Cities and Towns of Rajasthan*, op. cit., pp. 249-50.

[57]Availability of water in desert area is also valuable factor for the traders passing the town. Fascinatingly *qasba* Nagaur had seven *talabs* during medieval times. Even they are still alive.

[58]PKS. Choondavat, 'Trade Commerce and Medieval Routes of Nagaur', an article in proceeding of *Nagaur Ka Rajnitik Aur Sanskritik Vaibhav*, op. cit., p. 151.

[59]Ibid.

[60]*Rajasthan District Gazetteer*, Nagaur, op. cit., pp. 457-58.

[61]K.A. Nizami, *Some Aspects of Religion and Politics in India during the 13th Century*, p. 180 and comments no. 4.

[62]Yahya-bin-Ahmad, *Tarikh-i-Mubarakshahi* pp. 34,166,193,217. G.N. Sharma, *Rajasthan Studies*, p. 163. G.N. Sharma, *Social Life in Medieval Rajasthan*, p. 323. (Quoted by M.H. Siddiqui, *Madhya Kaleen Nagaur ka Itihas* (Book in Hindi), Jodhpur, 2001).

[63]K.A. Nizami, *Some Aspects of Religion and Politics in India during the 13th Century*, op. cit.

[64]Yahya-bin-Ahmad, *Tarikh-i-Mubarakshahi*, op. cit.

[65]Ibid. pp.192-193.

[66]Toda is presently located 63 miles away in the south-west of Jaipur on latitude 26°4' and longitude 75°39'. In a Rajasthani sources *Arhasatta*, it is mentioned as Toda Bhim under Rajputana Principality. Akbar also visited Toda, when started his journey from Agra to Ajmer (see an article of Jibraeil, "Contribution of Sufis in the Growth of Urban Centres in Rajasthan During the 18th Century", op. cit., pp. 62-75. Cf. Abul Fazal, *Akbarnama*, Translated into English by H. Beveridge, Vol.-II, rpt., Delhi, 1993, pp.510-511.

[67]*Tarikh-i-Farishta*, pp. 199-201.

[68]*Zakat Bahi*, No. 81, V.S.1807/AD1750, RSA, Bikaner.

[69]*Sanad-Parwana-Bahi*, No.25,V.S. 1838/AD.1781,f.77, Record of Jodhpur.

[70]*Sanad-Parwana-Bahi*, No.25,V.S. 1838/AD.1781,f.238, Record of Jodhpur (In my study, Ajmer was on the way of this route and comes after Merta, but scholars missed to plot it)

[71]Dasrath Sharma, *Rajasthan through the Ages*, Part-1, pp. 491-492 and 740.

[72]*Akbarnama*, Part-II, pp. 535-50.

[73]M.H. Siddiqui, *Madhya Kaleen Nagaur Ka Itihas*, op. cit., pp. 257.

[74]G.N. Sharma, *Rajasthan Studies*, p. 164.G.N.Sharma, *Social Life in Medieval Rajasthan*, p. 324.

Sufism in India and Central Asia 121

[75]Abul Fazl, *Akbarnama*, Translated into English by H. Beveridge, Vol.-II, op. cit, pp. 372-373.

[76]*Sava-Mandi-Sadar-Bahi*,No.11,VS.1822/AD.1765, RSA, Bikaner. B.L. Gupta also mentioned in details about the internal trade routes of Rajasthan in his book *'Trade and Commerce in Rajasthan'*).

[77]*Sanad-Parwana-Bahi*, No. 21, VS.1835/AD.1778, f.239 Jodhpur Records.

[78]*Sanad-Parwana-Bahi*, No. 19, VS.1834/AD.1777, Jodhpur Records.

[79]*Sanad-Parwana-Bahi*, No. 8, AD.1768, Jodhpur Records.

[80]*Byav-ri-Bahi*, No.158, VS1827/AD1770,RSA,Bikaner.

[81]*Sanad-Parwana-Bahi*, No. 8, AD.1768, Jodhpur Records.

[82]*Kagad-ri-Bahi*, No.6, AD1782, RSA,Bikaner.

[83]*Sanad-Parwana-Bahi*, No. 13,VS.1830/AD.1773, f.58, Jodhpur Records.

[84]*Sanad-Parwana-Bahi*, No. 9, AD.1769, Jodhpur Records.

[85]*Byav-ri-Bahi*, No.158, VS1827/AD1770, RSA,Bikaner.

[86]Khalil Tanveer, 'Nagaur Ke Sufi Aur Unka Yogdan' (Hindi Article) in proceeding of *Nagaur Ka Rajnitik Aur Sanskritik Vaibhav*, op. cit., pp. 75-79.

[87]Ibid and M.H. Siddiqui, op. cit., pp. 227-230.

[88]Ibid. Cf. *Ain-I Akbari,* Part-III, p. 367.

[89]Ibid. pp. 230-31.

[90]Ibid

[91]Mohammad Mujeeb, The Indian Muslims, London, 1967, p. 151.[When the governor of Nagaur requested the Shaikh to accept a gift in cash and a grant of rent free land , for cultivation, of which he would make an arrangements. The Shaikh refused. The governor mentioned the matter to the Sultan and was asked to press the Shaikh to accept 500 silver tankas and the grant of a village. When the governor come with this offer, Shaikh said nothing and went inside his house, he told his wife about the Sultan's offer. His wife suggested him to reject this offer, while she had nothing with which to cover her head. Shaikh was overjoyed at this reply and went out and told the governor that he would not accept the Sultan's offer].

[92]Khaleel Tanveer, op. cit., pp. 76-77.

[93]Ibid.

[94]Ibid. p.247. For more details see, K.A. Nizami, 'Shaikh Ahmad Maghribi As a Great Historical Personality of Medieval Gujarat', in Medieval India, Vol.-III., All the relevant chapters.

[95]K.A.Nizami, op. cit., p. 242.

[96]Ibid. pp. 242-251.

[97]M.H. Siddiqui, op.cit., pp. 248-49.

122 Chapter 8 Central Asia to India: Immigration of Sufis....

[98]K.C. Jain, op. cit., pp. 322-25.

[99]Ibid.

[100]Ibid.

[101]*Rajasthan District Gazetteers,* Sikar, edited by B.D. Agrawal, Jaipur, 1978, p.419.

[102]Ibid.

[103]Ibid., p. 420.

[104]Ibid., p. 431.

[105]M.H. Siddiqui, op. cit., pp. 245-46.

[106]Ibid.

[107]*Rajasthan District Gazetteers,* Jhunjhunu, edited by Savitri Gupta, Jaipur, 1984, p.382.

[108]M.H. Siddiqui, op. cit., pp. 246.

[109]Ibid.

[110]For more details see article of J.K. Ojha, 'Hazrat Deewanshah Sahib: Rajasthan Ke Ek Sufi' published in a seminar proceeding entitled *Sufi Movement in Rajasthan,* edited by S.M. Azizuddin Husain, Idarah-i-Adabiyat-i-Delli , Delhi, 2007, pp.220-231.

[111]*Rajasthan District Gazetteers*, Dungarpur, edited by K.K. Sehgal, Jaipur, 1974, p.347

[112]*Rajasthan District Gazetteers*, Dungarpur, op. cit., p.367.

[113]Ibid.

[114]Ibid. pp. 367-68.

[115]Ibid. p. 368.

[116]*Rajasthan District Gazetteers*, Dungarpur, op. cit., p. 367-68.

[117]Meenakshi Menariya, *Galiakot: Sanskritic Ekata Ka Pavan Kendra* (Hindi article) in *Sufi Movement in Rajasthan*, edited by S.M. Azizuddin Husain, Idara-i-Adabiyat-i-Delli, 2007, pp. 120-121. Also see the book *Galiakot Darshan* by Ravindra Pandya. (According to their works the *Urs* of Syedi Fakhruddin was attended not only by the people of India but abroad such as; Shri Lanka, Africa, Thailand, Malaysia, England, Karachi, Burma and Central Asia (Arab Countries like; Iran Iraq, Saudi Arabia etc.).

CHAPTER 9

Sufism in Bengal: Interactions and Impacts through the Ages

Mohammad Shaheer Siddiqui

In Bengal Sufism breathed through Sheikh Akhi Siraj, a great Sufi of Chishtia cult. The striking feature of Bengali Sufism is the exposure of 'Bauls', a traditional mystic culture of Bengal. They give emphasis on love as means to attain God. It's another form of Sahajiya path introduced Sexo-Yogic relations. According to him physical love leads to higher spiritual love. Out of such intermingling features the origin of 'Satyapir' cult in Bengal became a significant common cultural heritage of Bengal. Nathist and Yogic ideas were found mixed up with the Sufi ideas and prevalent in Bengal. The traces of degenerated Sufism or heterodox 'faqirism' in Bengal belong to 17th and 18th centuries. The historical role and contribution of great Sufi Masters AkhiSiraj and NurQutbAlam, during 14th and 15th centuries, shaping the spiritual atmosphere of Bengal cannot be neglected. In the 20th century Bengal the songs of QaziNazrul and Rabindranath Tagore filled the spiritual firmament of Bengal with ecstasy. Tagore's Gitanjali is the epitome of spiritualism. This paper is an attempt to find out some untouched features of Sufism in Bengal through the ages.

Sufism in Indian culture reoriented the spiritual thinking by amalgamating ancient Upanishadic pinnacle of virtues with the esoteric aspects of Islamic teachings. It was also a fresh lease to cultural transmigration and merger of two great civilizations in India. The culture of India is an amalgamation of different civilizations, castes, creeds, conventions, traditions, languages, religions, rituals, rhythms, reformations and beliefs. Despite it, beauty of diversity lies in cultural unity. In order to understand the nature of the Indian scene, it is necessary to take into account the long continuity of its cultural tradition. Its special difficulties and complexities as well as its richness, and note varied influences and streams of culture making its over the centuries.[1] As far as cultural and social interaction among the religious groups is concerned that Islam has predominantly developed and shaped itself in a new spiritual incarnation with the amalgamation of Indian spiritual traditions. One can realize this transmigration in the development of Sufism in India by the two treatises viz. Ali Hujwiri'[2] *'Kashf-ul-Mehjub'* and DaraShikoh's[3] *'Majm-ul-Bahrain'*. The writing of Hujwiri's work does not only mark the maturity of Sufism as a systematic body of belief and practices, but is also a firm announcement of the system's arrival in India. (Habib, 2008).By the end of 13th century there were 14 Sufi cults in India.[4]

Most of the Sufi saints established their seminaries in Northern India and started spreading the teachings of Islam, though they were highly influenced by the social, religious and spiritual environment of the country. Sufi movement in Bengal was the expansion of Sufi Deputy System or *'Khalifa'*[5] with the ousted of the Sena dynasty in the first decade of 13th century and the emergence of Sufi movement.The *Sahajiya* tradition in Bengal manifested itself into two interconnected streams: the *Vashnavas* spiritual traditions based on *Radha-Krishan Bhakti* led by Chaitanya and *Bauls* tradition based of divine singing for spiritual ecstasy.[6]

Development of Sufism in Bengal

In Bengal Sufism developed in two forms, one belonged to the established 'Sufi Cults' coming from North India as Chishti, Suhrawardi and Qadri, and second was developed within Bengal by the syncretism of two religions, called as *Pir* culture.

Traditional Sufi Cults

The first Sufis who came to Bengal were Shah Sultan Rumi in 1053 A.D. and Baba Adam in 1119 A.D.[7] Sheikh Jalal-ud-Din Tabrizi (1225 A.D.) was next Sufi to came Bengal after them. He came to Bengal just a few years before the Turkish conquest, and the downfall of Sena dynasty. Within a century or two Bengal became over flooded by the influx of Sufis from different orders.[8] Shaikh Jalaluddin Tabrizi introduced the Suhrawardi Silsilah in Bengal[9]. Sufi

Sufism in India and Central Asia 125

scholar Abdul Haqq Muhaddis Dehlavi mentions him in his *Akhbar-ul-Akhyar*. Chishtiya Silsila was popularized by celebrated Sufi Sheikh Akhi Sirajud Din Badayuni, who was a direct disciple of Hazrat Nizamuddin Auliya of Delhi. He arrived in Bengal around 1325 A.D. Sheikh AkhiSiraj established a Library with the books he took from the library of '*Mehboob-e-Ilahi*, Nizamuddin Auliya while coming to Bengal. He spread Islamic learning and Islamic Culture by his toiling efforts.

Another Chishti Sufi saint was Sheikh Nur Qutb Alam who was the son of Sheikh Ala-al Haqq, the most illustrious disciple of Sheikh AkhiSiraj.[10] Hamid Danishmand (d.1653) of Mangalkot, Burdwan introduced Naqshbandi Silsila in Bengal while Shah Qamis popularized Qadri Silsila, the last of all, in Bengal during the16th century.[11] Broadly the arrival of Sufi sheikhs in Bengal, as recorded is available in literature, reflects that Sufis came by an order of the sheikh as the deputies (khalifa) and established their *Khanqah* (Seminary) at different places as Pandua, Gaur, and Malda.

Celebrated Sufi saint Syed Pir GorachandRazi of Balanda's younger sister Hazrat SyedaZainub Khatun became renowned female Sufi saint of Bengal (d. 1342 A.D.).[12] She was born in Mecca in 1279 A.D. and came to India to preach Islam with her another brother Syed Shahdali. Her grave is situated at the Western Bank of the Ichamati River in the Taragunia village of Bashirhat, in West Bengal. She is popularly known as Raushan Bibi or Raushan Ara in the area.[13]

The striking influence of her spiritual aroma is reflected in the unity of love and harmony between two religions at the annual fair called *urs* near the *dargah* of Raushan Bibi, which is held in the Bengali month of *Chaitra*. It is significant to mention that a temple of Goddess Kali is also situated at the northern end of the *dargah*[14]. A large number of devotees of both the religions assemble here forgetting their religious differences to spread the message of spiritual joy and social amalgamation based on love, harmony and humanity. Details of some eminent Sufis that came to Bengal in different periods are given in Table 1.

126   Chapter 9 Sufism in Bengal: Interactions and Impacts....

Table 1: Eminent Sufis of Bengal

S.No.	Name of the Sufi Sheikh	Period	Tomb/Area
1	JalaludinTabrezi	d.1225	Pandua
2	Shah Abdullah Kirmani	d.1236	Birbhum
3	Shah SafiuddinShahid	d.1290	Pandua
4	Sheikh AkhiSiraj	d.1389	Pandua
5	Shah Anwar QuliHalbi	d.1375	Hoogly
6	Sheikh AlauddinAlaulHaque	d.1398	Pandua
7	Sheikh NuruddinQutb-e-Alam	d.1415	Old Maldah
8	Haji BehramSaqqah	d.1562	Burdwan
9	Sheikh Hamid Danishmand	d.1653	Mangalkot
10	Sheikh Mehar Ali	d.1868	Midnapur
11	Sufi Fateh Ali Waisi	d.1886	Howrah
12	Shah Abu BaqarSiddiqui	d.1939	Hoogly

Source: *Haque, Enamul (1975), Subhan, J.(1925), Khan, S. (1930), Nizami, K.A. (1966)*

Pir Culture in Bengal

The Persian word '*Pir*' means 'elder brother'. It took a special place in Bengali Sufism. *Pir* is the Spiritual Master who trains his novice called, *murid*, for the spiritual journey. *Pir* is considered by the followers to have super human powers. According to one legend of Qadri Sufi cult, celebrated Sufi Sheikh Abdul Qadir Jilani of Baghdad, popularly known as '*Bade PirSaheb*'is believed to attend the feast at the homes of his seventy disciples at the same time. But there is a wide difference between the implications of the meaning of *Pir* in case of Bengali *Pirism* and Qadri Cult. *Pir* is supposed to guide his disciples without physical presence. The idea comes from central Asia and reached Bengal via North Indian Sufism. In Bengal, it emerged as parallel to figure. The new converts in Islam in Bengal during 12th-13th centuries were the practical worshippers of Buddhist *Chaityas* and used to offer flowers, fragrance, and burning lamp. The *Avatarvad* belief strengthened the concept of deity in human body. New converts found a suitable and parallel tradition in *Pirism* and the followers increased in both the communities. Subsequently various local cults of *Pirs* emerged as *KumbhiraPir, MadariPir, SatyaPir, KhwajKhijr, Zindah Ghazi, PirBadar, ManikPir*, which were also propagated

Sufism in India and Central Asia   127

by Bengali Literature, Arts and Folk-Music. Credit of their popularity goes to the song culture of Bengal.

Interactions: Different Bhakti Cults and Sufism

Sufism in Bengal is the amalgamation of the interactions with established spiritual traditions having their roots in Indian mythology and cultural chronicles. This interaction gave birth to various legends, new spiritual sects and traditions based on communal and spiritual harmony. The impact of such interaction is very interesting and worth of noting which gave birth to a unique Sufi culture of Bengal.

The Sahajiya Tradition

Sahajiya philosophy in Bengal is precursor to understand the subsequent interactions with Sufism. During 8th century to 11th century, under the rule of Pala dynasty, the *Sahajiya*cult developed as the last tradition of *'sadhana'* in Bengali Buddhism after *Tantric-Buddhism, Mantrayan, Vajrayan and Kalchakrayan.*[15]

The *Sahajiyas* would proceed in opposite direction to advocated by sectarian scholastic scriptures. They would avoid all forms of institutional religion in which the natural pity of the soul was overshadowed by the useless paraphernalia of ritualism and pedantry.[16] *Dohadosha* and *Charyapada*are the authentic sources of *Sahajiya* philosophy in Bengali Literature. During the rule of Sena dynasty, two sects developed in *Sahajiyas.* One was *siva-sakti* who followed Lord Siva and other was Buddhist *Sahajiya* who followed Radha-Krishna bhakti. These gave birth *Nathism* and *Vaishnavism Sahajiya* cults in 15th century and by the middle of 17th century the impact of Sufism and *Vaishnavism* originated a unique culture of 'spiritual Singing' in Bengal, became popular as 'Bouls of Bengal'.[17]

The Islamic faith of the Bengali Muslims was basically influenced by Sufism and not by the orthodox Islamic scriptures advocated by *Ulema* (Islamic Religious Scholars). In turn, Sufism was also conditioned by its proximity to humanist *Sahajiya* tradition of contemporary Bengal. The Sufis came close to the *Sahajiyas* because both of them opposed the imposition of caste structure of Brahmanism, and both of them opposed the orthodox religious intolerance by the Hindu priests and Muslim clerics in the Bengali society.[18] The interaction with *Sahajiya* sect influenced Sufism in Bengal to the extent of its ultimate restructuring based on a 'reversal approach against the orthodoxy in religion.'

The Vaishnavism

In 12th century Bengal,*Vaishnavism* developed during the Senarulers, came from 'Kannda Country'[19] and brought with them '*bhakti* as a philosophical principal, as a way of life influenced by Ramanuja (d.1137 A.D.)[20] A synthesis of the '*vyuha*' and '*avatara*' doctrine might also have been affected in the 12th century.[21] The *bhakti* element in *Gitagovinda* of Jaidev is concentrated on the concept of Krishna as *avatar* of Vishnu and Radha as his beloved. Siegel (1978) finds in this manifestation of *bhakti*, a curious combination of sacred and profane love.[22]

The idea of contemplation or '*smarana*' of the sports of Krishna and his bliss attributes was later transformed into a basic concept of *Gaudiya Vashnavism* theology.[23] The prominent Sufi concepts of '*Zikr*' and '*Zuhad*' (Remembering and Praising Allah by His various Attributive names) got their parallel concepts in Bengali spiritual traditions. Like *Vaishnavism*, Sufis were also driven by the *spir*it of Love more than by fear of hell in the matters of divine contemplation and submission. 13th century's Krishna worshippers had to wage a long war against the '*siva-sakti*' worshippers of *Tantrika* Buddhism.[24]

Chaitanya's Movement and Sufism

During Chaitanya's (1485-1533A.D.) emergence in 16th century, Navadvipa was the greatest intellectual centre of Bengal. Despite it, society was trapped into rigid a caste system, dominancy of Brahmins and utter selfishness of autocracy of Hindu society. This led to mass conversion into Islam in North-East Bengal particularly in Tibeto-Burmese tribes and non-Brahmin class.[25] In 15th century Navadvipa, a group of scholars and intellectuals was desirous of both social and religious synthesis. To them, the old concept of *Bhakti* was only panacea. It was again revived by Chaitanya. The Sufi mystics of that time influenced the development of *Vaishnava* emotionalism and the *Vaishnava* cult of love.[26] The Sufi saints Nuruddin Akbar Rehman Jami (1414-1492 A.D.) was almost a contemporary of Chaitanya's movement. Most of the Advaitva songs were composed in the mass appealing and heart touching language of the popular *Bauls*. In all possibility, Advaitva followers were acquainted with the view points of the *Auls* and *Bauls*, who in turn were undoubtedly influenced by the Sufi concept of Mystic love (Kalna, 1923). There is a possible counterpart of Sufi concepts and similar *Vaishnava* concepts.[27] In spiritual traditions of both the cults are (Haq, 1957) as given in Table 2.

Table 2: Similar Sufi and Vaishnava Concepts

S.No.	Sufi Concept	Meaning	Vaishnava Concepts	Meaning
1	*Hal*	Ecstasy	*Dasa*	ecstasy
2	*Dhikr*	recitation of the names of God	*Krisnanama*	Recitation of the names of Krishna
3	*Sama*	religious gatherings where hymns are sung	*Kirtan*	Congregational singing of hymns

Source: Hujwiri's Kashf-ul-Mahjub, Jayananda's Chaitanyamangalmala

The influence of Sufism on contemporary *Gaudiya Vaishnavism* may be noticed in its emphasis on love as a source to Divine achievements and its liberal attitude towards prevailing caste system in the society. Muslim mystic poets like Sayyid Sultan desired a cultural conglomeration of various *Bhakti* cults. *'Avatarvada'* and *'Yogic Tantrik'* ideas of *Satchakra* were integral parts of his religious philosophy which emphasized the idea of a strong cultural synthesis by a Sufi.[28] But there is no evidence of any direct link between *GaudiyaVaishnava* philosophy and Sufi mysticism. Chaitanya had no contact with any Sufi nor did he read any Sufi literature. The Sufi influence in Navadvipa is debatable proposition (Chakraborty, 1985).

Spiritual Song Culture of Bengal

Poetry has emerged as a strong source of preserving traditional Vaishnavist culture. Buddhist revolution against *Vaishnavism* was neutralized by

Chapter 9 Sufism in Bengal: Interactions and Impacts....

accepting Buddha as the incarnation of Vishnu as mentioned magnificently in VaduChandidasa's *Srikrisnakirtana*. Vidyapati, the celebrated court poet of Mithila, composed 933 songs on the theme of love, Radha-Krishna and Siva –Parvati. In his poems, he used thirteen different attributive names to address Krishna – *Madhava, Kanha, Hari, Murari, Govinda, Damodara, Banamali, Madhusudana, Madhuripu, Gopa, Nandanandana, Kala, Radharamana and Mohana*. Madhava is used 175 times but Krishna is used only once.[29] Radha, as a central theme in Vidyapati's poetry, emphasizes that Murari (Krishna) is easily captivated by *prem* or love as says the poet using the symbol of Radha for love.Chandidas was another popular poet of Bengal using the theme of love. In 16th century he composed '*Bhavachandrika*'. Long before the advent of Chaitanya, the elite society of Bengal was highly impressed by the ideology of *Bhakti* through the poetic works of Vidyapati, Maladhar Basu[30], and Krittivasa.[31] Among the folk-culture three popular cults were *Vasuli, Manasa, Chandi*and *Dharma*. Some of these were musical cults and powerful media of mass entertainment.[32]

Muslims came to Bengal at a time when it had a strong cultural basis. The sultans of Delhi or Regional Muslim dynasty from IlyasShahi (1342-1413 A.D.) to Sultan Husain Shah (1493-1519 A.D.) there are no recorded attempt to destroy either Bengali language or Bengali bent of mind based on an expanded cultural sublimity.[33] Even after conversion into Muslim religion the masses in east Bengal remained culturally or mentally Hindu or Buddhist. They carried on the native Bengali traditions in literary activities, and social matters. The separatist tendencies among Muslims emerged only after communalist propaganda of Wahabi movement and political influence after 1880 A.D.[34]

There were some Muslims Saints like Sayid Sultan too who had the dreams of a cultural synthesis of Hindu-Muslim. They felt that Islamic ideas combined with Hindu elements would appeal to the minds of the local Muhammadans for whom the Hindu mythology was already known. (Tarafdar 1965)

Narottam Das or NarottamDutta[35] initiated the 'Classical Kirtan'[36] form of *Bhakti* sangit during the Kheturi festival with the approval of the contemporary *Vaishnava* leaders. While Kirtan, it is tradition that '*Gourchandrika*' (A hymn

Sufism in India and Central Asia

to Chaitanya) must be sung first to set the proper mood and to prevent any mis interpretation of the sensual imagery of the Radha-Krishna songs which are to follow (Mukhopadhyaya, 1990) *Dhap* songs were a new development in Kirtan. This was a simpler form in which the singer first delivered a short, prefatory lecture and then sang his song. The theme of the song was sung first.[37] It is important to note that the celebrated BaulLalan Fakir's songs on Krisna's childhood are similar to the *Dhap* songs in respect to thematic consistency and linguistic simplicity.[38] The *Baul* cultist specifically a song tradition which formed a unique culture of Bengal promoting the marvelous merger of Hindu-Muslim culture through music.

In the *Vaishnava* songs and devotional folk-songs in Bengal Krisna and Radha are the symbol of love and passion. Similarly these songs appeared as a bond of cultural and spiritual unity among the masses of two different religions in Bengal through their Saints and Sufis. In *'SrihaterLoksangit*,[39] the collection of *Vaishnava* folk-songs, out of 379 songs, one hundred and sixty songs are composed by Muslim Sufi poets. The folk songs of *Srihater Lok-s-angit* one can see the beautiful unification of wavy and easy pattern of Kirtan and the total dynamism of the Sufi devotional *spiri*t. Hundreds of Muslim poets including Sufis were highly influenced by *Vaishnavism* through devotional sang it. Some of the Muslim poets converted into *Vaishnavism*. Few of them include Akbar, Alawal. Ainuddin, Uchhman, NasirMahmood and Ashraf.[40]

The Kartabhaja

A good number of sects emerged and developed by the influence of Sufism in Post-Chaitanya period. *Auls* and *Bouls,* deeply influenced by Sufism, were popular even during 16th century Bengal. Some other orders such as *Darbesh, Gharpagla, Hazrati, Jaganmohani, Kartabhaja, Khusivisvasi, Sain*and *Sahebdhani* were profoundly influenced by Sufism based in Pandua, Decca and Sylhet. *Sahajiya* and Sufi were very close to each other. (Das Gupta, 1961).

Kartabhaja was one of the most popular sects developed in the Nadia district. Dulalchand, one of the founding father, was so popular that he was invited to attend the Parliament of Religions held in Chicago in 1893 in which

132   Chapter 9 Sufism in Bengal: Interactions and Impacts....

Swami Vivekananda participated, but the invitation was late by 60 years because Dulalchand had already died in 1833.[41] *Kartabhaja* sect is specially known for its exaggerated emphasis on '*Guruvad*'. If Saint Kabir emphasizes the need of Guru to find God, one step ahead, it proclaims Guru to be the incarnation of God. His philosophy is very similar to '*fana-fi-Sheikh*' (dissolve in the glory of Guru). It is obvious that the real founder of the *Kartabhaja* sect was Aulchand (1686-1779) who claimed to be trained and taught in the Qadiri order of Sufis.[42] Aulchand, a Muslim Fakir, is a legendary figure in the cultural History of Bengal. According to one widely accepted legend, "he was Chaitanya in disguise."[43] Another legend explain that Aulchand's identification as Chaitanya lent respectability to *Kartabhaja* sect and more important, the depiction of Aulchand, a Muslim Fakir, as Chaitanya's second incarnation made the *Kartabhaja* sect popular and respectable both among Hindus and Muslims.[44]

Bouls of Bengal and Fakir Cult

In the cultural background of *Sahajiyas*, *Vaishnavism* and *Kartabhaja* sects based on liberal way of spiritual ecstasy through music, dance and poetry were. *Baul* is the prominent culture of Bengal was developed as a reaction against all kinds of orthodoxy, bondages and external upheaval in the way of divine ecstasy. This freedom from every external compulsion is reflected in the name *Baul*, which means 'madcap' and it refers to a set of people who do not confirm the establish of social usage.[45] *Bauls* believe in the freedom of heart or they are the masters of their heart. Away from all types of discriminatory boundaries of religion, sects and castes, *Bauls* believe that God resides in man's heart. They follow the simplicity of Man's heart and propounded the theory of '*Maner Manus*' (Man of Heart).

Aulchand, a Muslim Mystic and Madhava Bibi, his companion is considered the founders of *Baul* tradition.[46] According to this cult, in order to gain real freedom, one has, first to die in the life of the world whilst still in the flesh. 'Those of the *Bauls* who have Islamic learning call such 'death in life' *fana*, a term used by the Sufis to denote union with the Supreme Being.[47] The

Sufism in India and Central Asia 133

philosophy of *Bauls* is very closely knit with the Sufi concept of suppressing '*nafs-e-ammara*' (lower self) in order to find the '*nafs-e-mutmainna*' (the purified self where God visits). The *Bauls* do not profess, like Pundits, to understand the *tat* in *Brahma*; rather they want a person of purified heart. So their God is the 'Man of the Heart' (*Maner Manus*)[48]. This 'Man of Heart' is ever and an on is lost in the turmoil of things.

Lalan Fakir has occupied a legendry place in the *Baul* culture of Bengal. He used to say that he was neither a Muslim nor a Hindu and the only religion he believed in was humanism.[49] The *Pir* worship was also a blend form of Hindu-Muslim harmony. In Medieval Bengal, Hindus were devoted to *Pirs* and regarded them as Gods as is reflected in literature like *Ghazi Vijay* and *Satyapir Vijay* of Faizulla (A Muslim Poet of 16th century), *Ray Mangal, Sasti Mangal* and *Sitala Mangal* of Krishna Das (17th Century)[50]. The tombs of *Pirs* are still visited by both the communities alike.The spiritual freedom was the basic source of wisdom in the cultural merger as Lalan Fakir describes the Brahmanical rituals as '*dark clouds generated by the Vedas*'[51], also, he criticizes the caste system and gender biasness in the society.

The Impact: Sufism and Cultural Merger

In Bengal, the Islamic tenets were not fully absorbed by the new converts as they were still attached to their old habits, beliefs, practices and ceremonies.' In a way their conversion in Islam was either due to the tantalization of the favour and facilities by the Muslim rulers or due to the suppression of lower strata people by the dominancy of upper caste people, and orthodoxy in contemporary religious rituals. A composite culture of Bengal was emerged there in which there was enough space for every cult, clan and class to bloom and flourish spiritually and culturally. Sushil Chaudhry (2013) explored in his intensive study that 'the fundamental concept of Islam was changed due to the Hindu influence. Prophet Muhammad was sometimes characterized as an avatar-an incarnation who endowed with supernatural power.

We see that *Vaishnavism* strengthened communal harmony in Bengal. There is a list of more than hundred Sufi poets who composed folk-songs on Radha Krishna, Chaitanya and other *Vaishnava* Saints. Many Muslim *Bauls* were fully absorbed in the spiritual harmony and wrote songs on *Vaishnava* themes. The Muslim mystics when exposed to the tremendous impact of Buddhism and Hindu mysticism unconsciously borrowed certain Indian elements, incorporating them into Sufism. Like the Indians, they began to tell the rosary while repeating the holy names of God. They borrowed the concept of *Nirvana* and the *Astangika Marga* from Buddhism and some elements of the *Raja Yoga.* Yogic practices like *Pranayam* (*Habs-e-Dum*) became common among Sufis.

Pir cult was a joint worship form of Hindus and Muslims. In Bengal, there is another manifestation of the religious syncretism.[52] The interesting fact, is that today's *Satya Narayan Puja* among Hindus is very close to the *SatyaPir* tradition in Bengali Sufism. The reverse is also applicable as Hindus have a deeper faith in *Pir* culture of Bengal. (Yamin, 2009)

There is a very close connection between *Bauls* and Sufi Fakirs. Firstly, they believe that Allah or *Paramatma* resides in the body of man. Secondly, self-realisation is the pivot of their *Sadhna* (spiritual practices) as Sufis follow the path of *Fana* through mystic union with God while *Bauls* make self-realization of *Maner Manus* (Man of Heart). Lastly, both of them avoid all types of rites and rituals which hamper spiritual journey.

The idea of *Maner Manus* is very close to Sufis as the *Bauls* believe that the Ultimate Reality resides in the inner recess of the heart of man in the form of *manus*. Likewise, Sufis give emphasis on *Tazkia-e-Nafs* (the process of purifying Heart and inner self). This spiritual unity originated a new cult in Sufism called Fakirs who sing, the songs of Divine Love along with the *Bauls*. Lalan Fakir is the celebrated Muslim *Baul* who is equally loved by both Hindus and Muslims. On the *Samadhis* (word used for Sufi *Mazar*) of *Fakirs* and Sufis, both *Bauls* and *Fakir* sing the songs all the night. Tomb of Data Saheb at 'Patherchapury' in Birbhum, is internationally famous for spiritual, cultural and social union. In the month of Chaitra (March-April) on the eve of annual fair (*urs*) huge number of *Fakirs* and *Vaishnava Bauls* visit and stay there for many days. They eat, live and sing the songs of devotion together with affection, love and passion for each other. This spiritual unity and social miracle is now here seen in the country. Many people from different religion visit many Sufi Tombs throughout the Nation, but it happens only in Bengal that *Vaishnava Kirtan* or songs of Krishna *Bhakti* and *Fakiri* songs of Islamic themes are sung together at one platform throughout the night. At *Poush Mela* and *Rathindra Mela* at Santiniketan many renowned *Fakirs* and *Bauls* visit and sing songs togetherly. *Poush Mela* and *Rathindra Mela* are officially organized by Visva-Bharati Administration.

The song culture of Bengal is so influenced by Sufism and *Vaishnavism*. The Literature of Bengal is predominantly rich in reflecting social and cultural unity, creating spiritual and cultural harmony and producing poetry of joy. We can find the deeper impact of *Masnawi* of Maulana Rumi, celebrated Sufi of Iran and *Diwan-e-Hafiz Shirazi,* in the spirit of 'Gitanjali' as it is obvious because Rabindranath Tagore's father Devendranath Tagore was a renowned scholar of Persian and a great admirer of Sufi Mysticism of Rumi and Hafiz. Most of his work has been translated into Persian. Devendranath Tagore so much loved the poems of Hafiz, the renowned Sufi poet of Shiraz. (Iran) He had memorised them and all for this reason it was called '*Hafiz-e-Hafiz*'. He used to recite his poems in holy temples.[53]

The popular Sanskrit work on Yoga *'Amritkunda'* written by a Hindu Yogi Bhujar Brahmin was translated in Arabic first time in Bengal by Rukn-al-Din Samarqandi under the title '*Hauz al-Hayat*' during 1210-1213 A.D. The Bengali Sufis experienced deeply the atmosphere of 'Yogic and Tantric' culture, and they were naturally influenced by it. Ali Rida's '*Jnan-Sagara*' and '*AdyaParichay*' by Sheikh Zahid are considered the renowned Sufi Yogic treatises in Bengali language. Many other Sufi books were also translated into Bengali and series of songs on Sufi themes were composed by many renowned Scholars. At the same time, Muslim *Fakirs* also composed songs on *Vaishnava* themes.

Conclusion

Sufism in Bengal has a specific shape, style and strength influenced by various sects and philosophical development through centuries. The Muslim society of

Bengal has been pointed out by Moinuddin Ahmad Khan (2006), a melting-pot for centuries in which various foreign and local influences were fused. With the blending of the various elements a complete socio-religious system had grown up in Bengal. Every custom usage or ceremony acquired a definite value through long practice. It is due to the interactions with various philosophical, intellectual and cultural cults and ideologies to produced a deeper impact on the Islamic Mysticism in Bengal. The song culture emerged with *Sahajiya* movement and passing through *Kirtan*, and *Bauls*, reached in 20th century to the songs of QaziNazrul and Rabindranath Tagore which filled the spiritual firmament of Bengal with ecstasy. Sufism in later period transformed into the unique Bengali culture based on the amalgamation of common cultural elements and spiritual harmony.

References

[1] Saiyidain, K.G. (1966) *The Humanist Traditions in Indian Educational Thoughts*, Bombay: Asia Pub. House, p. 4.

[2] Ali Hujwiri, the celebrated Sufi Saint, came to India from Ghazni after the invasion of Mahmud of Ghazni and settled in Lahore where he established a Sufi Seminary and lived till his death. He was the author of first Persian book on the principles and systems of Sufism. His Tomb is situated at Lahore (Modern Pakistan). He is popular as 'DataganjBaksh' among the people, cited in Laiq Ahmad, *Madhyakaleen Bharatiya Sanskriti*, Allahabad: Sharda Pub. p. 5.

[3] The Mughal Prince, son of Shahjahan and elder brother of Aurangzeb was a Sufi scholar who composed many books on Sufism as Sakinat-ul-Auliya, Safinat-ul-Auliya, Sirr-e-Akbar, Majm-ul-Bahrain, Risala-e-Haqnuma, Hasan-ul-Arifin. In Majm-ul-Bahrain he described the great mingling of two great culture and religions in India Hinduism and Islam. This book is the manifestation of cultural, spiritual and social harmony by the pen of a Sufi Scholar.

[4] AbulFazl, *Ain-e-Akbari* cited in Laiq Ahmad op. cit p.13.

[5] He is the disciple of Sufi Sheikh, called 'Mureed' who is given authority by his sheikh to spread the Teachings or way of life of the cult (Tariqa) by settling in any specific land area. In Sufi Hagiography, It is believed that Khwaja Moinuddin Chishti, the Propounder of Chishtia Sufi cult in India was given the order by the Prophet Muhammad (S.A.W.) himself in dream to go to India for spreading Islam by spiritual teachings. In Bengal most of the Sufis were the khalifa of Chishti Sufi Sheikhs of North India.

[6] Atis Das Gupta, 'Islam in Bengal: Formative Period' in *Social Scientist Vol32/Nos 3-4 March-April 2014, pp30-31.*

[7] Enamul Haque, (1975), *Sufism in Bengal*, p. 193.

Sufism in India and Central Asia

[8]Amit Day (1994) *Sufism in India,* Calcutta: Ratna, pp. 20-21.

[9]Sheikh Abdul Haq Muhaddis Dehlavi, in *Akhbar-ul-Akhyar cited in* Amit Day, op.cit.p. 25

[10]ibid p. 27.

[11]ibid p. 28.

[12]Bangla Pir Sahityer Katha, Girindra Nath Das, Calcutta, 1976, p.328, cited in Amit Day, op.cit. p. 8.

[13]Abdul Ghaffar Siddiqui, Balandar Pir Hazrat Gorachand Razi (Bengali) cited in Amit Day, 'Sufism in India' Calcutta: Ratna Prakashan,1994, p. 8 3.

[14]Bangla PirSahityer Katha, GirindraNath Das, Calcutta, 1976, p. 329, cited in Amit Day, 'Sufism in India' Calcutta: Ratna Prakashan,1994, p. 10.

[15]Raj Kishore Roy, Baul Sampraday Ek Parichay, *Visva-Bharati Patrika*, Vol.-II, April, 1968, p. 64.

[16]Dasgupta, Atis, 'Islam in Bengal: Formative Period' in *Social Scientist*, Vol. 32/Nos. 3-4 March-April, 2004, p. 31.

[17]Raj Kishore Roy, op. cit. p. 63.

[18]Das Gupta, Atis, op. cit. p. 36.

[19]The Deopara Prashasti of Vijayasen, Inscriptions of Bengal-III p. 42, cited in '*Vaishnavism in Bengal,* (1985), Chakraborty, R. Calcutta: Sanskrit Pustakbhandar, p. 6,

[20]Chakraborty, R. (1985), *Vaishnavism in Bengal,* Calcutta: Sanskrit Pustakbhandar, p. 6.

[21]Mukherjee, S.C. (1966). *A Study of Vaishnavism in Ancient and Medieval Bengal*, Calcutta: PuthiPustak.

[22]Siegel, L. (1978). *Sacred and Profane Dimensions of Love in Indian Traditions as exemplified in Gitagovinda of Jayadev,* London: Oxford University Press

[23]Chakroborty, P. op. cit. p. 8.

[24]Brahma Purana, Calcutta: Gurumandal Pub., 1954, Ch.56, verse 63-66, cited in Chakraborty, P. op. cit. p.17.

[25]Charaborty, R. op. cit. p. 46.

[26]Haq, Enamul (1935). *Bange Sufi Prabhav*, Calcutta: pp. 165-70, 171-78

[27]EnamulHaq, *Muslim Bangla Sahitya,* Decca 1957, pp. 149-50 cited in Charaborty, R. op. cit p. 51.

[28]Sayyid Sultan describes very vividly, the sports of Krishna (Lila) in his book *Nabivamsa* cited in EnamulHaq, *Muslim Bangla Sahitya*, 1957, pp. 149-50.

[29]BimanbihariMajumdar's analysis in 'Vidyapatir Padavali' introduction, p. 97 cited in Chakraborty, op. cit. p. 21.

[30]He was a Bengali poet of Kulingrama, Burdwan. He translated 'Bhagvadpurana' into Bengali in 15th century.

[31]He wrote 'Ramayana' in Bengali during middle of 15th century.

[32]Chakraborty, R. op. cit. p. 31.

[33]Sarkar, Binoy Kumar, (1941) *Bangalaya Desibedesi*, Calcutta, pp. 21-22.

[34]Chakroborty, R. op. cit. p. 37.

[35]He was the son of Krisnananda Dutta, the Raja of Gopalpur near Kheturi in North Bengal. He organized the famous Kheturi Festival sometimes during 1610-1620 A.D. In his festival the Vrindavan viewpoint finally dominated and Kirtan was appreciated as popular form of Vaishnava bhakti in Bengal. Cited in Chakrabarty, R. op. cit. p. 229.

[36]Kirtan belongs to probandha groups of Indian classical music which means well-knit structure of composition. It should not be confused with folk music. Almost all the ragas of Indian classical music are used in kirtan as Sri, Kamod, Dhanasri, Gandhar, Todi, Bhatiyari, Malhar, Pahadi, Behag, Kedar, Bhairavi etc. More than two hundred Talas are used in Padavalikirtan. It is tradition that 'Gourchandrika' (A hymn to Chaitanya) must be sung first to set the proper mood and to prevent any misinterpretation of the sensual imagery of the Radha-Krishna songs which are to follow.

[37]Atiskumar Bandyopadhyay, Bangala Sahityer Itivratta, Vol.-4, p. 408, cited in Chakrabarty, R, op. cit. p. 465.

[38]LalanGitika, Songs 341-373, Lalan Fakir. ed. Matilal Das and PiyushkantiMahapatra. Calcutta: Calcutta University, 1958.

[39]Folk songs of Sylhet collected by GurusadayaDatta and NirmalenduBhowmik.

[40]Muslim Padavali, in Mukhopadhyaya, D., (1990) ,Religion, Philosophy and Literature of Bengal Vaishnavism, Delhi: B.R. Publishing Corp. p. 131-133.

[41]http://nitaaiveda.com/Other_Scriptures_by_Acharyas/Apasampradayas/Kartabhaja.htm, , http://backtogodhead.in/part-four-kartabhaja-and-neda-nedi-by-suhotra-swami/,

TusarChattopadhyay, 'Kartabhaja O Chicago'rAmantran', Ananda Bazar Patrika, Sunday April, 29, 1979 p.4, cited in Chakrabarty, R. op. cit p.352

[42]Bimal Kumar Mukhopadhyay, Vol.-2, p. 7-12 as cited in Chakrabarty, R. op. cit p.353

[43]Chakrabarty, R. op. cit. p. 355.

[44]Misra, Manulal, (1911) BhaverGiterVyakhya. Calcutta pp.15-18.

[45]Tagore, Rabindranath, in '*The Religion of Man*' Visva-Bharati Publication, Calcutta, 1931, p. 117.

[46]Rajkishore Roy, op. cit. p. 64.

[47]Tagore, Rabindranath op. cit. p. 118.

[48]Ibid p. 122.

[49]Sushil Choudhry, 'Identity and Composite Culture: the Bengal Case' *in Journal of the Asiatic Society of Bangladesh*, Vol. 58 (I), 2013, pp. 5-6.

[50]Ibid pp. 6-7.

Sufism in India and Central Asia

[51]LalanGitika, Song No. 413.

[52]Sushil Choudhury, op. cit. p. 5.

[53]Extracted from the Address of Her Imperial Majesty Shahbanou Farah of Iran, at a special convocation convened on January 7, 1969 at Bareilly College, Bareilly, U.P. (India), appeared in 'Rang-o-Bu' Persian Departmental Megazine ed. M. M. Jalali, Vol. III, April, 1969, , p. 5 .

CHAPTER 10

Sufism and Religious Syncretism in the History of Central Asia

Laura Yerekesheva

During the mediaeval period of spreading and affirmation of the Islamic tradition, religion and socio-cultural systems of the region became inevitably linked with each other. Moreover, the religious factor exactly (Islam) had gradually become the ground for the process of consolidation and crystallization of the socio-cultural systems, could be termed as a civilization. Islam, particularly its various and yet interlinked traditions within the Hannafi *mazkhab* generally defined the appearance and specificity of Central Asian civilization. (Along the course of its affirmation, Islam faced the challenge of cementing and strengthening the already existing basis-carcass, of its filling with new doctrine which in turn had absorbed much from earlier pre-Islamic local traditions, and of suggesting new corresponding forms to become later the inevitable feature of this region.)

The result of this centuries-long process was the transformation of Islam into the dominant religious tradition and, at the same, the gradual download and almost oblivion of some of the previous ones, except Shamanic (though modified). In its own turn, Islam too became the subject of considerable modification. It acquired various forms, especially visible in nomadic and settled environment, and uneven spatial and temporal intensity.

The assertion of Islam, thus, paved the ground for defining in the Central Asian geo-cultural complex of the special contour, based on religion. This contour was still vague, unstable, differentiated at the centre and peripheries, leading to the diversity and mosaic. However, Islam and its significant part – Sufism – contributed certain orderliness in those processes, and bound itself with both religious and general socio-cultural tradition.

This had significantly paved a way to Islam finally becoming a stable and deep-rooted element of culture of the region. In this capacity, the next logical step for it was the preservation of these cultural symbols. In dealing with this task, Islam already had enough resources, one of which was the ingrowth into the structure of the political entities and the domination over the mind of the people, mainly in a modified, Sufi version. The issue of preserving the cultural symbols and even religion itself was become mostly exposed later at the periods of cardinal transformations of the societies of the region due, firstly, to Russian colonization and modernization, and later – to secularization.

In a more general plane, on the macro-level, the level of interaction among religion and socio-cultural systems, one can say about the integrative function of religion. It was mostly prominent during the process of the spreading and affirmation of Islam, or the so-called process of "gathering land" which was un-fold under the mottos of this teaching. However, it should be stressed here that on a micro-level to, *i.e.* within the religion itself, operational as well particularly the function of changes. The latter one could be traced in the development of different branches in Islam, along with the evolution of Hanafi *mazkhab* itself, which saw in various periods and due to various political events the formation of the ological thought, legal corpus *fikh*, Sufism, etc.

The spread of Islam in Central Asia was intrinsically linked with the affirmation of its mystic part – Sufism (*at-tasavvuf*), which in the region became the leading, though not the only paradigm of the religious perception of the world. But as a powerful life-asserting world-view was instrumental in widely spreading the ideas of Islam in the region; at the same time it acquired there a bright specificity. The key concept of Sufism -"unity of being" (*wakhdat al-wujut*) – significantly influenced the local religious beliefs and, being mixed with the local Tengrian-Shamanic religious constructions; it became the leading *modus Vivendi* and the form of the adaptation of Islam on the new territories.

Sufism and Religious Syncretism in the Region

At the beginning and middle of VII century the Arabs started systematic exploration of the region, especially since 705, the year when Quteiba ben Muslim was appointed the governor of Khorasan. At the beginning of its spreading Islam was one of many religious systems and like the others, aimed at fixing and spreading its influence particularly along the routes of the Great Silk Road. The spotted localization consequently led to its uprooting mainly among the settled population and city-dwellers, which further shaped the process of the following dichotomy -"oases-steppe" and "settled-nomadic" –resulted in contrast. For example, in the towns of the central Mavarannahr in VIII-XIII centuries the bright philosophical thought of the Hannafi *ulama* began to take shape, while the Kypchak steppe (Desht-i-Kypchak) up to XIII century (and in some places – even later) was marginalized in this respect and continued to stay at the periphery of the Islamic world. At the same time, the earlier religious beliefs of the local population continued to be the main form of their religiosity.

Along with the *tarikat* of Naqshbandiya, they were spread "what" the other ones like Qubraviya, Qadiriya, *Suhravardiya*. However, the biggest influence over the nomadic Turcik population within the course of their Islamization was played by the Yassaviya *tarikat*. All *tarikats* had to adapt their postulates to the already existed religious traditions, out of which the most vital were the Tengrian-Shamanic beliefs.

The process of Islamization became successful due to the similarities of the "*wahdat al-wudjut*" concept in Sufism (Absolut, Names, the Phenomenal world) and the Tengrianic-Shamanic ideas on the unity of the world and its three-partial division into Upper, Middle and Lower Worlds. The similarity was also seen in the acceptance of the universe and nature as crucial for individual and his spiritual perfection. In this regard, the Sufi thesis "all is God" and the importance of the numeric manifestations of the God including nature, was echoed and highly resonated in minds of the local population. For them the Tengrian-Shamanic holistic approach which saw the man as a small and yet integrated part of the nature only, was an extremely significant (this outlook was maintained partially through the nomadic way of life and activity). Thus, this conceptual similarity paved the way towards multiple interpretations of this thesis on the daily, mundane level became a ground for the ideological and spiritual closeness and approachment with Sufism. The result of this process was the symbiosis and new religious syncretism, which defined the new vector of the general socio-cultural synthesis and development in the region.

The conceptual similarity caused their mutual adaptation to each other. The preservation of the archaic layers in the new religious construction, the appearance of the so called "folk Islam" with the cult of saints (*auliye*) and the sacred places, linked with them; and the wide spread of the mystic flexible and unorthodox Sufi ideas which reflected this syncretism.

It is worth mentioning that this syncretism was seen both in the religious and socio-political spheres, which seems to go along the general concept of Islam to made no strict division between religious on the one hand and political, social fields, on the other. For example, some researchers highlight the coexistence and intermingling of Islamic thesis with the specific concept of power as taken shape among the Mongol-Tatars – so called "*chingisism*".

Islamization of the nomadic population of *Dest-i-Kypchak* was not the linear and continuing process. There were the geographical (spatial) and temporal inequality and sporadic character. The Sufi ideas have been penetrating into the Kazakh Steppe from Mavarannahr, particularly Bukhara and Samarkand. Specificity of the spread of Sufi ideas provided their rooting in contact zones, such as in Aral-Caspian region or in Turkestan (modern Western and Southern Kazakhstan respectively).

In modern Western Kazakhstan, for example, one could find the unique underground mosques and necropolis built along the old caravan routes from Mangyshlak, plateau Usturt, the lower parts of the river Emba towards Khorezm, along so-called old Nogai route that linked Central Asia with other parts of Eurasia. Among the underground mosques there could be mentioned Shopan-ata (end XII-early XIII c.), Karaman-ata (XIII c.), Beket-ata (XVIII-XIX c.) Shaqpak-ata (first century of XIV c.).

In the southern contact zone, one of outstanding exponent of the Sufi tradition was particularly in the town Yassy (modern Turkestan). During XII century, became the leading centre of Islamization for the nomadic Turkic population. The founder of the Yassaviaya *tarikat* – HojaAkhmetYassavi

Sufism in India and Central Asia

(Hazret Sultan) became the pioneer mission reviving high attention to the mystic ideas and highlighting their identity with the local Tengri-Shamanic beliefs. In the nomadic environment it was exactly the Yassaviya *tarikat* that became instrumental in spreading Islam and in turn, it even got the name of the "nomadic Turkic line of Central Asian mysticism".

Maximal adaptation of Yassaviya to the local environment was visible in the usage of the Turkic rather than Persian and Arabic language, and incorporation of the purely folk rites in the religious practice rituals (for example, such as ribbon binding on the trees, encirclement of the shrines by those wishing for a birth of a child, and other). One could also find the similarity stressed by Yassaviya between the Sufi and Turkic concepts of knighthood (*futtuva* and *batyr* respectively).

The syncretism is highly represented and visible in numerous monuments, artifacts, oral creativity. The specific forms of folk architecture such as necropolis, underground mosques, grave mausauleums-sarkofags-*saganatam, kulyptas, qoitas* -speak about this. One could mention, for example, underground mosques built in the rocks like the mosque-tomb Shopan-ata (end XII-early XIII c.), Karaman-ata (XIII c.), Beket-ata (XVIII-XIX c.), Shaqpak-ata (first century of XIV c.). Their specific designs, story of building testifies about religious syncretism and inter influence.

The various folk stories about Shopan-ata are representative. An theme that Shopan-ata was the disciple of hoja AhmatYassavi, and "after completing the teaching gathered his all disciples and told them to go those places their arrows could reach to preach Sufi ideas. The arrow of Shopan-ata landed at the Mangyshlak peninsula, not far from the small mountain, where after some time the underground mosque was built.

The other highly representative sample of the Sufi-Tengri-Shamanic fusion are the interior design of the underground mosque Shaqpak-ata, where on the walls of the portal and niche the lines from Sufi poems (written in Arabic) are intermixed with the drawings of the horses, cows, open hand (Fatima palm), tri-leaves. While the Fatima palm is considered to be a strong talisman and amulet against bad evil eye, then the pictures of animals – horses and cows

– as symbols of fertility refer us back to animistic and totemic symbolism. Alongside with this, the walls could be found the drawings of the kitchen utensils and vessels like kettle and plates what speaks about the continuing high role of the perceptions linked with the afterlife world. It is interesting that in the general course of this seemingly opposite fusion the Sufi elements are interweaved in a natural inclusive way rather than in an opposition. The Sufi poetic lines speaking about the burden of this mundane world and short earth life of the people are in a very harmonious and natural way contoured by the pictures and drawings of the animals.

In general, the ancient Turk tradition of depicting the animals as reflected throughout the long history of the region has not been interrupted even up to the XX century. The so-called grave monuments – *sagana-tams, kulyptas, qoitas* – and sometimes the sculptures of the sheep's (as a totemic and scarified animals) highly testify about this. It is interesting that under the influence of Islam the depictions of the sheep shave also been transformed by losing its realistic features and acquiring symbolical character thus becoming the prerequisite of such type of the grave sculptures as *qoitas*[23, p. 102].

In the process of interaction between Islam and local Tengri-Shamanic beliefs that their fusion and inter influence mostly vivid in culture. For example, the deny on drawing the human being and animals in Islam was echoed in a specific way in the stone sculpture figures *balbaly*, which starting from XIII century became depicted without the facial features. The other influence got reflected in the appearance of the new architectural forms –tent mausoleums, in spread of the blue colour in the décor art [more in: 137, p. 28-29].

The other important form of inter influence of Sufism and local traditions became the oral poetical creativity which in nomadic environment bears both cultural and social dimension. In nomadic societies the poets-singers *zhyrau* were seen as ideologists, representatives of the peoples' interests and even as leaders of social movements. Mahambet Utemisov – the poet, and leader of the popular uprising movement-was a bright sample of this approach. At the same time in the creativity of poets-singers *manaschi* and *zhyrau* the specific

Sufism in India and Central Asia   147

religious perceptions of the people were reflected, particularly, connected with the issues of moral behavior and *haj* to Mecca.

According to the researchers it showed the "nomads of the Kazakh Steppes which could equal to the positive moral actions and behavior with the pilgrimage itself" [95, c. 263]. Modification of performing the Islamic religious rites in a nomadic environment leads to the fact that along with the knowledge of the basic principles of Islam, however the stress was made on the individual spiritual-moral perfection. This could be found in the poetical songs of manaschi and zhyrau. For example Shal-akyn (XIX century) conveys that:

Could the man find a belief,

In a remote Mecca and Medina,

If to respect the parents and the guests,

Then the home is much better rather than Mecca [Cit. in: 95, p. 264].

The other sample of the influence of Islam in particularly, of Sufism, on the culture of the people's region is the creative works of Turkmen poet Makhtumkuli (XVIIIв.). He reflected the Sufi ideas of the Road and embodied his own Road of poet with the Road of dervish. The researchers mention the devotion of Makhtumkuli before the personality of sheikh (Hoja Akhmet Yassawi), his motifs of travels and discipleship as steps of cognition, his is in general [214, p. 267-269].

The Sufi philosophy are seen in the verses of Makhtumkuli in the following ways, traditional in the Sufi lyrics – addressing the God, using the epithets of lovers, rose-nightingale, mirror reflecting the feelings of mystical insight, approach to and dissolution in the God, enjoying the wine's bowl.

Since dervish gave me the bowl of eternity,

I started mixing *mehrab*and myself,

Fallen in love, I don't see, I am full of carelessness,

Whether the world is powerful or critically weak...

You are there, Fragi, where with the lush power

The *jigits* of the cheikhs dance freely.

In mirror I see my dearest,

I can't distinguish where there is water or *shirab*[Makhtumkuli, p. 176].

The temporal inequality of the process of Islamization paved the way to the fact that even in the XVI century one could find still continuing missionary activity of the Sufis. V. Yudin clearly showed this while analyzing the hagiography of the Sufi sheikh HojiIskhak (Hazrat-I Ishan) from Naqshbandi order and his missionary proselyte activity among the Kazakhs (in particular, Tavakkul-khan) and their subsequent turn into his own murids [Yudin, p. 167-178].

This syncretism became the remarkable feature to characterized the specificity of the process of assertion of Islam in the Steppe. The forms of Islamic way of life, particularly, of Sufi tradition were different in the region. On the one hand, there were the activities of the *tarikat* Yassawiya, embracing mainly the nomadic Turkic tribes and more fully incorporating the local pre-Islamic beliefs. On the other hand, one can see the activity of *tariqats* Naqshbandiya, Qadiriya, Qubraviya, is mostly popular among the city dwellers, the settled environment of Mawerannahr, and developed into the political force.

Along with Sufism, during the early period of spread of Islam in the region, there were also developments (especially in the town settled area) of the theosophical and theological thought that contributed to the formation of the *Hannafi Mazhab*. The latter one had its own distinguished features in various regions and the rich traditions of the Muslim legal scholars – *fakihs*.

CHAPTER 11

The Style of Persian Sufi prose XI - XIII centuries

Mehdi Kazimov

Persian prose as opposed to poetry in the Middle Ages did not receive such a large development, and it has not been represented by such brilliantly masters as a poetry. True, many famous poets also wrote prose writings, but compared with their poetic work they did not receive a large spread. The exceptions are perhaps *Gulistan* (Rose Garden) by Sa'adi or *Baharistan* (Spring Garden) by Abdar-Rahman Jami.

There are several reasons for this situation. One of them was related to the fact that the literary works in their bulk functioned in the courts of the rulers, major government officials, nobles. As rightly observes Z. N. Vorozheykina 'Yards were literary centres of urban life.'[1] And the preferences and tastes of the ruling circles focused mainly on the beauty and elegance of poetic production. In addition, the important role was played by the 'mobility' of the poetic word, its ability to respond quickly to events, to use these or other situations. It is known, for example, in the Middle Ages the art of improvisation, impromptu was spread, thanks to which poets could stand out from the fellow media writers, receive material rewards or strengthen their own position at court.[2]

Prosaic statement was deprived of such opportunities, and it was designed for the long term prospects, like 'mirrors', various anthologies, etc. However, in the Middle Ages in the Persian speaking region there existed works which were well-known in educated circles. Besides, the artistic elements were well represented in the historical, geographical, religious and philosophical prose, poetic treatises. In many, they are found in a vast reservoir of medieval Persian-language prose as Sufi. By combining a large number of works, Sufi prose, in addition to owning the content dominant, stood out with its stylistic features.

Starting with XI century Persian Sufi literature has been experiencing a period of rapid flowering. Sufi poetry is spreading rapidly throughout the near and Middle East. Not only the followers of the mystical reflections and experiences get acquainted with it, but all those who love and are interested in the poetic word. And names like Sanai, Attar, Rumi transform into symbols of Sufi poetry and gain fame far beyond the Persian-speaking region. Sufi prose in this sense, cannot boast of a vast readership, and by virtue of its specificity becomes a subject of study primarily in religious circles. However, some works, such as Ansari's due to poetic language and elegance of style, the works of hagiographic character, including literary themes and scenes, entertaining details from the life of the Sufi sheikhs and ascetics, are gaining popularity among the different social strata.

In the XI-XIII centuries Persian Sufi prose was represented by such names as Hujwiri, Abdullah Ansari, Muhammad bin Munavvar, Najm al-Din Razi, Fakhr al-Din Iraqi, and others. This period is associated with the appearance of hagiographic work by Farid ad-Din Attar *Tazkirat al-awliya'* (Remembrance of saints). The works of all these authors of differ with their genres and can be differentiated as prayers, Sufi allegories, lives, and theoretical works. Such a division is to some extent arbitrary, since these or other structural elements are found in all genres, and work by Hujwiri generally represents a synthesis of the life and theoretical work. In addition, the theoretical works themselves fall into any kind of leadership or treatises.

There are no special terminological designations for certain genres of Sufi prose. Often in the names of the works the words '*kitab*' - 'book' or 'risale'- 'treaty' are found. Only hagiographic writings are allocated, commonly referred to as *Tazkirat* (remembrances) or *Tabaqat* (bits); or, for example, the well-known essay by Ansari called simply '*Munajat*' (Prayers). The allegorical nature of some of the works can be indirectly judged by their names, such as '*Lama'at*' (The sparkling) by Fakhr al-Din Iraqi or, conversely, allegorical meaning denote a particular genre orientation of the work, as, we can say, *Nafahat al-uns min Hazarat al-Quds* (breath of friendship from the palaces of holiness) by Jami, representing a model of living.

Among the prose works of Persian Sufi the main volume is accounted for theoretical works, which is not surprising, as the rapid spread of Sufism in the

Sufism in India and Central Asia 151

XI-XIII centuries throughout the Near and Middle East required a corresponding ideological support in the form of theoretical development of basic provisions of the Sufi. This kind of works deal with the problems of doctrinal character, such as the nature and attributes of the Almighty, the role of God as the creator of the universe, the manifestation of the divine essence, the knowledge of the visible and the hidden worlds, place and purpose of man in the world; questions of Sufi rituals and rules, such as the need for *zikr*, seclusion, following the mentor; issues of ethical orientation: purification of the soul, living conditions, behaviour and quality of *murid*, education and improvement of human flesh and the heart in accordance with the laws of the *tariqa*, etc. The authors of theoretical works were famous Sufi leaders such as Najm ad-Din Razi, and others.

Najm ad-Din Razi owns several Sufi treatises, including such well-known as '*Marmuzat-i Asadi dar mazmurat-i Davoodi*' (*Asadi* Symbols in Davud's Psalms), 'Manarat as-sayerin' (Lighthouses of travellers) '*Risalat at-teyr*' (Treatise on birds), '*Siraj al-kulub*' (Light of hearts), '*Eshk-o aql*' (Love and intelligence). But he became famous in the Sufi environment and among educated circles undoubtedly due to his fundamental work '*Mirsad al-ibad min al-mabda ila-l-ma'ad*' (The Way of the servants of God from the source to return), referring to one of the most reputable Sufi sources. Consisting of five chapters (*bab*) and forty sections (*fasl*) it is dedicated to the complex of questions of the theory and practice of Sufism. However, as in other theoretical works, literary components correlated with the general development of Persian prose are clearly seen in it. In the *Mirsad al-Ibad* 'is, above all, the story of Adam's creation, false stories. There are also general poetic fragments which are typical for the medieval Persian-language fiction in the whole.

The history of the creation of Adam and his expulsion from paradise has parameters of mediaeval feature story, in which an invention, series of events, the author's interpretation of a familiar story present. The story in it develops from the string to the end, and it deals with the characters of the highest celestial spheres. Their behaviour in spite of that is of a down to earth character and is consistent with ethical issues, affected along with others in the story. Contrasting Adam with *Shaitan*, whom the last misled and who was for this reason expelled from paradise, Najm ad-Din, as if wants to indicate the universality of the opposition of dark and light starts, good and evil, followed by superior forces of good.

The story of Adam is close to the artistic prose for a lot of techniques and tools used in it, peculiar to the style of this prose. The author always resorts to personalization, extensively uses the vivid imagery, often enters dialogical structures into narration. As actors, along with God, the angels, Adam, Shaitan serve the earth, love, heart, spirit. They are actively involved in separate episodes, acquiring the status of competent characters. Describing their behaviour or the circumstances they face, Najm ad-Din uses visual tools. Here, for example, what appears to 'the spirit of eyes' when he enters the body of Adam, '... He found his shelter very gloomy and terrible, the foundation of which was laid on four opposing bases; He realized that it will not be durable. He saw a dark and narrow house with several thousand insects and pests [from among] snakes, scorpions, dragons; [Saw] a variety of predators: lions, panthers, leopards, bears, wild boars; different beast: donkeys, cows, horses, mules and camels.[3] The human body, as can be seen, is compared with the dark and narrow housing prone to destruction (*khane-yi tang-o tariq*), housing which is very dark and terrible (*khane-yi bas-i zolmani wa ba vahshat),* in which temporarily a pure spirit will remain, and animals represent the basest human qualities, defects, its negative aspects, actions deserving censure.

Actors in the story of Adam in the *Mirsad al-ibad* are chalked out superficially, there is no need to speak about their development, but it is symptomatic that features of psychologising are shown through the image of Adam, he pours out his spiritual experiences in verses, and his passionate pleas to the Lord for their expressiveness are similar to the soulful strings of *Munajat* by Ansari. One of its appeals is as follows: 'O God! Again, I saw that all of us are powerless and you are the powerful, we are all mortal, and you are the eternal, we are all in misery, but You saviour, we are all alone, and you are someone for everyone. Do not leave the one who you took, and do not crack the one who you called. Do not disgrace those who you made welcome for yourself, do not aggrieve those who you brought up in joy. Since you took us,

Sufism in India and Central Asia

you bless us; do not leave us to ourselves. Forgive us for this misunderstanding, for it is you who planted the seed, and you who needed the clay.[4] In these lines is felt heartache and despair of person who has committed a mistake, who is experiencing the horror of loneliness and at the same time hoping for a favourable turn of fate for himself.

Consistently turning events in the history, Najm ad-Din justifies their move not with natural cause-effect relationships, but only with the will of the Creator, who controls and directs all processes both in the universe-the macrocosm and in the individual-the microcosm. In the epenthetic stories there is no similar preset and other accents are placed in them. They are intended for illustrative purposes only, to confirm some of the author's thoughts, but are designed to do it not with a simple statement, but in a simple, entertaining way. In this respect they are similar to medieval novels with their unpredictable ending. So, in the epenthetic stories about the sister of Mansur Hallaj, the question of a respectable husband about why she does not cover her entire face, but only a half of it, is followed by such an unexpected answer: 'Show me a man, so I cover my face. In the whole Baghdad there is only one half a man, and he is-Hussein (*i.e.* Mansoor Hallaj - M.K.). If it were not for him, I would not close even this half of my face'.[5] Also unexpected phrase ends with the story of the plug-Shaykh Muhammad Kuf. In both cases, the moment of surprise only underlines the intention of the author, and enhances the perception of the correct thought. The epenthetic story about sheikh Muhammad Kuf also ends with an unexpected phrase. In both cases, the moment of surprise only underlines the intention of the author, and enhances the perception of the correct thought.

Epenthetic stories by Najm ad-Din can be divided into two groups. The first deals with the historical characters. In this group act such ruling such persons as caliphs of Abu Bakr and Omar, Sultan Salakh ad-Din; famous Sufi preachers, Sheikhs of Abu Saeed Meyheni, Abu Ali Dakkak, Junayd Baghdadi, Mansur Hallaj, etc. In the second group are presented Quranic characters: Ibrahim, Musa, Suleiman, Davud. A few stories are associated with the Prophet Muhammad.

The sources of epenthetic stories in '*Mirsad al-ibad*' are Muslim traditions, folklore; part of the story is taken from written sources. For example, Najm ad-Din included in the composition the story of Abu Said Meyheni and Abu Ali Dakkak, available in '*Asrar at-tawhid*'.[6] It tells the story of how Abu Said asked his teacher about the divine manifestation and how he behaved when heard his answer. But if in '*Asrar at-tawhid*' the story is followed in the general stream of stories designed to show the personality of Abu Said and its inclusion in the book is not caused by an explanation of some of the theoretical units, then for Najm ad-Din, it is directly related to the previous statement and is shown for clarifying 'the manifestation of the attributes of magnificence.

In many stories an edifying meaning emerges as well. They speak of modesty, chastity, honesty, truthfulness, frankness, but at the same time, these concepts are always infused with religious motives and suggest mandatory aspiration to God. For example, in the story about Davud and a poor man, the latter sees his everyday hard work, one dirham earned per day, as a special privilege of serving and nearness to God and refuses Davud's pittances.

Epenthetic stories are found not in all Sufi works or not always in large quantities. In the same '*Mirsad al-ibad*' they are relatively few, very few of them are in the '*Lama'at*' by Fakhr ad-Din Iraqi, and not at all in '*Esh-o-aql*' by Najm ad-Din Razi and '*Munajat*' by Ansari. In the latter it was caused by the specifics of the presentation. '*Munajat*' in general has not any scene rod or semantic breakdown of text into chapters and sections, and has a different logic of construction. It is a stream of references to God, called to demonstrate the firmness and the main goal of human spiritual quest. Interrupting these appeals by epenthetic stories would knock the rhythm of presentation down; suspend the increase of emotional state and prevent the concentration of religious impulses.

However, in some genres of Sufi prose epenthetic stories dominate. This applies primarily to hagiographic works. The essence of the life was to convey to the reader the true story of the saint's life, tell about his amazing deeds, deeds worthy of imitation, of the miracles performed by him and occurring after his death. And epenthetic stories could not be better suited for this task.

One could touch the most various aspects of the life of the saint in them; they showed the strength of his faith and love for God, affect its relations with the followers of the Sufi brotherhoods, the people as a whole. Stories could be used anywhere in the exposition; they could be easily interchanged or replaced by others, recalling in this sense, the stories from the most common in the Middle Ages framed novels, between the epenthetic components of which there is usually no logical sequence.

In '*Kashf al-mahjoub*' by Hujwiri the epenthetic stories are mainly included in the biography of sheikhs and mystics; they are quite lot. In '*Asrar at - tawhid*' there are 277 of such stories. They are all somehow associated with the image of Sheikh Abu Said, to whose life the work is dedicated. Muhammad bin Munavvar was not a Sufi authority or an experienced writer. Besides '*Asrar at-tawhid*,' he wrote nothing else. But this work is one of the most significant in the history of Sufi thought. Author was prompted to take up the pen by several reasons. He wanted to recreate as far as possible, the full image of the sheikh, because, in his words, 'from the traces of our sheikh, except the grave and Mashhad, there's nothing left,' and preserve for descendants 'favour of his sayings and deeds.'[7] Besides describing his pious deeds and actions, he tried to influence the people, to guide them on the path of faith, as well as provide spiritual guidance to those who wished to become a Sufi.

The composition of '*Asrar at-tawhid*', covering diverse materials is unusual. The first chapter tells the story of the life of Abu Said, from birth to death, and it is a coherent narrative, when events follow one another, forming a continuous chain. The second and third chapters include several sections each. At the same time the principal amount of epenthetic stories appear in the second chapter. There are prayers of Sheikh in it, his calls, letters, and poems spoken by him. The last third chapter, along with the description of the death of Sheikh, transfer of his wills also contains stories about him, even though their number is not as much as in the second chapter.

Epenthetic stories of '*Asrar at-tawhid*' can be divided into several groups. These are, firstly, the stories associated with the extraordinary abilities of Sheikh, in particular, with his astounding insight, the ability to read people's minds, his knowledge of their past and guessing the future. They are a lot in *'Asrar at-tawhid'*, as it should be in the work about the life of a Sufi sheikh; secondly, the stories about the initial non-recognition of the sheikh and a hostile attitude towards him, changing with a subsequent recognition of his excellence and the establishment of friendly relations with him; thirdly, stories that speak about the influence of the sheikh, about the authority he possessed, the respect and reverence that the people gave him.

Though part of stories is dedicated to the Sheikh, but carries a didactic cautionary load. Their main purpose is to bring up on the example of Sheikh's deeds high human qualities, love towards people, compassion, willingness to help, sacrifice, desire for companionship, loyalty, purity, etc.

Some stories are simply devoted to some real episodes from the life of the Sheikh, and some has a fantastic, fabulous nature and can be explained by the influence of folk elements. These are stories about meetings of *murids* with snakes, lions, dragon, who appeared to be friends of Sheikh, about a gazelle, who sacrificed itself for the sake of Abu Said and his students and others.

Folklore plot[8] often found in medieval literatures, lies at the heart of the story about a man who asked the sheikh to tell him some of the mysteries of God. In response, Sheikh gives him a box with instructions not to open it. However, the man could not stand, and opened the box, and a mouse runs away from it. Behind this plot move follows a comment of this kind that if you just could not keep the mouse in the box, how you will be able to keep the secret of God.

Literary treatment of the plots, the use of artistic means and techniques, mythological and fictional characters, the description of landscape, portrait and voice characteristics, and dialogical structure give *'Asrar at-tawhid'* features of artistic prose (fiction). Some episodes are processed so that they appear in the form of small art miniatures. All features of the medieval novel, as well as the above-mentioned stories of *Mirsad al-ibad* has, for example, the eighth story, the hero of which tells of his first meeting and acquaintance with Sheikh Abu Said. It also has a consistently unfolding plot and an unexpected ending, provides the performance of characters, and describes their appearance, state of mind, feelings and experiences.

Sufism in India and Central Asia 157

The medieval novel is reminded also by 261th story. It states that the eldest son of Sheikh Abu Tahir did not want to go to school. He did not know the Koran, but at the direction of his father, learnt by heart Surah *'Al-Fath'* (Victory), beginning with the words 'Inna fatahna'. Many years after the death of Abu Said he once was at a reception of the famous vizier Nizam al-Mulk, and here he was accused for not knowing the Koran. Not believing it Nizam al-Mulk, offered to the man accusing him to ask Abu Tahir to recite any *surah* of the Koran. And the prosecutor chose for the son of Sheikh precisely the *Surah 'Al-Fath'*. This story was supposed to demonstrate the foresight of Abu Said, but also the author's idea got a brilliant implementation in the short story ending. In the story, there is also a moment of entertaining inherent in other stories as well.

In the epenthetic stories *'Asrar at-tawhid'*, especially in those which are devoted to Divine Powers (*Karamat*) of the Sheikh, fantastic events and incidents are mixed with the real; fairy-tale characters act along with the ordinary people. However, in such a mix the author's desire to draw a distinction between them and comprehend what is happening in terms of the real logic of things is still felt. So, the 104th story narrates that a certain woman in the sermon of Sheikh was captured by an ecstatic state, and she threw herself from the roof. Sheikh made a sign, and she hung in the air. Thereafter, the women who were on the same roof, pulled her back. But then they looked and found that the edge of her dress had been caught on a nail, so she remained still alive. Miracles of the Sheikh during the rescue of the woman are nothing to do with, and she remains alive due to the banality of the circumstances. In some episodes, even in the words of the sheikh emerges a desire to avoid a fantastic explanation. For example, by the end of the 74th story it is noted that he deliberately sent men to the people of Nishapur, to tell them what happened to him - was not a miracle, but the usual case. Muhammad bin Munavvar notes that miracles ability to read the thoughts were a considerable phenomenon to others, ordinary people, but for the sheikh they meant nothing. The main thing for him was the inner spiritual connection with God, his special position.[9]

158　　　Chapter 11 The Style of Persian Sufiprose XI-XIII centuries

In '*Asrar at-tawhid*' emerges the image of Abu Said, endowed with traits of sanctity and piety. This is a man, sometimes overly idealized, enthusiastically welcomed and respected by people. Nevertheless, he is not transformed into some kind of scheme befitting hagiographic genre. Although Berman's comment on that the life describes not just what is 'due' and not the supreme ideal of life, but the ascetic life, gives the image of the ideal incarnation requirements to the earthly reality[10] and finds confirmation in the Persian Lives nonetheless unlike many other medieval works, in which it is too difficult to see a certain person behind the images of the characters a particular person, '*Asrar at-tawhid*' transmits the image of Abu Said. For example, in one of his stories Muhammad bin Munavvar describes him as 'a tall, white-skinned, stout man with big eyes, a beard till the abdomen, wearing a Sufi *muraqqa*, with a stick and a jug in his hands, with a prayer, thrown over his shoulder, Sufi hat, worn on the head and chomchomas on his feet'[11] Some details of this portrait are then repeated several times.

Likhachev, examining the ancient Russian literature, noted its inherent realism, which is displayed in a number of symptoms.[12] A similar way of description is characteristic for Sufi hagiography. The same characters in '*Asrar at-tawhid*' look like alive people. Thus, the 96th story tells: 'There was a dervish in Ajdjdakh named Hamza; he was engaged in trade, was murid of our sheikh and very precious [to him] a man, loving, hot, restless and passionate.[13]

Sheikh Abu Said is the protagonist of the work. He is a real person, for example, he is not deprived of the same feeling of subtle humour, often expressed through his words and expressions. Among his many exhortations and instructions there is an anecdote: 'Some farmer told his wakil;' Buy me a donkey which is not too big and not too small to be able to hold me on the descents and ascents and not to turn out to be powerless when there are difficulties, and to pass through stones, and bear if the grass is finished, and if I gave it a lot (of food), he would have multiplied it [food]- wakil said – hey Hodja! I have not seen such qualities, except for Abu Yusif al-Kazi's. Ask your God to transform Abu Yusif into the donkey' for you. His disciples, like Hassan Muaddab, children, grandchildren and close relatives, friends and enemies and people with their own characters, habits and interests, weaknesses and praiseworthy qualities. They are easily recognizable and can be represented in a picture of social relationship which is displayed by Muhammad bin Munavvar.

However, despite of the realism '*Asrar at-tawhid*' is a medieval writing, which clearly shows stereotypes of situations, actions and performance. Emotions of people at the sight of Divine Powers of the Sheikh are always described in the same words. They cry with delight, scream or faint. The young man and the wise Imam of years, an eminent Sufi and a rich merchant, Shihna, *muhtasib* and scientist - all behave the same in the presence of Sheikh; in the case of their own short-sightedness, hostility or committing errors they fall at his feet and ask for forgiveness, seeking his friendship and patronage. Characters often see prophetic dreams, after which they get convinced in the power of the sheikh; this situation is often repeated: the Sufis and their feasts, which are told about the miracles, the words and deeds of Sheikh, all at once rise to their feet and bow towards Meyhene – Sheikh's homeland.

There are also stereotyped phrases and expressions in the text. In this respect, the initial phrases of stories are interesting. If the information is given on behalf of the sheikh, such an expression follows: 'Sheikh-i ma goft' - 'our sheikh said' or 'Sheikh-i ma Abu Said *gofte ast*'-'our Sheikh Abu Said.' and then the story itself or its description. Similarly, certain statements, the sayings of Abu Sa'id are included in the text.

If the author knows exactly who transmitted the story, from whom he heard it or where he had read it, for example such a phrase is provided: 'Khoja Hassan Muaddab goft'-'Khoja Hassan Muaddab said' or '*be khatt-I Sheikh Abu-l-Kasem bin Ali ash-Sharmagani ke Didam neveshte bud* 'I saw a writing written by the hand (handwriting) of Sheikh Abu-l-Qasim bin Ali ash-Sharmagani'.

In case the absence of information about the storyteller or transmitter of messages these words are given: 'avardeand ke' - 'say that'; and finally, if the message is told by the author himself, for example, such a phrase is used, in the 19th story, which 'I heard from Sheikh *Zayn at-Taif* Omar Shavkani, who said that he heard from Imam Ahmad Malekana. Names in the chain of transmitters may change; it may consist of one or more elements, but it is not as important as the purpose of all these phrases is the same: to refer to any particular name, and thus give credence to the presentation.

Stereotyped phrases and expressions are found in the writings of the Sufi's work. But among them dominate the religious formula. After mentioning the name of Muhammad, as a rule, this phrase is given: 'May God bless and welcome him'; after the deceased the holy Sheikh follow these words follow: 'Let peace be upon him', 'May Allah have mercy on him' or 'May Allah sanctify his place of rest.' Often, after the presentation of some events the following words are added: 'Allah knows the best.' In the '*Mirsad al-ibad*' almost every chapter ends with the expression: 'May Allah bless Muhammad and all his family.'

The author of the work, speaking of him, diminishes his value. This feature is characteristic for medieval literature. In the Persian-language poetry, especially in the Masnavi, poets highly assessed the merits of predecessors in the field of art and poetry at the same time very modestly and even disparagingly mentioned their own abilities and skills. In the Sufi prose the writer, as if doesn't want to interfere in what is destined, only traces what is happening, or offers an explanation, based on his own capabilities. In the 'Asrar at-tawhid' he calls himself 'the prayer ascender' referring to God in 'Munajat,' he says, 'Oh my God! I am aware of my weakness and witness of my helplessness.[14]

While mentioning Shahs and crowned heads, opposite, with the help of traditional epithets and comparisons their names and deeds are exalted. This usually occurs in the introductions of the works. Such parts have a normative nature and contain binding fragments of comprising praise to God, to the Prophet Muhammad and the prophets, and saints, shahs and rulers. They also report on the circumstances of writing the work, its name is given, historical and autobiographical information is provided.

In smaller works, such as '*Eshq-o aql*' and '*Lama'at*', some parts are missing; there are no historical and other data. Hujwiri, on the contrary, included additional chapters related to the authorship of the text or wearing didactic sense into the introduction part. The full adherence to the canon appears in the introductions to '*Asrar at-tawhid*' and '*Mirsad al-ibad*'.

Sufism in India and Central Asia 161

Introductory parts stand out with solemnity and grandiloquence. Long, flowery proposals sentences, abundant in graphic means, which nevertheless do not create any particular image or visible environment, are used in them. Muhammad bin Munavvar, for example, referring to the Shah and praising his qualities, uses, as was customary, fanciful hyperboles, lush and flowery epithets and florid comparisons. Expressions like 'were the sun of the sky of faith and stars of the horizon of certitude,' 'to grasp perfection', 'with sublime judgment of the highest immortality' and others are deprived of the special information content and are designed to maintain the elected narrative tone. Such an abstraction and remoteness from reality conformed to the aesthetics of description, when not a visual image was required to be created, but conditionally - exalted, surpassing everything else. Especially important was this way in the presence of a particular recipient of work or solving a specific ideological task.

Abstractness of description in the introductions prevails in some parts of the text. But it may have a functional significance. It is often used by Fakhr ad-Din Iraqi. For example, in '*Lama'at*' the morning is coming to describes as follows, 'The morning sighed, the sun of favor shone, breeze of happiness blew and the sea of generosity came in motion. Description does not show any real picture, but images of the 'morning appearance', 'the sun of favour', 'breeze of happiness,' 'Sea of generosity' alienate it from concreteness and representation, and seemed only to 'brighten' it, making it more attractive to the reader.

But the following sentence gives the key to understanding the whole fragment, translating it into the plane of symbolic interpretation. In this case nothing comes not in the morning, but a divine blessing is expressed, giving the lover or aspiring to God to the chance step on the right path of seeking and discovery of true being: 'The cloud of generosity so much rain,[15] then shed its light on the ground of talent, that 'the earth will be lit with light of his own Lord's'[16] the lover drank plenty of water of life, awakened from the sleep of nothingness, dressed Gaba of life, hoisted on the head of contemplation, girded with a strap of passion, set foot on the path of seeking, and from knowledge came to the entity, and from heard to embrace. In '*Lama'at*' abstract description does not include individual fragments or episodes. In fact, they are just pieces of a single symbolic painting of work. Its ideological core passing through all the twenty-eight chapters, each of which is called the 'sparkling'-is the interpretation of the Sufi concept of love.

All the basic concepts are concentrated around three semantic centers – symbols of *'Lama'at'*; *'eshk'* - 'love', *'Mashuk'* - 'beloved', *'Ashik'* - 'lover.' Already in the first chapter Fakhr ad-Din sets the correlation between them: 'The essence of love through the lover has become a mirror of love, so that he could learn his beauty in it and by the state of love it became a mirror of the beloved, so that it could see its names and attributes in it ...' Despite the apparent differences, all three images, according to Iraqi are the unique embodiment of the essence of the Absolute. About this he wrote repeatedly throughout his whole work, reinforcing his thoughts with poetic accents:

Beloved, love and lover-all three

are the same here,

Since there is no link [between] them, then what

Can separation do?[17]

Each chapter of 'Lama'at' in one form or another contains interpretation of the essence of love, the actions and state of being in love represents his relationship with his beloved, in fact the behaviour of the Sufi, seeking to find out the divine truth and union with the Absolute. The symbolic subtext can be easily read in other writings. It was caused by an initial orientation of Sufism on the symbolic perception of the environment. The real world was considered a transient, being false, only a reflection of the true life belonged to forever mere and single Creator. Comprehension of the theory required the development of special terminological device and imagery that could reveal the essence of the depicted. Besides that, some Sufis wanted to hide their mystical illuminations from the profane, describing them in an inaccessible allegorical language. All these led to the symbolic 'filling' of individual texts and the whole works.[18]

In Sufi literature, especially poetry, one of the most striking examples of the allegory by Farid ad-Din Attar *'Mantiq at-teyr'* (Conversation of birds).

Sufism in India and Central Asia

It tells about how the birds were looking for their Sultan-Simurg. And after all the difficulties of a long journey, which claimed the lives of thousands of birds, only thirty flew to him (in Persian simurg means thirty birds), and they were that Simurg. The mystical subtext of the statement here reflects the basic Sufi concept of connection and dissolution of a traveler- seeking in God, and the birds in the 'Mantiq at-teyr '-these are the same Sufis, following by divine searching and spiritual development, aimed at ultimate achievement of God.

'*Mantiq at-teyr*' played a significant role in the development of Persian Sufi medieval literature and the creation of a special language, appearing including in poetry. In poetic lines could be more emotionally and vividly reflected the mystical experiences of persian poetry not by chance but exactly gave the world the greatest Sufi poets. The abilities of a poetic word, associated with his particular expression were widely used in Sufi prose and beyond. Almost in every prosaic works whether its historiography, literature of *adab* or religious work, not to mention artistic prose, there are poetic inserts in a variety of them: individual Misra, baits or even whole poems of small genres. So, almost every page of the manuscript of a small historical work of a prominent medieval historian, geographer and public figure Hamdallah Mustaufi Qazvini *Zeil-i tarikh-i-gozide* (Supplement to Favourite History), written in XIV century, contains poetic fragments, some of which are important in terms of presentation of historical events.

The authors also often resorted to Saj – a rhymed prose, created such brilliant examples of it as the *Gulistan*. However, long before the *Gulistan* Sufi prose featured the great works which write by Saj. In this regard, of course, merits of Abdallah Ansari should be admitted. Some researchers believe that he is the creator of rhymed prose. M. Bahar mentioned him as a pioneer of the Persian *musadzha*.[19] Another Iranian scientist Z. Safa believed that Ansari sought to distinguish his speech from ordinary prose, and, moreover, wanted to make it more pleasant and catchy.[20] One way or another, Ansari often uses in his prosaic writings saj, and his *Munajat* is entirely written in rhymed prose.

Compositionally *Munajat* is organized so that the pleas to the Lord are followed by a single stream, subdivided into small paragraphs, each of which begins with an appeal: *Ilahi* - 'Oh, my God.' Then the prayers themselves are pronounced, standing out with a delicacy of the language and a subtle imagery, showing the depth of artistic thinking of Ansari. In some appeals prayers alternate with the glorification of God, mention boundless love to Him, the third, exalts His essence and attributes. Sometimes Ansari writes about his own condition, experiences, hopes and anxieties, tying his thoughts with God. His Sufi views gain vivid, emotional realization, followed by a guessed passion and altitude of the soul.

The rhymed lines of *Munajat* are often interrupted by poetic accents. Basically they are two or three baits, the value of which fits into the theme of prosaic excerpts. The verses explain or supplement the already initiated idea and the entire paragraph looks as a complete independent fragment. The following lines may serve as an example of this: 'Oh my God! In each of the two worlds, I have chosen the love To You, I tailored clothes of unhappiness and tore curtain of prosperity.

> Oh God! Intoxicate me with the wine of love,
>
> And with Your love destroy me and [again] give me a life.
>
> In everything but love, make me poor.
>
> Once and for all fascinate me with fetters of love.[21]

This fragment is curious to contains two references: one - 'Oh My God' in the prosaic part, the other - 'Oh, God!' - in a poetic. What is more plea-prayer is not given in the prosaic part, but in poetic. It looks quite natural. Since in prose Ansari speaks of his love to God, and in his verses asks him to strengthen love. Love is a key concept in the teachings of the Sufis - serves as a link between the two parts, and in the lines of poetry other two famous Sufi images are featured with it - the symbols 'intoxication' and 'wine'.

The connection between the two parts is created not only due to the image of love. Here is used another Sufi symbol-poverty (*faqr*), the lack of property. In the prosaic part Ansari says that he tore 'the curtain of prosperity,' but in verses, he asks God to make him poor. Thus, the semantic interdependence ensures a close contact of both parts within a single segment.

Sufism in India and Central Asia   165

The principle of the use poetic lines in the Sufi sources being considered by us is basically the same. But the frequency of their uses varies. So, in the works it's approximately similar in terms of volume-*Munajat, Eshk-o aql* and *Lama'at* the leader on the occurring poetic fragments, of course, is '*Lama'at*'. It contains 139 fragments, comprising 206 baits, whereas in '*Munajat*' and '*Eshk-o aql*', their number is respectively equal to 61 and 28; the number of baits in them is 115 and 84. In addition, in the *Lama'at* there are more complete poems in terms of genres. Among them there are three gazelles, ten *kitas* and nine *rubais*.

There no rules exist for the use of poetry in Sufi sources. The quantity and quality of poetic passages depended mostly on the abilities and desires of the writer himself. The author of 'Lama'at' -Fakhr ad-Din Iraqi was himself a poet, owner of divan of poems, consisting of gazelles, rubai, qasidas, tardzhibbands, tarkibbands, kitas. Aside from the small-form poetry, he created a masnavi, with the volume of slightly more than 1000 baits. It is called 'Ushshak-name' (The Book of Lovers) and is devoted to Shams ad-Din Muhammad Juveyni-grand vizier (sahib-divan) of Ilkhans, the brother of a historian Ala ad-Din Malik Ata Juveyni. Poetry of Fakhr ad-Din differs with a higher emotion and at the same time is written in simple, accessible and melodic language. Ya Ripka, describing the work of Iraqi, noted that it was entirely penetrated by ecstatic moods.[22]

On the poetic field Fakhr ad-Din was not a novice. He was known as a skilled poet and apparently this fact left an imprint on his prose, giving it greater in comparison with other writings focus on the poetic dimension. Other authors, in particular, Najm ad-Din Razi and Ansari also wrote poetry, but their poetry did not gain a wide acceptance. V. Zhukovsky, referring to Haji Halfa, noted that Ansari had three divans of Persian poetry.[23] But in fact, what reached to our days, are poetic fragments from his prose works.[24]

The same is true about Najm ad-Din. His poetry does not represent an independent reservoir, and all his poems are included in the prose writings. They are written primarily in the genres of *Rubai, Gazelles* and *Qasidas*. The compiler of texts for verses by Najm ad-Din, Mahmud Modabberi estimated that the volume of them comprises 391 baits. Their contents are mostly Sufi motives, philosophical reflections on the transience of life; there also occur social and moral themes in them.[25]

Religious poetry prevails in the *Mirsad al-ibad*. In general, the total volume of poems in the work is quite significant and is more than 500 couplets. They are mostly scattered baits, lines of poems, excerpts from qasidas, gazelles; there are various rubai and the whole gazelles. Some of them are owned by well-known masters of the poetic word, such as Rudaki, Ferdowsi, Sanai, Khagani, Anvari, Nizami, Khayyam, *etc.*; part is written by Najm ad-Din. By the time of writing *Mirsad al-ibad* solid *Hadikat al-haqiqa* (The Garden of Truth) by Sanai, poems by Farid ad-Din Attar, examples of Sufi poetry have already been created. Their influence is especially Sanai, who accounts for almost a tenth of all the works of poetic lines, traced in the poems by Najm ad-Din.

As for the *Asrar at-tawhid* except the 172 couplets in it, scattered throughout the whole work, has a special chapter called: 'Scattered baits, spoken by the mouth of our sheikh.' It also contains 75 baits. As it is seen from the name of the chapter all the baits used in the composition, are associated with the name of Sheikh Abu Said. He himself is the author of, most likely, only a few rubai. [26] But, as in the 'Asrar at-tawhid' the Sheikh knew poetry well, understood it and knew by a great number of poems in Arabic and Persian languages. Therefore, it is not surprising that Muhammad bin Munavvar, was acted virtually as a biographer of the Sheikh, tried to save as many verses which had a direct relation to it.

From a poetic point of view, Hujwiri composition has the lowest interest contained only a few small fragments of poetry. Hujwiri was not particularly a 'decoration' of the prosaic part and his main focus was directed on the statement and discussion of theoretical questions.

Talking about the style of medieval Persian Sufi prose we would also like to mention one of the features associated with its religious color. It was the presence of Qur'anic verses and hadiths in the text. In some works their number is quite significant. But in the 'Mirsad al-ibad' by Najm ad - Din each of forty sections begins with a verse from the Quran, followed by one or two

Sufism in India and Central Asia 167

hadiths, and the section ends with a blessing to Muhammad. His other work 'Marmuzat-i Asadi dar mazmurat-i Davoodi' consisting of ten chapters has a similar composition.

Najm ad-Din verifies according to the Quran almost every thesis and strongly emphasizes his commitment to the Quranic tradition. H. Algar right when he pointed out that one of the features of 'Mirsad al-ibad' was a clear demonstration of the Quranic roots of Sufism and that the Quran for Najm ad-Din and other Sufis was a solid and harmonious universe.[27] Numerous excerpts from the Koran, the hadiths were to show the solidity of the work and serve as evidence of the validity and fidelity of thoughts and sayings by the writer, and his boundless love for God and worship of the Prophet Muhammad. They should have also emphasized the 'orthodox' essence of Sufi piety and the way of life.[28] In addition, the author not only drew his arguments in them, and sometimes inspiration, but also used them as a starting point for subsequent presentation of events which were more evident in hagiographic writings.

Verses and the hadiths contained in the works were cited in Arabic language. Actually, for the medieval Persian-language prose the use of the Arabic language can be regarded as the norm already. Authors included in the texts in Arabic short expressions, proverbs, sayings, as well as the whole baits,[29] a fairly large fragments and even stories. Occasionally they performed some translations into Persian. So, Muhammad bin Munavvar owns several translations from the Arabic language. Among them there is a well-known expression: 'Some of the sages said:' To this world you came crying and people were laughing, so try to die laughing, and people would cry for you[30] or the following proverb:' And even a fire does not fuel a fuse as the enmity incites the tribe, Najm ad-Din has also translations; for example, such sayings: 'If there would be no passion, no one would have the way to God.[31] The use of the Arabic language, considering its role and influence in the Muslim world, was to become an additional indicator of learning and education and once again pointed to the connection of works with Islamic values.

Persian Sufi prose of 11-13th centuries is a complex and multifaceted phenomenon. Appearing as a product of creative activity, it naturally developed in line with the religious - ideological, literary - cultural processes in the Middle East. This prose is characterized by not only a literary component, but first and foremost by a religious orientation, and sometimes the presence of the historical reservoir. All these could not affect its style, which preserved its uniqueness, not only at this stage, but also in XIV-XV centuries.

References

[1] Z.N. Vorojeykina, *Isfahan School of poets and literary life of Iran in the pre-Mongol period XII - beginning of XIII centuries*-M., 1984, p. 54.

[2] One of these impromptus associated with the poet Unsuri is shown in E.E.Bertels, also see, E.E.Bertels, *History of Persian - Tajik literature* -M., 1960, p. 331.

[3] Najm ad - Din Razi, *Mirsad al-ibad min al-mabda ila-l-ma'ad*/ Translated from persian, foreword, note and denotation by M.D. Kyazimov - Baku, 2014 , p. 93.

[4] Ibid, p. 99.

[5] Ibid, p.115.

[6] Muhammad bin Munavvar, *Asrar at-Tawhid fi Makamat ash*, Sheikh Abu Said / Translated from Persian, foreword, note and denotation by M. D. Kazimov - Baku , 2010, p . 86.

[7] ibid, p. 36; 34.

[8] N.P. Andreev. Directory of fairy stories according to Aarne-Leningrad system, 1929, p. 54, No. 790.

[9] Muhammad bin Munavvar. *Asrar at-Tawhid*, p. 446.

[10] B. I. Berman. *Life Reader* (Hagiographic canon of Russian of the Middle Ages and its tradition of perception), In the book, *Artistic language of the Middle Ages*, 1982, p. 173.

[11] Muhammad bin Munavvar. *Asrar at-Tawhid*, p. 100.

[12] D.S. Likhachev, *Poetics of old Russian literature* - Leningrad, 1967, p. 135.

[13] Muhammad bin Munavvar, *Asrar at-tawhid*, p. 220.

[14] M. D. Kazimov, *From the history of Sufi thought*, Baku, 2001, p. 23.

[15] A phrase from *hadith* (see Ahmed b. Hanbel, Musned, *Kahire*, 1313, s. 176.

[16] Koran/ translated from Arabic and commented by M. - N. O. Osmanov, *Kum*, 39 : 69

[17] *From the history of Sufi thought,* The significance of this bait is that since the beloved, love and lover- are united, between them cannot be a connection, there is no need for it , and without a connection separation becomes unnecessary.

[18] A. D. Knish. Muslim mysticism - M., 2004, p. 116.

[19] M. Bakhar, *Sabkshenasi ya tarikh- i tatavvor - i nasr - i Farsi*, Jeld - o dovvom - Tehran, 1338, p. 240.

[20] Z. Safa. *Tarikh i adabiyyat dar Iran. Jeld - i dovvom Tehran*, 1367, p. 882.

Sufism in India and Central Asia

[21]From the history of Sufi thought, p. 23.

[22]Ya. Ripka, *The history of Persian and Tajik Literature,* M., 1970, p. 246.

[23]V. Jukovskiy, Songs of Herat old man - Oriental notes, St. Petersburg, 1895, p. 81

[24]V. Zhukovskiy himself translated and published his poems, included in "Manazil as-sayerin" (see V. Zhukovskiy. Songs of old Herat man).

[25]Najm ad-Din Razi. Ash'ar/ Be kushesh - i M. Modabberi - Tehran, 1363, p. 4.

[26]For details, see . M.D. Kazimov. Foreword-In the book, Muhammad bin Munavvar, *Asrar at - Tawhid,* p. 18-20.

[27]Kh. Algar. Foreword - in the book by Najm al-Udin Razi. The path of God's Bondsmen from Origin to Return/Translated by H. Algar - North Haledon, New Jersey,1980, p. 17-18.

[28]A.D. Knish, *Muslim Mysticism,* p. 136.

[29]In *Mirsad al-ibad* by Najm ad-Din there are poems in old dialect. See Najm ad-Din, *Mirsad al-ibad,* p. 99.

[30]Muhammad bin Munavvar. *Asrar at-Tawhid,* p. 288.

[31]Najm ad-Din, *Mirsad al-ibad,* p. 163.

CHAPTER 12

Significance of Abd-ur-Rahman Jami's Sufi-Poetic Discourse in the Literary Legacy of Medieval Persia

G.N. Khaki

The history of Medieval Persia is full of secrets and mysteries. Legends, poems and anecdotes profoundly supplement rich archaeological findings and historical documents. During its long march of literary developments, the region produced scholars of eminence in almost all branches of knowledge and learning which left indelible mark on the history, culture, traditions and character of Persian society. The region continuously maintained itself over the famous saying of Ibn Khaldun (*undoubtedly non-Arabs have been the torchbearers of knowledge and learning.*) March of scholars in far off lands, dissemination of knowledge and learning, establishment of *madrasas* and *maktabas*, the process of migration, encouraging interconnectedness at doctrinal and practical levels are some of the salient attributes of Medieval Islamic heritage which inter alia greatly benefited the Persian civilization. This historical process of cultural interaction and assimilation gave birth to a significant development of acculturation and enculturation. Islam exposed this region to the global process of literary and cultural growth and threw its corridors open for diverse socio-cultural activities.

The civilizational and cultural profile that emerged as a result of these developments could not confine itself to Persia alone but influenced and engaged the surrounding regions of Central Asia and India as well. Consequently contributions made by Central Asian, Iranian, and Indian Scholars to the enrichment of Asian culture and civilization reached its zenith. Persia thus emerged as a grand civilization owing to the innumerable developments in the literary landscape of the region.[1] Since Persia has been both an imbiber of new influences and a vector of the most novel trends. It is rightly pointed out that out of the several strands which provided the warp and woof of Muslim civilization in Central Asia; the most dominant was the influence of Persia. Medieval Persia forged its identity through the cultures which have enriched them. Their sense of worth and personal dignity lies in the recognition of their celebrated scholars viz-a-viz their special contribution have made to weaving the rich tapestry of the world's civilizations.[2] The contribution of Persian litterateurs to language and literature played a prominent role in shaping the cultural diversity of Iran and made a significant and everlasting contribution to its originality. Having remained as a glittering star among the literatures of their times, Persian poets imbibed and incorporated the universalistic features of poetry in their compositions. Consequently this part of the globe became the torchbearer of the dissemination of knowledge, religious philosophy and world view and value system. The prominent literary figures like Rudaki, Firdausi, Hafiz, Nizami, Rumi, Sa'di and Jami became the torchbearers of sufistic perspectives and literary ethos, the manifestation of which is found in their celebrated works.[3]

In the backdrop of these introductory remarks present in chapter would be an attempt to;

(i) Identify the role of Islam in the promotion of scientific ethos of Medieval Persia,

(ii) Unfold the literary legacy of the region to identify the place and status of Mawlana Jami, (iii) Sketch the position and poetic vision of Jami and refer to the similarities' that exist between him and celebrated scholars of the world and

(iv) Explore the contribution of Jami in the Sufi-Poetic discourse of the region.

Literary Legacy of Medieval Persia

It is an admitted fact that the history of Persia is that of the cradle of mankind and the study of literary ethos in this region is fundamentally the study of a historical process. Whatever the extension and depth of Islam's penetration in numbers and quality may have been characterized by tremendous amount of contribution by Muslim scholars in the field of literature as well as nat-

Sufism in India and Central Asia 173

ural and religious sciences. Great centers of learning emerged in Tashkent, Bukhara, Samarqand, Nishapur, Khawarizm, Khotan, Yarkand,Kashghar Nasph, Tirmidh, Merv, Hussair, Marghinan, Maa-i-margh and Farab.[4] The secular diffusion of Islam and the formation of neo-Islamic communities in Central Asian region were further strengthened as a result of the activities and efforts of distinguished Sufis. The *Risalah* of Abul Qasim Qushaire, *Ihya-al-Ulum* of Ghazali, *Kashf al-Mahjub* of Abu Ali Hujwiri, *Tabaqat-al-Sufiyyah* of Abdul Rahman Sulami and *Fu'ad-al-Fu'ad* of Shaikh Nizamuddin of Delhi, *Awarifu'l Ma'arif* of Shaikh Shihabu'din Suhrawardi and *Fususul-Hikam* of Mohi-ud-din ibn al-Arabi were the most important classics of Sufism produced in the region.

The Persian literature in fact represents one of the high water marks of their cultural and civilizational history. The older forms of Persian poetry that had developed as a result of cultural assimilation in the Muslim era started receding with the passage of time and the genre developed in an entirely new direction and adopted a changed discourse, which though thematically Islamic, essentially represented Persian lore and local cultural ethos.[5] The literary legacy of Persian language is highly colorful and complex in nature. Their literature in general and the genre of *Mathnawi* and *Dastan* in particular embodies the essence of the Persian poetic discourse during the seventeenth and eighteenth centuries displaying its fullest range in the intimacy, intensity, and precision. It represents many aspects of social change, behavior patterns, hopes, repressed wishes, creative thoughts, unconscious yearnings and collective dreams. It analyses the social drama in the geographical frame and with reference to its beauty, diversity and complexity of interpretation. This literature received the attention of distinguished scholars of varied fields of learning.[6] This poetic zeal was further promoted and encouraged by Timurids as rightly referred to by Losenski that poetry was a crucial part of the Timurid project "of cultural mastery and assimilation."[7] The genre of choice in composing poetry during this period was the lyric, especially the *ghazal* while the *qasida* was the genre of choice for the court poets and *mathnawi* was too lengthy for social gatherings. *Ghazal* was the favorite of the era because it provided more options

174   Chapter 12 Significance of Abd-ur-Rahman Jami's Sufi-Poetic ....

for expressing emotions and philosophical or religious thought. Jami also regarded *ghazai* as the best kind of poetry and spent at least fifty years of his life, writing lyric poetry, which he compiled in three sections of a *diwan*.

It is an established fact that Central Asia in general and the populace of Persia in particular, forged their identity through the cultures which have enriched them. Their sense of worth and personal dignity lies in the recognition of their celebrated scholars viz-a-viz their special contribution have made to weave the rich tapestry of the world's civilizations. The contribution of Persian litterateurs to language and literature as such played a prominent role in shaping the cultural diversity of Iran and made a significant and everlasting contribution to its originality. Having remained as a glittering star among the litterateurs of their times, Persian poets imbibed and incorporated the universalistic features of poetry in their compositions. Consequently this part of the globe became the torch bearer in the process of dissemination of knowledge, religious philosophy, worldview and value system. The prominent literary figures like Rudaki, Firdausi, Hafiz, Nizami, Rumi, Sa'di and Jami became the torch bearers of sufistic perspectives and literary ethos, the manifestation of which is found in their celebrated works. They set the stage upon which Firdausi (d.1021) was, in about 1980, to begin his long epic march by gathering together in some 60,000 couplets the legends of Iran, to form the *Shahname*, (the Book of Kings) which remained a reminder of the possibility of national unity and integrity. It has been the inspiration of all generations of Iranians down to present day and served to hold the nation together in the memory of Shared legends about shared sufferings and glories. [8] There was the zest for novelty, first in the language itself, then in the art of penning it; finally, the quest for novelty in striking off new and startling images whereby to move afresh the heart and titillate the mind in taking up perennial and basic human topics of love, separation, sorrow and joy. Shaikh Sa'id Shirazi, (b.1213), a versatile poet brought Persian prose of the high Islamic period to the apogee of perfection, albeit in an intricately stylized form of rhyming prose. In verse and prose, notably in his early middle age works, *Bustan*, (orchard) and *Gulistan* (the flower garden), he inculcated magnanimity' especially in tyrants, repentance, tolerance and other virtues through the artifice of entertaining and easily memorized poems and prose anecdotes. His fellow-citizens of Shiraz, Hafiz (d.1390), used the instrument of the lyric, *ghazal*. He inherited from Sana'i (d.1130) which had been skillfully continued by Sa'di to carry much of the imagery which pointed Rudaki and the earlier poets in their the example. Hafiz's *ghazals*, susceptible, like scripture, to interpretation of many different levels, also have the appeal of a song, to please their reader.[9] While Sa'idi composed the great text of mysticism, tapestry of allegories about human deprivation of the greatest of human needs, apprehension of God and about how this aching separation and dissolution may be bridged, so that the contentment and freedom of living in God are achieved. Rumi (d.1273) having in his *Mathnawi* brought to fullness the spiritual and allegorical literature of which Sana'i and 'Attar had earlier been exponents when social and political hardships had led the people of Iran increasingly to seek the solace of the inner life.[10]

The lyrical and mystical traditions attained another flowering in the fifteenth century in the poetry of Jami who inherited both development of epic strain beyond the use which Firdausi had put it. The long episodic allegorical poem perfected by 'Attar and woven into a vast corpus by Jalal ud-din Rumi. Nizami altered the epic from the' factual' narrative of legendary episodes which is in the *Shahnameh* to make it present episodes as symbols, heroes as paragons, so that the whole mechanism of the epic was lifted on to a more abstract level, and a strong spiritual element introduced.[11]

Similarities between Jami and Celebrated Litterateurs

In the galaxy of Persian poets and scholars who tirelessly contributed to the growth and development of Persian literature in all its manifestations, Mawlana Nurud-din Abd-ur-Rahman Jami managed to occupy special status in the Sufistic traditions and Persian language and literature. Jami (1414-1492), a towering scholar of 15th century, born and brought up in Persia is deemed as a bedrock and representative of high styled contemporary Persian poetry, language and literature. This formidable poet of Persia developed a realistic style of writing to attained the heights of popularity and which eventually earned for him the title of *"Khatam-ul-Shura"* (seal of poets) [12] most cherished of all times. Persian literature in fact came to limelight and assumed its full glory and due to recognition after the emergence of Jami. As against the philosophical treatises, more akin to Persian poetry, Jami went beyond the conventional limits and used the format of Persian national poetry and its epic traditions. The profound quality of his poems has dominated the minds of not only the Persians, but all populace living in the vast region from the Oxus to the Transcaucasia. His diligent mind, poetic style, Sufi precepts and eloquence influenced his predecessors to such a degree that he is revered not only as a poet but a saint in disguise and is rated among the tallest and versatile poets with sound spiritual dimensions. Jami's poetry by and large remained unknown to the western scholars till the translation of his poetic compositions into English. Abd-ur-Rahman Jami is in fact a culminating figure in Persio-Islamic culture whose reputation and influence have remained undiminished throughout the Eastern Islamic World. Primarily celebrated as a poet, Jami was an accomplished Islamic scholar and Arabist, a Sufi of great standing and an acerbic polemist and social critic. [13]

Jami was associated with Naqsbandi order and belonged to Ibn Arabi's school of thought. His long didactic poems belong to both Sufism and Greek philosophical traditions. Jami who was known for his extreme pity and mysticism created a distinction between two types of Sufis, now referred to as the "Prophetic" and the mystic" spirit. It is said that Jami started his poetic journey probably at an early age. Many of his poems are devoted to his people, ideals of the human being and the love to his country. He is in fact one of the prominent scholars in the frequent use of the Arabic language and poetry. The concepts of patriotism, love for native language and idealism is reflected in a similar fashion in the renowned poems of Lebanese poet Gibran Khalil Gibran (1883-1931), "Dead are my people" and "My Countrymen". In conformity with Jami, Khalil Gibran often uses native and formal language with frequent spiritual terms. He used to say *"Spare me the political events and power struggle, as the whole Earth is my homeland and all men are my countrymen".*

Jami also describes the devastating effects of tragic, social and political events, as war and conflicts on the lives of ordinary people.

Jami is believed to have written on an enormous variety of subjects which appeals to various strata of Turkic people. The human suffering and social injustice which he witnessed around himself made him pay attention to worldly matters. He became more interested in the concept of the happiness of his people. In a similar fashion Moulana Jalal-ud-din Rumi (604-672), a thirteenth century Iranian mystic poet known throughout the world for his exquisite poems and words of wisdom wrote on variety of subjects and devoted himself for the cause of joy and happiness to be administered among the masses. He says *"Every objectis being a jar full of delight and happiness"*. In view of their compatibility both Abdur-Rahman Jami and Jalal-ud-din Rumi attained the status of spiritual leaders and teachers with extraordinary capabilities. Even to some they are patriots and guides leading their people to prosperity and happiness.

The compatibility and juxtaposition of Jami's poetry viz-a-viz its style, format and thematic approach with prominent and renowned poets around the globe demonstrate his vision, genius, versatility and extraordinary status. Viewing life from the point of view of human morality, Jami's poetry becomes an embodiment of love and compassion for his people. As a result of this he never reconciled the corrupt and unjust of society. Makhtumkuli (1733-1813) a prominent scholar of 18th century Turkmenistan gives in a similar fashion an account of a destitute as follows:

The poor man, vows barefoot, showing his need,

At meetings they will seat him low indeed,

While if he rides a horse it's called an ass,

A rich man's ass of course, is called a steed.

This poetic exposition and vivid account of the sufferings inflicted on poor has been the theme and subject matter of Great Iranian poet and philosopher Sa'di Shirazi (1200-1292) as well. Sa'di says *"All human beings are like organs of a body; when one organ is afflicted with pain, others cannot rest in peace"*. His best known works *Bostan (the orchard) and Gulistan (the rose garden)* consist of stories aptly illustrating the standard virtues as justice, truth, liberty and modesty. Jami like Sa'di attached great importance and significance to truth and the concept of a perfect man. There is, in fact, conformity of thought between the two in so far as the thematic approach to poetry is concerned.

Persian authors often compare Jami to Shakespeare. Like Jami, William Shakespeare (1564-1616) was master in exploring the multiple facets of nature. Without doubt the exploration of human strengths, sufferings and weaknesses is the key to the popularity and survival of Shakespeare's literary genius and its applicability across cultures and times. Even John Milton (1608-1674) in his "Paradise Lost" affirms an ultimate optimism in human potential-a concept found in the major part of Jami's poetry.

Jami like Allama Iqbal (1877-1938), a renowned poet of Lahore Pakistan persuades for national unity and integration. Iqbal's renowned works like *Baang-e-Dara (1924), Baal-e-Jibraeel (1935),Zarb-e-Kaleem (1936) and Armaghan-e-Hijaz (1930)* by and large represent the same ideology. Jami insists on remembering past, doing well in the present and preparing for the future while emphasizing love, enthusiasm and energy to fulfill the ideal life. Iqbal like Jami believes that an individual can never aspire to higher dimensions unless he leans of the nature of spirituality. Like Jami Iqbal's poetry is often highly personal but also takes up universal themes. Jami praise of Prophet, belief on *Khatam-i-Nubuwat,* praise of religious figures with special reference to twelve Imams is found in the poetic composition of Allama Iqbal:

Zindah haq az quwat shaberi ast

Batil akher dagi hasrat meri ast

(Truth is alive because of the courage and power of Hussain (Shabir) and falsehood perishes at the end.)

Malwana Jami on the other hand in his praise to *Ahl-i-Bayt* says: "O breeze of morning, visit the hills of Najd for me and kiss them, for the fragrance of the friend comes from those pure camping grounds".[14]

Sufism in India and Central Asia

Some of the prominent happenings in the life cycle of Jami, not to talk of his poetry are also akin, similar and most compatible to the events and episodes of some of the distinguished Sufi poets of sub-continent. It is believed that Jami as a Sufi and follower of Baha-ud-din Naqshband sought the blessing of the known Sufi Khawaja Muhammad Parsaand, Jami showed greatest veneration and homage to his spiritual teachers and to those who guided him in the mystic's path. [15] In a similar fashion Amir Khusro (1253-1325), urged to meet his Sufi master KhwajaNizam-ud-din Awliya at Delhi India. On his refusal Khusro took recourse to his pen. The poem finally confirmed his permission and resulted in everlasting bonds between the two.

Tu an shahi ki bar aiwan-iqasrat

Kubutar gar nasheenad baz gardad

Faqiri mustamandi bar dar a'mad

Beyayad anorun ya bahar gardad.

(Thou art such a king that when a pigeon perches upon the top of thy palace, it becomes a falcon. A poor and distressed person is standing on thy threshold. Is he permitted to get in or go back?)

Jami is believed to have experimented both with new and old forms of poetry as a consequence his mosty poems became popular and familiar in Persian region. In a quiet similar fashion the famous poets of Kashmir Sheikh ul-A'lam (1376-1431) and Lala Arifa (1301-1367) made a frequent use of new forms of poetry which eventually attained the status of folk songs. These poems like Jami's poetry are presently known to ordinary Kashmiri people, not to talk of men of vision and comprehension. It is quite interesting to note that Sheikh-ul-A'lam's *"Shurk"* and Lala Arifa's *"Wakh"* bear the same value and merit in poetry as that of Maulana Jami. George Bernard Shaw has rightly said *"Great men think alike"*. Jami, Sheikh-ul-A'lam and Lala Arifa share a common style and have a great compatibility as all are widely revered as Holy among their countrymen and their poems are often quoted as proverbs in their respective regions.

Jami and Sufi-Poetic Discourse

Although Abdul-Rahman Jami has been target of critics for excessively following the footsteps of his predecessors.[16] He "tried to save the literary tradition from crumbling down and being wiped out when state was coming up the ladder of history and falling down deep into the abyss of nothingness".[17] Jami's *diwan* or collection of poetry, includes *qasidas, ghazals, ruba'is, tarji'-bands, tarkib-bands,* and *qit'as,* Although Jami tried his skill in different genres of poetry. He emphatically stated "a work lives not by its form, but by the profundity of its content". Since Jami appeared after what literary scholars consider the "zenith of Persian Poetry," he had no doubt little new to offer little new, following some extra-ordinary works of previous masters. He felt a sense of urgency to keep the light shining, and in order to rejuvenate the field. He embarked on re-introducing some of the previous works in new forms. He states, "put old stories to new tunes," thus opening him up to being accused of plagiarizing or indulging in too much imitation. [18]

Among the prominent *diwans* of Jami, the first *diwan, Fatihat al-Shabab,* is the most voluminous and perfect as compared to two *diwans*; where the poetry is more colorful in terms of theme and subject matter. It covers subjects such as philosophy, life, friendship, humanistic issues, and morality. The other two *diwans* mostly cover mystical themes. The first one hundred *ghazals* of Jami's *diwan,* frequently responds to Amir Khusraw and Hafiz.

Although the apparent theme of Jami's *ghazals* is *'ishq,* either divine or mundane, he occasionally inserts some praises or advice. Usually the theme of Jami's *qasida* is either praise of God, the Prophet and his household, or is descriptive of a structure.

Imam Al-Ghazali's admonishes to the last king of Saljuq rulers Sultan Sanjar in his renowned book *Nasihat-ul-Mulk* to implement Justice among the needy. Likewise in one of his *Qasidas,* Jami advises the Sultan to implement justice and be fair to just his subjects. Though these *qasidas* are regarded as panegyric lyrics composed for Sultan Hussein, Jami intentionally gives instruction to the Sultan to rule justly in his domain. Jami's *qasidas* as compared to his *ghazals* are more difficult owing to the frequent use of Arabic phrases or unfamiliar expressions. *Tawhid, na't va munajat,* praise of God or the Prophet, or fervent prayer, advice, biography, complaints, response to his predecessors, description of gardens and buildings, and praise and eulogy of elites and nobles are some of the major themes of Jami's *Qasidas.*

Jami's celebrated work, *Mathnawi Haft Awrang,* refers to the constellation of the Great Bear. As the title indicates, it is a collection of seven works, wherein Jami attempted to create an equal, if not better, work compared to the famous work, *Khamsa,* which Nizami composed three centuries earlier. Yet, only two sections of *Haft Awrang* (*Layli va Majnun* and *Khirdnama-i Iskandari*) are found in *Khamsa.* The first book of *Haft Awrang* is *Silsilat al-Zahab* (The Chain of Gold) composed in 1485. The next is *Salaman va Absal,* another didactical love story, which Jami imitated from the structural type similar to the one presented by 'Attar'. The mystical allegory work, *Yusuf va Zulaykha,* is substituted for the secular pre-Islamic love story of *Khusrau va Shirin* written by Nizami. Jami left out Nizami's *Haft Paykar,* another pre-Islamic story about a Persian king, Bahram-i Gur; he instead added a second didactical poem, *Tuhfat al-Ahrar, (The Gift of the Nobles).* His other work, *Subhat al-Abrar, (The Rosary of the Pious)* is also regarded another imitation of Nizami's work, *Makhzan al-Asrar.* It is because of *Haft Awrang* that Jami gained recognition, and was said to have had a "commanding influence over Ottoman literature." Consequently, *Haft Awrang,* besides its literary value, became an important source for the social and political history of the era.

Although Jami's poetic oeuvre makes him the most prolific poets in the classical traditions. His *Nafahat al-Uns* in prose earned fame for him for including biographies of six hundred-fourteen male Sufi saints and thirty-three female Sufi saints. The work is deemed as a valuable master piece for the history of Sufism, Sufi teachings, and philosophy. Jami's *Baharistan, (The Spring Garden),* a work in mixed prose and verse is authored following the footsteps of Sa'di's *Gulestan.* The thirteenth century Christian era is deemed as a significant period in the promotion of mysticism and Sufi orders. The era, of the later Middle Ages, as Marshal Hodgson rightly points out, was a period that religious creations and earlier cultural identity were stabilized; in addition to new institutions which went on to affect the future centuries.[19]

Although, Jami does not a name of any particular order where he expresses disapproval of Sufis in general, it appears that he was not happy by some practices of the Naqshbandi Sufis in particular, with whom he dealt the most. Like Hafiz, he was so frustrated with the hypocrisy, insincerity, and pretense of various Sufi groups, that he articulated his frustration through subtle language of poetry. He writes:

Thank God that I am neither a sheikh nor a follower, neither seek knowledge, nor teaching and tutoring. I am free from the bondage of the world, either impure or bright; I shall sit in a corner of a shack, lone and solitary.[20]

References

[1] Ziauddin Sardar; *"Islamic Science or Science in Islamic Polity: What is the Difference?"*, *Journal of Islamic Science*, Aligarh Vol. 1, 1985, p. 40. Muslim contribution to physics, chemistry, medicine, astronomy, navigation, mathematics, geology, geography, botany, zoology, sociology and philosophy is well known to the historians of science and human development.

[2] A. J. Arberry; *Revelation and Reason in Islam*, London, 1957, p. 29.

[3] Keeping in view the importance and significance of history and civilization of central Asia, UNESCO, as recommended by its international editorial committee, the history of central Asian civilization beginning from the earliest eras to the present times is to be projected in a series of six volumes. However, volume IV, the age of achievement (circa 750 A.D. – end of 15th century) covers the most flowering period of Islamic civilization in central Asia. For the purpose of this project, "Central Asia" is seen in its wider historical cum-cultural setting as including eastern Iran, Afghanistan, Pakistan and adjoining regions of northern India, the Soviet Central Asian Republics, the Chinese "Central Asia" and Mongolia.

[4] (One needs to be abreast of the fact that the medieval central Asia unlike its modern connotation includes the whole of Khurarsan province that by definition meant contemporary Eastern and Western Turkestan. *Mu'jam al Buldan* of Yaqut al Hamavi as explicitly included the centres of religious learning in Iran with Central Asia).

[5] Jinger, H. (ed.), The *Literature of the Soviet peoples: A Historical and Biographical Survey*, New York, F. Ungar, 1970, p. 130.

[6] K.H. Menges, *The Turkic Languages and Peoples: and Introduction to Turkic Studies,* Two Wiesvaden, 1995, p.169.

[7] Afsahzed A'lkhan, *A Critical Study of Jami's Bibliography and Writings,* Tehran, 1999, p. 27.

[8] John A. Boyle, Persia, History and Heritage, Henry Melland Limited, 1978, p. 69.

[9] John A. Boyle, Persian - History and Heritage, p. 71.

[10] John A. Boyle, Persian - History and Heritage, p. 71.

Sufism in India and Central Asia

[11]John A. Boyle, Persian - History and Heritage, p. 71.

[12]Encyclopaedia Iranica, p. 338.

[13]E.G. Brown, *A Literary History of Persia,* Vol. IV, Cambridge University Press, Cambridge, London, 1978, p.26.

[14]E.G. Brown, *A Literary History of Persia,* Vol. III, Cambridge University Press, Cambridge, London, 1978, p. 545.

[15]E.G. Brown, *A Literary History of Persia,* Vol.-III, Cambridge University Press, Cambridge, London, 1978, p. 510.

[16]Fulian Baldick, *Mystical Islam: An Introduction to Sufism*, I.B. Tauris & Co. Ltd; New York, London, 2012, p. 111.

[17]Fulian Baldick, *Mystical Islam: An Introduction to Sufism*, I.B. Tauris& Co. Ltd; New York, London, 2012, p. 111.

[18]Fulian Baldick, *Mystical Islam: An Introduction to Sufism*, I.B. Tauris & Co. Ltd; New York, London, 2012, p. 111.

[19]Marshal Hodgson, *The Venture of Islam*, Vol.-2, Chicago: The Chicago University Press, 1974, pp. 371-372.

[20]Marshal Hodgson, *The Venture of Islam*, Vol.-2, Chicago: The Chicago University Press, 1974, pp. 371-372.

CHAPTER 13

The Understanding of Self and others in Teachings of Sufism: Najmuddin Razi (1177-1252)

Usmonali Kamolov,

Sufis are the people, who were travelling around the world for the search of knowledge and bring the peace. One of them was Najmuddin Razi, the famous representative Sufism of XII-XIII of Tajik – Persian people was born in 1177 in Rai (Iran). He wrote a lot of books, such as *"Mirsod-ul-Ibod"*, "Ishqvaaql" etc. which made great influence in theoretical and practical Sufism and its representatives. After conquest of Mongols, he travelled around the world, Central Asia (during the time of Muhammad Khorazmshah), Iran, Rome, and Arabia, Iraq and died in Iraq. Razi had the greatest influence on the thinkers throughout all Central, South Asia and Middle East.

In his spiritual teachings, self-consciousness, cognitions of God and existence, the theory of Sufism, was brought up a great number of great Persian speaking Sufis, as Jaloluddin Balkhi and many others. Even, till today we can see his influences in modern Sufi teachings of Central Asia, Iran, India, Iraq, Indonesia and Europe.

According to his teachings, the person is a holy creation to the is a purpose of the universe. The Purpose of the making the person, in accordance with teaching Sufism in general and in teaching of Najmuddin Razi in particular, is self-consciousness of person and cognition of the God. Without self-consciousness, as he considers not only be impossible orientated of the person in life ways, in life problem, but also it is difficult to distinguish most from animals, since last he will not get to know the sense of its existence. Exactly self-consciousness, ability to get to know add the person a sense to humanities. This idea is illuminated by thinker in context of the analysis of the problems of existence and cognitions.

In teaching of Najhmuddin, the person found not only whole divine creation as essence existence, but also teaches us not to lose this essence multiplying human value in the centre. It is correct to use their own possibility and always not losing hope to fight for the sake of full of life and complete life. One of the importance's of the teaching of Razi for modern world is that it can help us to challenge more spreading radical interpretation of fundamental principles of Islam and its diverse cultures.

Najmuddin Razi - the prominent representative of Sufism XIII of century, special attention gave to a problem of the person and its place in a society. According to his opinion, the person is the sacred creation providing with special qualities for the universe's purpose. The purpose of creation of the person, according to the Sufism doctrine in general, and in the doctrine of Najmuddin Razi in particular, are the self-knowledge or self-consciousness of the person and cognition of the God. He considers that without self-knowledge not only it is impossible to be guided for the person on a life's ways, in vital problems, but also difficult to distinguish him from an animal as the last does not learn sense of the existence. Namely to self-knowledge as a final goal not only subordinated all ontological system of the thinker but also puts forward the person to perfection. On the one hand, the self-knowledge gives to the person sense of humanity, expresses its aspiration to true achievement, and with another it improves the person to deity level. In the doctrine of Najmuddin Razi, the person is in the centre of all divine creation, as essence of life. Razi teach has us not to lose this essence, multiplying thus human values, correctly to use the spiritual possibilities and always, without losing hope, to struggle for the sake of full value and perfect life. These ideas of Najmuddin Razi, promote for the decision of many modern problems, especially it can bring the powerful contribution to eradication of one of the sorest problems of XXI century and in spiritual crisis it can bring up youth in the spirit of kindness, justice, honesty, decency, tolerance and internal perfection of the person.

According to Razi everything in the world was created for the sake of the person. If the person was not the purpose of the creation, the world and of all the multi-collared existence hardly would be created. And if to investigate thoroughly into existence, it is possible to notice that the creation purpose is hidden in the essence of existence of the person.

Чаҳонробаландивупастӣтуй,

Надонам, киҳарчиҳастӣ, туй.

(Height and lowland of the world – it you, I do not what you are, but what there is – it you.)

The person, having such status, constantly should improve itself, his mind and should rise to degree of General Reason or Mind. But the person possesses it between spiritual and physical, animal and heavenly nature simultaneously, because there is a constant enmity. At whom the animal party wins, that will not reach at all degree of General Soul (or Mind). In opposite side at whom the heavenly nature gets the best level, he/she can learn essence of the Creator, and he/she even becomes identical to him.

The correlation between the Human and the Cosmos is like the analogy of Microcosm and Macrocosm; for example, in comparison with some other Sufis, according to the doctrine of Jaloluddin Rumi/Balkhi, the person become like a microcosm, being diminutive copy of a macrocosm:

Гартуодамзодайчунӯнишин,

Чумлазурриётродархудбубин.

Пасбасуратоламиасғартуй,

Пасбамаънйоламиакбартуй.

If you from a human race sit down as he,

And all universe contemplate in himself.

Hence, on a form you are a microcosm,

And on a sense you are a macrocosm.

The true and correct cognition of an essence and qualities of God was possible to nobody, except to the person. From all creations of Omnipotent God only the human soul has wished to be mirror of qualities of God. The human soul constantly should be brought up and improved. It will find out in oneself all qualities of True (God), to learn the soul and be informing for the sake of what he (person) was created. And only after that will open the true

188   Chapter 13 Shaikh Sharfuddin Bu Ali Qalander Panipati's....

maintenance of expression «Everyone who organized himself will recognize the God», the paraphrase of the saying in Holly Qur'an "*Man arafana fsa*.... When the person will organize himself and God, will open the sense that who is he and for the sake of what he was created and for what secret has got such magnanimity and generosity. Najmuddin Razi concludes that this is in his opinion, rather rich in content or pithy and profundity verse. The Human being is a creation of God like his book, he illuminate the God's beauty. According to him, in order to reach the perfection and become like pure mirror, the person should follow and then overcome step by step the ways of *Shariyat, Tariqat and Haqiqat*. Only then the person will be worthy that true trust and honor, which God merit him. Out of the person there is nothing what is in both worlds, and the person should search in himself everything what he wishes from existence and a non-existence:

Эйнусхаиномаиилоҳӣ, китуй,

В-ейоинаиҷамолишоҳӣ, китуй.

Берунзиту нестҳар чи дар олам ҳаст,

Дар худ биталабҳарончи хоҳӣ, ки туй.

You (person) - a copy of a true deity,

You a mirror of display of a divine face.

There is no out of you all what is in the world,

Search in yourself for all what is necessary for you.

Since the Human person as the last creation of the creator, he is considered as his deputy. The person among all real lives surpasses all creations and it is considered essence and sense of existence as existence was created for the sake of the person. Because the person is a mirror displaying God and a macrocosm copy. God beholds himself in shape and an image of the person.

According to Sufi doctrine of Razi, the self-knowledge of the person consists also in achievement of worthy and laudable human qualities and clearing of obscene qualities, or blamed tempers. The unique or sole way of clarification of the heart, the Sufi see in disposal of all not approved person

Sufism in India and Central Asia

qualities and blamed tempers. According to Razi, each succeeding person should counteract, first of all, to his soul (*nafs*) and under the direction of the leader (Sheikh) must to transform his blamed tempers and not approved qualities into worthy behaviour and approved qualities. Correspondence to thinker, the belief is a rupture and connection, *i.e.*, to be released from not approved qualities and to dress up with laudable tempers. The traveller of Tariqat in a result of the efficacious desire, effort, and upbringing of the perfect improving instructor and, necessarily, the expiry of the divine good fortune will eliminate from himself not approved qualities peculiar to animal's world, but will dress up good desired qualities. He attached to this important mystical with special significance and a main goal of Muslim mysticism is connect with a true Beloved after separation with him. It is reachable by two ways: elimination blamed and acquisition of laudable qualities (изалатисифатизамимаваикт исабисифатихамида).

According to thinker, elimination blamed and acquisition of laudable qualities is a love to the true beloved. For achievement of divine attractions (*джазбатиулухийат*), it is necessary to eliminate blamed and to get laudable qualities. Followings are the mystical ways.; The true beloved wants to display himself, however, the appearance of God to the person, the ophany (*таджалли*), is possible only in the pure and cleared heart, but the nasty and bad heart is unworthy for divine cognition. The mirror of heart which the display the object of display of divine essence and divine attributes has grown dull from a rust of human sediments and murk's. Therefore it is necessary to clear it by removal blamed and acquisition of laudable qualities to reach external and internal cleanliness.

Achievement of external and internal clarification from all bad qualities, such as anger, rage, envy, hatred and animosities, and love of all of other, except God is possible. The heart will find his rest namely thanks the love to Supreme. Having cleared of bad qualities and having dressed up in good qualities, heart becomes healthy. From disasters of this and a next world it is impossible to escape, except with healthy heart. It is necessary for the traveller that internal has assimilated to his external, without plans, envy and trick and ruse.

As we can see the main focus of Razi is the moral condition of the human being and society. He that states about is concerning bad qualities and possibility how to overcome them. These bad qualities are: unbelief, stinginess, avarice, envy, slander, malicious gossip, ridicule, an abuse, mockery, a refutation of prophets and saints, lie, tricks and ruse, ridicule of people of True, evil thoughts, adultery, drunkenness and trade of wine, shed of blood of innocents, the use and acceptance of in persistence, trickery, disobedience of parents, rupture of related communications, insult concealment usury.

Najmuddin Razi considers as the worst quality, after disbelief, avarice and stinginess (*бахили*). According to his opinion, after belief nothing will be similar on clemency to generosity. The reason of infernal torments is covered in two things: in no acceptance of belief and in avarice and stinginess. According to *Hadith*, avaricious, what devout he was, will not enter into paradise and generous, what debauchee was, will not enter into a hell.

The next bad quality is envy (*хасад*). The believer should not be at enmity with the divine friends and look with envy at them, because of, they have pupils (*муридан*) and friends (*дустан*); not to be envious and to reconcile to the divine fate; not to feed envy for people of True.

Other bad quality is the slander (*суханчини*). The thinker writes that «the Slanderer goes among people, disseminating contention seeds between them, and he will not enter in paradise.

The believer should refrain from malignant gossip (*бадгуи*),ridicule (*хаджвкардан*) and an abuse (*гийбат*). Then, it edifies the reader, to refrain from malignant gossip on Moslems, seeing Supreme present and observing and not to deride anybody.

Sufi should be engaged constantly in divine service (*таат*), observation (*муракаба*), diligence (*муджахада*), the self-report (*мухасаба*), to avoid mockery *(хазл)* and lack of knowledge (*гафлат*), to be careful of a refutation of prophets and saints (*takзiбанбийаваулийа*). The believer should avoid lie (*батил*), and sarcasm to people of True (*истехзабаahlHak*).

Sufism in India and Central Asia 191

The believer should wake up from blunder dream, not to be carefree and to address to divine service. When the person remembers God, the devil departs from him and as soon as he becomes careless, again comes back to him, inspiring to human heart bad thoughts, like adultery прелюбодеяния(*зина*), drunkenness's and shed of blood of innocents.

The believer should not get accustomed to trickery (*кампаймайандаги*). It is necessary to stop similar occupations and to repent. If it will not stop and considers its permitted then such person is the non-believer and its place - in a hell.

In night of greatness (*Lajlat* is *scarlet-shot*) God, having looked at believers a mercy look, has forgiven their sins, except sins of five groups. The believer should confess from the five bad acts not to remain without destiny in night of greatness. The first of these acts is a drunkenness and wine sale (*шарабхаривашарабфуруши*), the second–to offend parents (*azurdanmadarnadap*); the third to interrupt related communications (*кат '-ирахм*), not observance of relationship rights, the fourth-to conceal insult, to feed hatred (*кинагири*), the fifth-usury (судхури).

Sufi should avoid the bad friend and bad companions. The bad friend is worse than a snake. Najmuddin Razi expresses along with blamed, bad qualities as well as on some worthy, laudable qualities, such as stability, clean food, a good temper, occupation of good professions, conversation, exhortation and sermon conducting.

He says it is necessary to be refrained even from drinking water from a bowl belonging to the orphan. The thinker subjects to the sharp criticism of those contemporaries *Ulema* and sheikhs for whom fat meat and a lot of property is more important, without a difference, they are permitted or not permitted, rather than piety. He also asserts that in the Doomsday, nothing is better than a good temper (*khulqineku*).

The believer should talk (*sohbat*) with sincere enamoured in supreme to become from their number and to avoid enemies divine and sacred and not to talk to them. Najmuddin underlines that the true scientist should conduct *the sermon (ваъз)* even if it is not pleasant to debauchees and cheats, they do not take advantage of it. According to him, it is not necessary to refuse sermon and exhortations conducting. The believer should not turn away from the sermon and conversation of true preachers and instructors, not to avoid them and not to feed in a shower enmity for them. Believer and searcher, constantly is in search of exhortations and admonitions: in the beginning parents, then at the teacher, sheikh, divine inspirations. The preacher should on a direct way and take pity on those who does not recognise it.

Important place in суфийских products have edifications and exhortations of Razi (*pandunasihat*). To this genre has given special significance not only in practical Sufism, but also in theoretical Sufism. Razi, basically has two products - in *Mirsod-ul-ibod* and in *Ishq-va-aql.* edify and preach on a direct way Sufis, Gnostics, believers, scientists, enamoured, preachers, people of True, Muslim jurists etc.

If it collect togetherly and to group all edifications and exhortations of Razi, scattered, mainly, in its two specified products it will turn out some kind of the independent didactic collection, being expressed by modern terminology, the moral code of the Moslem.

According to other exhortations of Razi, sufi, first of all, should:

– Only appointment with the God should be his required desire in order to receive honour of travel in God. Razi advises Sufi to observe *Sheriyat*, avoiding heresy and ignorance. According to manuals Razi in *Mirsod-ul-ibod,* the mystic should:

– To observe external and internal stability, to reach more divine cognition and knowledge.

According to these manuals the mystic should:

– To clear heart of human attachments, whims of soul and instigations of the Satan; the appearance to dress up according to Sheri installations attached to sacral life and to become its beloved, because «the Allah love those who addresses to him and those who contains himself in cleanliness;

Sufism in India and Central Asia 193

- To release itself from blamed qualities and to begin the shine laudable qualities; to observe for the words, acts and conditions that they did not contradict Its consent; to consider itself noble and not to pay attention to pleasure of this and another world, and to feed attachment only for the Lord.

Then after interpretation of other divine names, he edifies of the mystic, that he:

- Efforts made for a moral of people. "to deduce from heart hypocrisy".

- To be engaged in studying of the obvious and latent knowledge, and to be careful of his objection as He knows and sees.

- To clear his interior from external meanness and to do kindness for a smallest fellows and greats»; to avoid rage and revenge;

- To forgive sinned, referring to amnesty of God»; to refrain from whims of soul, desires, anger»;

- To try the benefit creations giving them food and exhortations of their souls to Islam»; to try to facilitate difficulties of creations.

The Gnostic should be quicken to belief on divine knowledge (улумиладуни). The mystic as can render favour to all creations, look at them a mercy and goodwill look; to accept apologies dissolute; despite plurality of the sins not to despair and hope for the Divine favour. The mystic should make frankness and straightness his motto; to prepare himself for fulfillment of good deals for the sake of the other world; the favour expect namely from him, resort to him at disaster; by his knowledge and exhortations indicate a way to ignore muses and to facilitate their burden; beauty and delights to consider proceeding from him; to love him and to distract from other, except him.

So, summarizing, the Sufis doctrine of Najmuddin Razi about self-knowledge it is possible to come to such conclusion that he considers achievement of a main objective of Muslim mysticism connection with the true loved with possible two ways: elimination blamed and acquisition of laudable qualities.

CHAPTER 14

Shaikh Sharfuddin Bu Ali Qalander Panipati's Contribution for the Development of Composite Culture in Panipat during 14th Century

S.M. Azizuddin Husain

Shaikh Sharfuddin Bu Ali Qalander Panipati (1208-1323) laid the foundation of sufi movement in Panipat. He started shaping it as a centre of Islamic learning and culture from 13th century and by 18th century. It became one of the leading centers of *Tasawwuf*, Islamic learning and culture of India. He was followed by Shaikh Amanullah Panipati, Qadiri Panipati, Saadullah, Khwaja Shibli, Shaikh Usman, Masih Panipati, Jalaluddin Kabirul Aulia Panipati, Qazi Shaikh Nizamuddin, Sanaullah Panipati, Saiyid Ghaus Ali Shah Panipati, Shaikh Abdus Salam, Shaikh Nizam, Maulana Altaf Husain Hali and others.

Those, who have written on Panipat, whether Indian or Irani, like Zakaullah[1], Deh Khuda[2] and others, mention the three battles which, took place in Panipat. The three battles of Panipat were fought between Babur and Ibrahim Lodi in 1526, between Akbar and Hemu in 1556, between Marathas and Ahmad Shah Abdali in 1761. K.A. Nizami writes, "If the neglect of cavalry brought disaster at the battlefield of Tarain (1191), then neglect of artillery received severe punishment at Panipat (1526)"[3]. However, they do not talk about the role of persons who worked for peace, harmony and learning, that is the Sufis of Panipat from 13th century to 18th century. It is quite surprising that K.A. Nizami who has worked on Sufism and covered 13th century, does not comment on the contributions of the Sufis of Panipat.

Sufis influenced Indian society and culture. They worked for the welfare of people. Never did they discriminate on the basis of religion, caste or colour. They preached the religion of Islam but at the same time paid full attention to learning and education. They opened new vistas in Indian society and culture. Persian became the language of state and culture. Chronicles, *Tazkiras*, *malfuzat*, poetic compositions, *dastavezat* etc. of this period form a great cultural heritage. Prof. Dodwell comments on these contributions of Muslims in India, "The advent of Islam begins a great series of Indian chronicles – the Muslim chronicles are far superior to our own (British) medieval chronicles. They were written for the most part not by monks but by man of affairs, often by contemporaries who had taken part in the events they recount.... The Muslim period is one of vivid living men whereas the Hindu period is one of shadows".[4]

Panipat became a part of the Sultanate of Delhi, but it flourished in the true sense during the period of Shaikh Sharfuddin Bu Ali Qalander. Panipat became the centre of his *vilayat* and this enriched the socio-cultural scenario of the place. In due course of time, it became an important centre of sufi movement in India. *Khanqahs, madaris, takias* came up in various parts of Panipat and its adjoining towns.

Bu Ali Qalander's father Fakhruddin Salar came from Iraq to India in 600/1203. Bu Ali Qalander was born on 604/1207 in a village Budha Khera in Panipat.[4] However, another tradition opines that he was born on 605/1208 at Panipat.[5] His mother's name is not known. According to Mohammed Ghausi Mandvi, his mother was the sister of *Maulana* Saiyid Naimatullah Hamedani. His teacher was *Maulana* Sirajuddin Makki. After spending 40 years in Panipat, he came to Delhi and started teaching in Delhi in the vicinity of Qutub Minar. The place he taught in was the *Madrasa-i-Moizi*. In a short period, he became very popular among the elite and *umara* of Delhi. He was appointed as *Qazi* and continued in this position for a period of twenty years. During his stay in Delhi, a section of *ulema* joined his opponent's group which was led by *Maulana* Sirajuddin and *Maulana* Amir Ali. But on the other hand a larger section of people and eminent *ulema* like Maulana Sadruddin, *Qazi* Hamiduddin, *Maulana* Fakhruddin Naqila and others had great respect and regard for him. He got annoyed and resigned from the teaching position and the office of *Qazi* and then he joined Sufi movement. He became so involved in Sufi spirit that he threw his books in water.[7]

شرف الدین پانی پتی اور ابوعلی قلندر نیز گویند از مشاهیر مجاذیب اولیاءست می گویند که در اوائل حال تحصیل علم کرد و در طریقت مجاهده و سلوک و ریاضت نمود۔ در آخر مجزوب شد۔ کتابہا را در آب انداخت۔''

اخبارالاخیار۔ص:124

Ghulam Sarwar Lahori writes in *Khazinatul Asfia* that Bu Ali Qalander was among the eminent Sufis of Chishti *silsilah*. In his early age, he concentrated on acquisition of knowledge but when he was inclined towards *Irfan* (knowing God), he had thrown his books in the river and joined the Chishti sufi order.[8] (Persian). Amin Razi holds the opinion that after getting involved in *Irfan*, he always got himself involved in that spirit and never talked to any one. If anybody could by chance see him he used to feel lost.[9] there is a tradition that Bu Ali Qalander knew Khwaja Qutubuddin Bakhtiyar Kaki and Hazrat Nizamuddin Aulia but Shaikh Abdul Haq is of the view that he had no relationship with these two Sufis.[10] But Allahdiya Chishti writes in *Sairul Aqtab* that Bu Ali Qalander was devoted to Khwaja Qutubuddin Bakhtiyar Kaki and received *Khilafat* from him.[11]

There is the tradition of *Hukum Nama* that Bu Ali Qalander did *Baiyat* with Maulana Jalaluddin Rumi (1207-1273) and he met Shaikh Shamsuddin Tabrezi but his meeting is also not well accepted. Mirza Sangin Beg in his work S*airul Manazil* also mentioned this union of Bu Ali Qalander with these people and his later retirement to Panipat[12]. Accordiing to the tradition of *Hukum Nama,* Bu Ali Qalander came with fifteen hundred murids and settled down in Panipat on 14th Muharram around 1267 A.D.

Among Bu Ali Qalander's contemporary *ulema, mashaikh* and poets like *Maulana* Ziauddin Sanami, Khwaja Shamsuddin Turk, Nazimuddin Qalander, Kabirul Auliya, Shaikh Jalaluddin Panipati, Shaikh Nizamuddin Auliya, Amir Khusrau and others, it is believed that Khusrau met him and he recited his *ghazal*.

He had good relations with the Sultans of Delhi, like Jalaluddin Khalji (1290-96), Alauddin Khalji (1296-1316), Qutubuddin Mubarak (1316-1320) and Ghiyasuddin Tughluq (1320-25). The author of *Khazinatul Asfia* is of

198

Chapter 14 Shaikh Sharfuddin Bu Ali Qalander Panipati's....

the view that both Sultan Jalaluddin Khalji and Sultan Alauddin Khalji were devotees of Bu Ali Qalander.[13]

علاءالدین وجلال الدین پادشاهان دهلی هم حلقه ارادت آنحضرت بگردن خود داشتند ـ (خزینة الاصفیا ـ ج:ا،

ص:327

It is recorded in *Miratul Konain* that one of Alauddin Khalji's *Khwaja Sara* Malik Nayab teased one of the *darwaish* of Bu Ali Qalander. When Bu Ali Qalander came to know about it, he was very angry and wrote a letter to Alauddin Khalji regarding the incident. In this letter, Bu Ali Qalander addressed Alauddin as *shahna* of Delhi and warned him that if he did not punish the culprit then the former shall appoint another *ruler* of Delhi who will replace Alauddin in this position.[14]

Bu Ali Qalander wrote a *Qasida* in which he praised Sultan Ghiyasuddin Tughluq (1320-25). It was Ghiyasuddin Tughluq who was responsible for removing a tyrant ruler of Delhi, Khusrau Khan. So everybody was praising him. In the same spirit Bu Ali Qalander also praised Ghiyasuddin Tughluq which was a great honour for him. Bu Ali Qalander addressed him as *Shah-i-Azam*. He compares him with the four caliphs. Bu Ali Qalander was not only a sufi but he was also an eminent scholar of his age. He was also an eminent poet. In prose, his letters addressed to Ikhtiyaruddin and *Hukum Nama-i-Sharfuddin* is his valuable contribution. Abdul Haq writes that his letters are a great source of *Irfan* (mysticism).

Bu Ali Qalander was not only *Sharaf* (prominent) by name but he was a prominent poet as well. He excelled in all the branches of poetry such as *Qasida* (elegy), *ghazal* (language of love), *qitat (*verse), *Rubai* (verse of 4 hemisticks) and *Masnavi* (Sufi poem in a pair of rhymes).

Bu Ali Qalander is the author of two *masnavis* and one *Kulliyat* (collected works). *Masnavis* are entitled as *Kanzul Asrar* and *Ishqiya*. *Kanzul Asrar* is a collection of several *hikayat* (stories). *Ishqiya* has 362 verses. His *Kulliyat* is a collection of 1700 verses. This collection consists of *Qasayed*, *Rubaiyat*, *Qitat* and *Ghazaliyat*. *Ishqiya* is one of the important contributions of Bu Ali

Sufism in India and Central Asia

Qalander in the field of *Irfan*. Every verse is full of *Irfan* and a great source of *Irfan* for Sufis. The author of *Nuzhatul Khwatir* has given the sub-titles of this *masnavi*. *Darvaishi Cheest* (what is saintness?) *Nafs kushtan, Talsam-i-Hasti* (How you can kill your desires, Magic of life), *Do Atish-i-Mohabbat Ikhtiar wa Khakistar Shudan* (burning in the fire of love and ultimately turning into an ash). Bu Ali Qalander has covered all such topics which were addressed by the Sufis in the Islamic world. These verses cover topics like *Ishq-i-Ilahi* (love of God), *Mardan-i-Khuda* (people of God), sufi (mystic), *zahid* (pious), *arif* (person having gnosis), *Fiqr-o-Faqa* (resourcelessness and hunger) *Qanaat* (contentment), *Yad-i-Khuda* (remembering God), *Miskini* (poverty), *Tawazeh* (humility), *Isar* (bestowing), *Mujahida* (striving), *Riyazat* (suffering from hardships), *Zuhd-o-Taqwa* (devotion and piety), *Shah-i-Gada* (leader of the Sufis), *Halal-o-Haram* (allowed and prohibited), *Tark-i-Dunya* (abstaining from worldly luxuries), *Hirs-o-Havas* (greediness and lust): Bu Ali Qalander has covered almost all those subjects which are dealt or practiced by the Sufis. These verses of Bu Ali Qalander tried to comment on all such problems of society. In poetry he has explained the sufi terms very well. His emphasis is on the distance from worldly luxuries.[16]

In his poetry he has clearly defined the ideas of Mansoor and Bayazid Bustami. He has clearly defined his ideas on *wahadatul wujud*. If we compare his discussion on *wahdatul wujud* with Maulana Jalaluddin *Rumi,* we would find a similarity in the ideas of Jalaluddin Rumi and Bu Ali Qalander. Bu Ali Qalander basically became the spokes person of Jalaluddin Rumi's ideas in India. How did Bu Ali Qalander get so much influenced by the ideas of Jalaluddin Rumi, it is not known. How he consulted the poetry of Rumi is also not clear because Rumi and Qalander were born in the same year in 604/1207? Rumi lived for sixty six years and Qalander survived for one hundred fifteen years.

In his *Risala,* Bu Ali holds opinion that, "For enjoyment of life and governance, God had created Adam. He named him as *Khalifa.* He created his own qualities in Adam and declared that I have sent my Caliph on earth".

Bu Ali Qalander seems to be very clear on these issues. Bu Ali Qalander holds opinion that God created Adam to enjoy life and for the governance of the world. Governance becomes an important aspect of Islam because without governance management of various aspects of life becomes difficult. So governance becomes one of the obligations of a Muslim, like *Namaz* (Prayer) *Roza* (fast) *Haj* (Pilgrimage) etc. God had assigned this duty to his Caliph. *Malfuz* literature is silent on such issues. Prof. K.A. Nizami an eminent historian, who worked on Sufism and the role of Sufis in India, holds opinion on this issue that, "The Muslim mystics of the early middle ages, particularly those belonging to the Chishti *silsilah*, cut themselves off completely form kings, politics and government service. This attitude was based on various considerations; psychological, legal and religious. First, they believed that government service distracted a mystic from the single-minded pursuit of his ideal which was 'living for the Lord alone. Secondly, as *Imam* Ghazali puts it: "In our times, the whole or almost the whole of the income of the Sultans is from prohibited sources". .... Thirdly, all Muslim political organizations from the fall of the *khilafat-i-Rashida,* were essentially secular organizations, having little to do with religion or religious ideals. Fourthly, if a mystic associated himself with the governing class – which by its very nature was an exploiting class – he isolated himself from the main sphere of his activity, the masses".[19]

What K.A. Nizami has said to do nothing with the fundamental spirit of Islam. Secondly Bu Ali Qalander belongs to the Chishti *silsilah* and he holds opinion totally contrary to what K.A. Nizami has said. My ancestor, Mir Saiyid Ali Hamedani,[20] a 14th century sufi belonging to kubravi *silsilah,* wrote a book – *Zakhiratul Muluk,* which is based on his political ideas. In this book, he advised Muslim rulers to follow Islam and do justice with the people. Prophet Muhammed was also the head of the Islamic State from 622 to 632. Then he was followed by his Caliphs. But in 661, Muawiyah declared himself as Caliph and then nominated his son Yazid as his successor. In this way Muawiyah converted Caliphate into hereditary *mulukiyat.* Later on *ulema* also justified it by dividing caliphate into two categories: (1) *Khilafat-i-Rashida*

Sufism in India and Central Asia 201

(632-661) and (2) Khilafat. There are no such two categories in Quran. There is only one, that is, *Khalifa*. Naturally all institutions of Islamic state w.e.f. 661 got corrupted. But K.A. Nizami contradicts his earlier statements by saying", "Amir Muwiyah organized the Umaiyads into a governing class. But with the developments that were taking place in the political life of the Musalmans, had become almost inevitable. An empire, without an aristocracy or a governing class was an anomaly in the medieval context of things[21]. Bu Ali Qalander had good relations with the Sultans of Delhi and Mir Saiyid Ali Hamedani also had good relations with the Sultans of Kashmir. Bu Ali Qalander was available or approachable to *Salatin, Umara, Ulema, Mashaikh* and the common man. Bu Ali Qalander did not write a book on polity but his small comment on polity is very significant. He holds opinion that governance of the world was one of the objectives of God for sending Adam on earth. With the result like other prayers, governance is also the part of the directions given by God. God sent his Caliph to govern. Governance is the basic part of Islam. So we should not denigrate this aspect of human affairs. Governance comes under the obligations for a Muslim. But we are expected to do justice with the people. This significant remark on polity and especially from a Chishti sufi of 14th century is very significant.

His thought was becoming popular in the Indian *Khanqahs*. If we study *Risala-i Ishqiya* and *Masnavi Kanzul Asrar*, we will find clearcut impact of Maulana Jalaluddin Rumi's thought on the verses of Bu Ali Qalander. Some verses of *Kanzul Asrar* appear to be that of Rumi. Not only poetic composition but also the *hikayat* of Bu Ali Qalander are under the influence of Jalaluddin Rumi. Some are *Dastan-i-Mahi-o-Magar, Almas-o-Pisar-i-Maldar, Ustad-o-Shagird, Dastan-i-Qalander, Mohaqiq Naseeruddin-o-Afzal, Mard-i-Jahil Dar Mahfil-i-Danayan, Do Nabina wa Chahar Rafiqan Ke subute Yaftend, Shair Pisar-i-Bul Havis* and *Shaikh-i-Sada Loh Muridan*. These *hikayat* are very informative and full of lessons. In *Risala-i-Ishqiaya* he has discussed topics like *hikmat-i-arifan-i-Ishq* (art of the love of Sufis), *Ashiq-i-Iman-i-Kamil* (lover with perfect faith), *Iman-i-taqlidi* (faith with allegiance), *Zahir-o-Batin* (face and inner), *Istidlaliyan* (analytical) *Ahwal-i-Jahan* (position of the world), *Khassan-o-Amiyan* (special and ordinary), *Zat-i-Bari* (God), *Ilmul Yaqeen* (Perfect knowledge), *Ainul Yaqeen* (visible perfection), *Haqqul Yaqin* (real faith), *Haqiqat-i-Zat-i-Haq* (Reality of God), *Shikwa-i-Dunya* (grievance of the world), *Azadi* (freedom), *Khud Shanasi* (recognition of self). Questions addressed by Bu Ali Qalaner are of great importance. This is not only a poetry but it also reflects Bu Ali Qalander's thought provoking comments on sufi philosophy. Both poetry as well as his thought in these *masnavis* reflects the impact of Maulana Jalaluddin Rumi.

Qalander is of the opinion that whole life rotates around *Ishq*. Everybody is involved in *Ishq*. He opines that it is *Ishq* (love) which can fly without any feathers. It is *Ishq* which can put Sultan's crown on your head. It is *Ishq* which gives you an empire. It is *Ishq* which can give your heart a mission. But it is also *Ishq* which finishes your wisdom. It is *Ishq* which can make you forget everything. Those who are thirsty of *Ishq*, it can provide them the other life.

Lovers are basically inside hundreds of curtains. *Arif* has made it his habit to know the God. Lovers are deeply involved in love and they can't see anything big or small. When lovers hear the name of God they disturb their faith and worldly interests.

Lovers are lost in the love of God. Every beggar can't understand the essence of love. Lovers do not need guidance. They are only for drinking the syrup. A person is lost from the reality and has nothing to do with stitching clothes. As sun has nothing to do with stitching of clothes.

Basically Bu Ali Qalander wants to convey that a person who has lost himself for the love of God and a person who becomes successful in knowing God, becomes a different being altogether. These lovers of God, basically called as men of God delink from worldly affairs and they are lost in the remembrance of God. Maulana Jalaluddin Rumi considers remembering God, as the highest prayer of God. This remembrance makes the status of an *Arif*, very high. Bu Ali Qalander also considers it very important. He says that

When God creates his presence in the heart of his slave. Basically a thorn of separation from worldly affairs goes into his heart. As a drop falls into the

Sufism in India and Central Asia 203

river, it results in the gnosis with the river. When drop comes to know about river, then the process of distinction starts. This gnosis is something very different. When one comes to know the reality then everything becomes meaningless. You clean your heart from *La*. You tear your chest with the sword of love. When his name is engraved on your heart, then you can mint the coin of love. When every figure becomes *La Ilaha* then my heart does not accept any figure except that of God.

Wisdom has no relationship with love. A person, who is completely involved in love, knows everything. How one gets wisdom, it is not known? Even wisdom does not give any source for that. Love of life has again come into the world. Wisdom is only under the protection of this or that. Love is basically very serious and minute observer. Wisdom considers you ignorant and lost. Wisdom looses its basic relationship forever. Love is the host custodian of good people. Love knows the secrets of the unknown world. Wisdom is amazed with this control. Love sacrifices life every morning and evening. Get up with the order of God, get this message every time. We find the same ideas in the poetry of Maulana Jalaluddin Rumi. Bu Ali Qalander considers that whole world is basically under the obligation of God. Everything of this world is under the influence of the beauty of God. This basically reflects his faith in *Wahdatul wujud*.

Whatever fragrance I smell, is basically his fragrance. I am basically intoxicated and wandering in his lane. Flower of Odoriferous is basically happy from the fragrance of that. Tulip's cheeks become red and bloody just because of him. He has used hundred praises for lily. Rose bud teared his clothes for having hundreds desires. Narcissus, who is having ailment in her eyes, also opened her head. She served while in a golden glass. Cypres tree has an elegant height just because of his beauty. He becomes green and happy. Nightangle and ring dove laments in the garden, whosoever is having a heart in the courtyard, can talk to him. O! you have heard the song of *Chang-o-Rabab*. Chest becomes roasted and due to heat, heart becomes the *kabab*. The last verse takes us to Maulana Jalaluddin Rumi's verse

Bu Ali Qalander also got influenced from the sufi concept '*Hama Oost*' (Everything belongs to Him). He wanted to be drowned in the river of '*Ho*'. By this act he wanted to loose his existence for him. Sufis are drowned in the river of God. There is no respect for an *alim*. These *ulema* are having scarcity of bread. Sufis have passed it in the world. For *ulema,* it is just like the daily wages. Sufis are basically old lovers. What do you know about the condition of a Sufi? Sufi is he who is having right statement.

There are several stories in the *masnavi-i-maanvi.* There is one story related to a teacher and a student. Bu Ali Qalander also gives a story of a diamond seller and a student. Student of Maulana Jalaluddin Rumi looks in two mirrors instead of one but the student of Bu Ali Qalander considers diamond just like a stone. Both say it is basically the result of misjudgement of an eye. Bu Ali Qalander says

Maulana Jalaluddin Rumi in his *masnavi-i-maanvi* described a story of a "grain merchant and a parrot". He conveys his ideas through parrot. And it is amazing that Bu Ali Qalander is having parrot as the main symbol. Parrot is very important for him. Bu Ali Qalander conveys his ideas through parrot. And it is totally different from Maulana Jalaluddin Rumi's ideas.

Bu Ali Qalander followed the words and idioms of *Maulana* Jalaluddin Rumi in his poetry. He has also copied some of the terms used by Rumi in his *masnavi.* How Bu Ali Qalander has used Rumi's word '*So Fistai*' in this verse? How Bu Ali Qalander accepted so much impact of Maulana Jalaluddin Rumi on his thought and poetry? If we accept the tradition of *Hukum Nama,* so Bu Ali Qalander did *baiyat* with Maulana Jalaluddin Rumi and Rumi had also assigned the *Khirqa-i-Khilafat* to Qalander. But whatever may be the reason Rumi's impact is quite obvious on Qalander's poetry and his thought.

Bu Ali Qalander raised a very well debated question among the *ulema* and *mashaikh* on the position of a *kafir* (pagan). Whether *kafirs* will be punished by God? Bu Ali Qalander holds opinion that they will not be punished by God because in the eyes of God Muslims and Kafirs are equal. He guides both of them.[22]

Bu Ali Qalander out rightly rejected the idea that all *kafirs* will be punished by God. Not only he stopped on that point but he further clarifies the point that Muslims and *kafirs* are equal, before God and he guide both of them. In contrast majority of *ulema* out rightly declare that *kafirs* will be punished. It shows that Bu Ali Qalander had taken a different line of action on this issue. This makes Sufis different from *ulema*. This spirit of Sufis made them popular among Indian masses that they are not against Hindus at all and everything will be decided by God on the day of judgement. We can not pass judgements on behalf of God.

Bu Ali Qalander raised another question whether *kafirs* will be punished and hell is created for them. Bu Ali Qalander holds opinion that Pagans and Muslims will make their own way. God has created both *Bahisht* (heaven) and *Jahannum* (hell). Paradisiacal will go to heaven and hellish will go to hell. God has said that for you is your religion and for me, mine.[23]

سوال ۔ کافران را دوزخ آراستہ و عذاب فرمودہ است یا نہ ۔ جواب ۔ در دنیا اسم داشتہ اند کافر و مسلمان براہ خودی رود و بہشت و دوزخ دو مقام کردہ است ۔ بہشتی در بہشت خواہد رفت و دوزخی در دوزخ خواہد رفت ۔ چنانچہ فرمودہ ۔ لکم دینکم ولی دین ۔ (رسالہ بو علی شاہ ۔ 34)

Bu Ali Qalander holds opinion that heaven is not only meant for Muslims or hell is not only meant for *kafirs*. *Behishti* (Paradisiacal) is he who followed God's direction. He will go to heaven. *Jhannami* (Hellish) is he who did not follow God's direction. He will go to hell. Question of being a *Muslim* or a *Kafir* has nothing to do with it. Merely religious affiliation of a person has nothing to do with his entry into heaven or hell. It will be decided by God on the basis of his actions. This shows the concept of justice and openness of Bu Ali Qalander. All these factors made the Sufis popular and acceptable in Indian society.

Tomb on othe grave of the Bu Ali Qalander was built by Muqarrab Khan. His name was Mohammed Hasan and was among the descendants of Khwaja Jalaluddin Kabirul Aulia. He was the *mansabdar* of Jahangir's reign (1605-1627). There is an inscription on the tomb which also bears the chronogram. Choronogram gives the date of its contruction. 1071/1660.

It bears another inscription which proves the geneaological table of Bu Ali Qalander upto Imam Abu Hanifa.

بسم الله الرحمٰن الرحیم ۔ نسب نامہ حضور قلندر صاحب رحمتہ اللہ علیہ سید شرف الدین بو علی شاہ قلندر بن سالار فخر الدین بن زبیر بن سالار حسین بن سالار عزیز بن ابو بکر غازی بن فارس بن عبد الرحمٰن بن عبد الرحیم بن نعمان ابو حنیفہ کوفی امام آعظم رحمتہ اللہ علیہ ۔

Adjacent to his tomb there is also the tomb of Shaikh Mubarak Ali Shah who was the teacher of Shaikh Bu Ali Qalander. At a very short distance there is the tomb of Muqarrab Khan the builder of Shaikh Bu Ali Qalander's tomb. It is also surrounded by a verandah and topped with a dome. It is built of red sand stone. It is having the graves of Muqarab Khan's family members also. Later on Shaikh Rizquallah constructed a mosque of red sand stone but recently that was demolished and a new mosque was constructed. In other corners of the campus there are some graves of stones but those graves does not bear the inscription. Adjacent to the main entrance of the tomb there is a grave of Altaf Husain Hali, well known Urdu poet of 19th century.

References

[1] Zakaullah – *Tarikh-i Hind*, Matbai Shamsul Mutalia, Delhi, 1898, vol. III, pp. 82, 83.

[2] Deh Khuda – *Lughat Nama-i-Deh Khuda*, Tehran, 1338, vol. V, P. 576.

[3] K.A. Nizami : *Some aspects of religion and politics during 13th century*, Delhi, 1974, p. 87.

[4] C.H. Philips – *Historians of India, Pakistan and Cylone*, Oxford University Press, New York, 1961, pp.115.

[5] Saiyid Muhammed Mian – *Panipat Aur Buzurgan-i-Panipat*, Al-Jamiat Press, Delhi, 1963, pp. 35.

[6] Sabahuddin Abdur Rehman – *Bazm-i-Sufia*, Matba Maarif, Azamgarh, 1971, p. 278. Sabahuddin Abdur Rehman – *Tazkira-i-Aulia-i-Kiram*, Adabistan, Lahore, 1982, pp. 116.

[7] Saiyid Muhammed Ghausi Shattari – *Gulzar-i-Abrar*, Islamic Foundation, Lahore, 1395, p. 100.

[8] Shaikh Abdul Haq – *Akhbarul Akhiyar*, Matba-i-Mujtabai, Delhi, 1280, p. 124.

[9] Ghulam Sarwar Lahori – *Khazinatul Asfia*, Nawal Kishor, Lucknow,1280, Vol. I, p. 326.

[10] *Haft Iqleem*, P. 461.

[11] Abdul Haq, op.cit., p. 125.

Sufism in India and Central Asia

[12]Allah Diya Chishti – *Sairul Aqtab*, Nawal Kishore, Lucknow, 1913, p. 190.

[14]Mirza Sangin Beg – *Sairul Manazil*, Ghalib Institute, Delhi, 1982, p. 50.

[15]*Hukum Nama* – (Aligarh Manuscript). f.2a

[16]Ghulam Sarwar Lahori, op.cit., Vol.-I, p. 327.

[17]*Miratul Konain*, Nawal Kishor, Lucknow, pp. 337, 338.

[18]Muhammed Iqbal – *Asrar-o-Rumuz*, pp. 23, 24.

[19]Khwaja Abdul Hai – *Nuzhatul Khawatir*, Dairatul Maarif Osmania, Hyderabad, 1962, Vol. II, P. 4.

[20]Risala-i-Bu Ali Qalander, Aligarh, Ms.f.2a

[21]K.A. Nizami, op.cit., p. 240.

[22]His grandson Mir Kamluddin Hamedani came to Jalali, Distt. Aligarh (UP) during the reign of Mughal emperor Humayun (1530-1555) and laid foundation of the Khanqah of Kubravi silsilah at Jalali. I am one of his descendants.

[23]K.A. Nizami op cit. p. 19.

[24]Risala op.cit.f3b

CHAPTER 15

The Theme of Sufism and Perfect Human

Mukhayyo Abdurakhmonova

Sufism, from one side, is religious and *sharia'*, from the second side, particular doctrine developed by means of philosophy and khidmat (wisdom). But it is to say, Sufi people had always been against to the philosophies and the scholars of *sharia'*. Why? Because scholars of *sharia'* didn't go away on explaining the verses of the Koran, the *Hadith* of the Prophet (p.b.u.h.) outward, and they fought to accept both Islam and *iman* (religious faith) with an external brainpower and to maintain the traditions and customs of the sentences firmly. So Sufi people had called the scholars of *sharia'* as *"muqallids"*, that was imitators and dogmatists to the passed people. And philosophies (for instance, as Farabi, Ibn Sina, Al Kindi and Ibn Rushd) researched the nature, the human being and the society through the experiences and observations, logical analyses and common conclusions of Greek philosopher whose names were Aflatun, Arastu and others. It is clear, moral-logical science, experience, enlarging knowledge lead to both scholars of *sharia'* and wise men.

Philosophies knew the God on this way; they described him as the reason of before, the first motive presenter or Javhar (Jewel). Although according to Aflatoon and his disciples the God is an absolute spirit, the spirit is a primary base in human being and in the world, but it is seen without feelings as if they depicted the spirit as an "objective world" and as an instrument. There are following ideas in philosophy *i.e.* Human being which the highest vision of development, the God is an Absolutely Completed and Honourable Being. These ideas are frequently spoken in the works of Farabi and Ibn Sina. In the Sacred Koran there is an aggrandizing verse related to human being "We have honoured the children of Adam" (Koran: 17:70) and the prostration of angels to him is written as well.

Sufism accepted such kind of ideas about human being. Human being contains two bases — body and spirit. In the body of human being, there are four elements such as — water, fire, air and soil, the specificities of the four elements are found in him. According to some Sufi *Shaikhs*, human being with his spirit dates back to the angels and with his body to the nature, *i.e.* animals.

But all of them are analyzed in different purpose and in a particular way in Sufism doctrine. Let's look through, in what things are seen?

At first, it is seen to this world on viewpoint of anthropocentrism. That is, knowing human being as an "axis of the world", observing all the actions in human being such as events and changes news of the world. Jaloliddin Rumi said in his *Masnavi* "Human being has all the inner oppositions and developing, growing and miracles of the spirit". It is implemented by understanding the essence of the Jewel, Names, Might of God who created the World and human being as well as learning and the peculiarities of human being's spirit.

Secondly, it is difficult to know the God, his might and his miracles and the world of *Ghaib (God's secret knowledge, only He knows)* not only with a mind of human being. I emphasized underlining the word only. Because it has been a tradition to describe the (*Irfan*) gnosis that is the knowing theory of Sufism, like an irrationalism or myth in some works. It's true, in Sufism doctrine the irrational *(wajd — 'finding' or 'feeling' spiritual ecstasy in 'finding' Allah Almighty)* knowing leads. But it is not an idea that the mind is not completely disclaimed in Sufism. Both mental knowing and power of mind are admitted in Sufism. According to Sufi men, the mind is worthy for worldly knowledge which might be proved with a fact. Our mind is incapable to perceive the *Ghaib* knowledge. Sufi man perceives the *Ghaib* knowledge, unrestricted-un-territories knowledge in the God's world with a thought of feeling *(wajd)*, as well as the marvel *(karamat)* beam descended into his heart. For this reason, following concepts such as *mukashafa, kashfu-karamat, hal-sukra* are taken into consideration in Sufism.

In this place, the third peculiarity in Sufism doctrine appears. That is, without satisfying of mental development, possessing all knowledge, but tempering the spirit, striving to the perfectness by purifying the soul, self-perfecting, possessing new spiritual grades (*maqom-mertabas*). As to Sufi men, it can't be executed not only with a theoretical preparation but an education-study. To perform it, first of all, one must pass a certain spiritual way, undergo steady restriction and losses. If one doesn't perform like this, the spirit isn't able to prevail the body, the self *(nafs)* and the nature. In order to act upon it, human being ought to approach to his origin — Absolute Spirit and join Beloved.

So, striving to the perfectness, possessing the peculiarities of angel and even leaving behind them are widely publicized in Sufism. Practical courteousness *(adab)*, traditions and customs, codex has been produced and they have been accumulated in the conception of spiritual path, Sufi order *(tariqa)*.

It is known, that *tariqa* has served to the development of society as a social case. In the base of *tariqa* some view points of Sufism have become existence such as good and ideal society. For instance, the people who have no kings, *i.e.* society of good-mannered people are spoken in the epic poems such as *Khiradnamai Iskandari* by Jami and Saddi Iskandari by Navai. Sufism considers that it isn't true to achieve such kind of society is the way of violence and revolution, but it might be achieved this thing by ethical bringing up each human being.

Achieving desires of human being for absolute reality, absolute justice and pureness were incarnated in Sufism. This need, dream, strong pleasure and enthusiasm come into sight the love which caused forgetting himself and unsteadiness So, the fourth peculiarity is — in Sufism the idea of becoming purer through the Divine Love and joining the God, the Pure (that is, Human being and the God become one). The God is — ideal, his world is absolute world of pureness. And to become purer, one must possess unrestricted and never-ending Love to the God, the symbol of Pureness. This Love is not an abstract feeling. The beauty in the passing world which was created by the

God, reaches — through the things reflected the God's words and His vision and the love for the human being who is the wreath of him. so wordless and divineness connect in this way. The Divine Love — is a gnosistic feeling, and an enthusiasm which appears from the knowing and understanding to the idea and *marifa'*. In the idea, the Sufi man burns in the fire of Love, as if getting rid of the materiality and becomes one idea — a part of *marifa'*. So, if we give a description to Sufism from this point of view, such a sentence becomes: "Sufism is an emotional thought which came into existence in the fire of Love". So then, the idea of knowing human being as an axis of the world becomes visible with its essence. Because enormous thought leads to inventing an unknown glosses and views of the spirit and going from the image to essence. For no reason, the collection of psychological knowledge which are seen in the works of the present philosophies of the West remind the ideas of *arif* ('one who knows' — the knowledge of the self, the Gnostic, the knower) **Sufi men and F.Attar, J.Rumi, Ibn Arabi** with the most features.

But we mustn't say that Sufism is unfamiliar eclectic collected doctrine which accumulated different knowledge. Sufism used on the way of purpose from the diversity of lineages; from the religious-literary sources and it developed them by adapting own outlooks. But grieving for the human being, thinking his spiritual perfectness is a permanent root issue of Sufism. Although different genealogy and estates had exchanged in the history of Sufism, the issue of human being's spirituality has never been neglected by the people of *tariqa'*. Especially, Sufi men were much more interested in the inward world of human being, inner oppositions, the war between spirit and body. They underline that human being has two old contrasting powers — divine and satanic strengths Human being as a slave must win the saitan's treachery and possess divine dignities. Both the place of human being in life and the living orders as a society were taken into account from this status; for instance, social contrasts, war-arguments, the core essence of property inequality and Sufism look for the top reason from the nature and interior world of human being, to improve the moral values of human being, according to the Sufism doctrine, negative and brutal strengths must be liquidated firstly. Sufi people

Sufism in India and Central Asia

213

call the negative strengths in the human nature as *"nafs" ("self")* or *"nafsi ammara" (bad self)* and announce it a war. In Sufism following matters are analyzed such as gathering the wealth, living for the need of *nafs*, longing for the passing world are categorically blamed, saving the human being (as well as the mankind) from imperfectness and misfortunes. The unique way is — to kill the *nafs*, to live honestly with a contentment, to temper the spirit-will, to celebrate the humanity as well as the divinity in the human being.

Such kinds of ideas are definitely expressed in the description notes of great Sheikhs' to "Sufism" conception. For the question of "What is Sufism?" Sheikh Nuri answered: "Sufism is — refusing the amusement of the *nafs*" or Sheikh Safi Alimshakh said so: "Sufism is — stepping the destinations of the *nafs*". Sheikh Ravim's words: "Sufism is — refusing the *nafs* in the way of the God". Well-known Sufi poet Baba Takhir answered for this question clearly: "Sufism is — the life without death, the death without life", *i.e.* dying in the life of *nafs*-brutal, living in the humanly life". Some of them the Sufism draw an analogy to vagabond dog or dirtiness which adhered to the hem of the skirt, and others draw an analogy to greedy a dragon or Dajjal, symbol of deception.

According to the religious doctrine, Dajjal appears in the Doomsday, showing all the wealth of the world, turns back the people from the way of the God, the people forget themselves as well as the God, go behind the Dajjal to the hell. So then, the *nafs* kills the humanity, it is a reasoned of making great sins and makes a human an ill-starred person. According to the Koran in the sura of "Khumaza" there are some verses such as: Who amasses wealth and considers it a provision (against mishap); He thinks that his wealth will make him immortal. Nay! He shall most certainly be hurled into the crushing disaster, (Koran 104:2-3-4). In the most verses of the Koran the disastrous fate of a legendary stingy richman Qorun. It is a sample for the treachery of *nafs*. He had become a hero of the literature as a symbol of treachery (He accumulated uncountable, a lot of gold, but he didn't give anybody, so the Earth gulped him down). It is clear, that *nafs* is a thing which puts an obstacle to enter the Paradise: according to the religious doctrine, Adam Ata (pbuh) was deceived by Satan, he ate the wheat corn, which was prohibited by the God. For this reason he was driven to the Earth, because the Paradise is a place of pureness. There is no place for the *nafs* in the Paradise. In the former Soviet system, we refused such kinds of religious stories and ridiculed on them. This event is given in the Koran (Koran 2:35-36). In this story, the human being is aggrandized because he had been pure and had no sins in the beginning. So there is a call that he must return to that pureness.

The *nafs* calls the philosophy of selfishness. If a person lives with *nafs*, he isn't ashamed, doesn't hate the prohibited things, and thinks to live in good condition in favour of others. In consequence, he becomes a tyrant, merciless, hypocrite person. So Sufism requires following things such as keeping himself from *nafs* and sins. Contentment, patience-poorness (on the way of the God) is very useful for mankind. There is a philosophical idea which has been clear for everybody for a long time: "You come to the world one time, take everything you want". The purpose the same: find an opportunity in order to live good, do not think others, think only yourself. The philosophy called "Everything is permissible" separate from the belief makes one embezzlements and pogrom, and strengthens the instinct of savagery. Maybe this is the influence of this dogma which opened as a discomfort of the ethical crisis in the different groups of our society at present time!

We want you to pay attention for one Sufi saying, this is — "Human beings are friends for each other", and also there is an idea, in particular, the rich and the poor are also friends. According to this idea, following people are responsible for their people: king for his people, rich for his servants under his control, khwaja for his slaves, they must live friendly each other and the wealth which they find must be distributed equally. There is a *qit'a* (poem) in "Gulistan" written by Sheikh Sa'di:

Bani odam a'zoyi yakdigarand,

Ki dar ofarinish zi yak gavharand.

Chu uzve ba dard ovararad rozgor,

Digar uzvhoro namonad qaror.

Tu k-az, mehnati digaron beghami,

Nashoyad, ki nomat nihand odami.

Adam's people are the organs of each other, because they were taken from one pearl when they were created. When life gives pain for one organ, others suffer from it. So if you are unaware of the torture of others, you are not worthy to be called a human being!

This *qit* is given in some researchers and analysed at the same meaning, *i.e.* Sa'di Sherazi with his seething and philanthropic words summoned all the people of the world to live friendly. We do not say this kind of description is not true because there is a hint this meaning. In that situation, if we discuss the *qit'a* without separating the meaning of the story given by the author, everybody understands that as if the author said about a friendship and a needy between *amir* (a managing level under the king's control) and citizen, the rich and the vagabonds. The meaning of the story as follows: One day Sa'di was sitting near the mosque of the prophet Yakhya (pbuh), one of the kings of Arabians came to visit and addressed to Sa'di, he said that there was a threat of a strong enemy and then pleased him to pray for him. Then Sa'di said to him: "If you mercy upon your people you do not suffer from the enemy" and explained him that oppressing the people was the same oppressing himself and he added the *qit'a* given above. According to the conclusions of Sheikh Sa'di, if the Adam's people are the organs of each other, though, with the want of the God, one is a king, another one is a vagabond, one is a rich, another one is a poor, when the vagabond suffers from the starving, the body of the rich must also suffer from it, then a mercy awakens in his soul and must help him; and the king has the same body with his people when they separate from each other, become enemies, the country ruins inevitable. In this place have a look at the following meaningful lines:

If you heard, maybe you remember the kings used to have a habit: on the left side of them the athletes (strong warriors) sat, because the heart is on the left. Officials and poets and writers sat on the right side of them, because a letter and a composition are written with a right hand. And Sufi men sat face to face in front of them, as a mirror, because the Sufi men are the reflections of the soul, they are better than the mirrors. Hey son, *Hajibs* — the people who hold the curtains, they look with a simple and disinterested, free, pure glance. Their souls are brightened with *zikr* (remembering the God) and idea, so their soul mirror is also pleasant. Who was born pure and out of ghastly ideas, a mirror must be put in front of him. Good face is lover of the mirror, such kind of the mirror (*darvesh* – vagabond on the way of the God) is a bright of the soul and the adornment of the soul. Whoever is a beautiful and has good face is a disciple of the mirror, and it is enough.

Sufism — is a doctrine about the perfectness of human being and mentally purifying

The ideal person that the Sufi people adore is a Perfect Human being. He is originally an ideal of the people and the literature. When we look through the works written by the sacred people of this doctrine, the poems inspired with the Sufism ideas, we become eyewitness to the contradictions such as brightness and torture, goodness and evilness, perfectness and imperfectness, kindness and ignorance. Sufism Sheikhs look like the athletes (strong warriors) who entered the battlefield in order to fight for the forces of torment and darkness as if holding the *marifa* (knowledge of Allah, gnosis) as a weapon. (Tustari: "*Marifa* is a fight for the spite (illiteracy) and ignorance"). They admit the soul as Ka'ba, they called the people who know the world through the soul, and worship for the soul is the lovers of Allah. From the work of Alisher Navai's "Nasaim-ul muhabba'": "Ismail Dabbas said, having intended to go to Khaj, I reached to Shiraz. I entered a mosque. I saw Sheikh Mumin he was sitting and watching his *khirqa* ("cloak", usually patched garment representing renunciation of worldly value), greeted and sat down. I was asked what I wanted. I said: I have an intention to go to Khaj. He said: Do you have a mother? I said: Yes, I do. He said: Go to mother and serve for her... I did Khaj fifty times — with bare head, barefoot, without any fellow-traveler. I'll give you all; give me the enjoyment of your mother's soul!"

These people were the living conscience of the society. Other people used to be vigilant when they looked attentively at their souls , the penance actions which they did for their sins. Their (Sufi men's) dispositions and actions were the power of the soul of the human being, devoted a beam for the eyes.

Speaking in essence, the short kernel of the concepts about the perfect human being consists of what we told above. But there are important and precious outlooks and ideas of the great intellectuals related to this matter. The perfect human being was spoken a lot in the Sufism literature, it caused discussions and some special books were written about it. It's specially spoken Sayid Abdulkarim Jilani and the pamphlet called "Insani kamil (Perfect human)" by Aziziddin Nasafi (XIIIth century). It must be noted the conception of the perfect human which was firstly used by the famous scholar Mukhyiddin Ibn Arabi (1165-1240). According to Ibn Arabi the conception of the perfect human is synonomous for the words such as *aqli avval or nafsi avval* and *aqli kull.* Because The God created initially *Aqli avval* from the divine beam, then his vision and form appeared as a perfect human. So, there is a *Hadith* (The Prophet's words) "Xolaqallohu adama ala' suratar Rohmanu" (Meaning: "Allah created the human like an image of Rakhman"). They say perfect human from this time, possessed the belongings of Rahmonu Rahim names of Allah (Sayyid Sadik Gukharin. Sharhi istilohoti tasavvuf, 1st volume, p.125.)

According to Ibn Arabi, the symbol of the perfect human in the Earth is the Prophet Mukhammad (pbuh). He possessed mentally, spiritually perfectness, worldly and heavenly knowledges. The Prophet (pbuh) was a person and a messenger between the people and the God. So we are not allowed to call the people and the other prophets and holies and wise men as a perfect human. If this name is used comparatively to other people besides Prophet it must be accepted as a conditionally description or the sign of respect and esteem for the higher level. According to Sayyid Abdulkarim Jilani each person is a copy of the second who replaces the another one and a mirror standing in front of each other. The peculiarity and feature of a human reflect on the second one. But there is a difference, this reflection appears by character and attempt in some people, and other people can be seen by *quvva* that is, qualities and peculiarities. So then there are a lot of people who look like each other's such as according to talent and ability, peculiarity and quality. We can call them with the general names such as people, humans and men. Having looked at a person we can estimate the one according to the ethics and grades. But there are such perfect humans in the world, in perfectness they are not only differentiated from the other people, but they differ from each other. We call them prophets and holies. They have some grades such as: some of them are perfect, some of them are most perfect, some groups are scholars, others are preferable, and another group is preferable and perfect. Jilani having told this classification, he adds following words: "A perfect human is Muhammad (pbuh) and the other prophets' and holies' perfectness is comparatively combined with him".

Sheikh Amili says, according to the honest scholars, the world is steady because of a Perfect human, because the skies round with his breath, all the creatures get knowledge from him. They say on this grade the Perfect human is a mirror of the God. The God finds his names and properties only in a perfect human. And they also underline the following ideas: perfect human is only person who eyewitnesses the greatness and endless of the power of the God.

If we pay attention to the outlooks of Ibn Arabi, Sheikh Amili and Abdulkarim Jilani, Perfect person seems to be a heavenly creature; his properties do not look like the properties and peculiarities of the definite mortal people of the Earth. On this way we observed the compilations of all the extraordinary strengths because in this place, of course, a physical strength isn't considered, as a matter of fact. If we speak about the divinity, physical strength is not influential because the God's creatures are unworthy and incapable pictures at the presence of the divine power. According to the scholars the Perfect human is a great spirit who occupied the entire world and can influence all the living things and human beings, run the mankind.

But the issue of the perfect human is illuminated on the other way in the works of Sheikh Aziziddin Nasafi such as "Perfect human", *Maqsadi Aqsa*, "Zubdatul khaqayiq" (The cream of realities) and others. In these works this conception is analyzed with the combination of the appearance of the human being, development, achieving grades. In consequence, we see the signs, mental properties concerning with the definite living human being in the descriptions of Aziziddin Nasafi. To add this thing, Nasafi compares the outlooks and attitudes of a number of sciences in Islam. He researches the human being as both heavenly body and the creature of the Earth.

Sufism in India and Central Asia   219

The conception of the perfect human and spirit are densely examined. The grades of the human being are explained as well as the grades of the spirit. So there can be seen the conceptions passing to the exact ones. One of the reasons of this matter, Aziziddin Nasafi understands the *kamala* (perfectness) on the base of *uruj* (ascending) and *nuzul* (descending) theories. This theory is combined with the conceptions of great and small worlds. Because Nasafi joined Ibn Arabi and called the human as *alami saghir* (small world), heavenly world and mortal world together called *alami kabir* (great world). — All the things and peculiarities in the great world exist in the small world, he said. So the human being is considered to be diminished the copy of the great world (*alami kabir*).

Aziziddin Nasafi giving a description to the perfect human and writes: "Know it, Perfect human is a person who achieved the *sharia'*, *tariqa'* and *haqiqa*" and if you don't understand this description, let me say another meaning: know it, perfect human is a person whose four things must be obtained to the perfectness such as: good word, good deed, good ethics and *maorif* (gnosis)".

The three properties which are called by Nasafi good word, good deed, and good ethics are taken from "Avesta" written by Zardusht (Guftari nek, kirdari net, raftari nek). The human being who is brightened with these properties withdraws from lie, hypocrisy, scoundrel, all the time he is ready for good intention as well as good actions. Aziziddin Nasafi added a word "*maorif* (gnosis)" near the words of Zardusht, *i.e.* he added the requirement of the pureness in Sufism. According to him, the disciples *(salik)* who entered the *tariqa'* have to achieve these four dignities. Their tasks and purposes are the same. Whoever "increases those properties, he achieves".

Following description of Nasafi there are two conclusions. One is, according to the scholar, the perfect human is not an abstract person who is out of life, but he is a real man. A person, who has been achieving good properties, can ascend such grade. The second conclusion is that, according to Nasafi, the grade of the perfect human is a high status which can be gained it by *tariqa* and on the way of difficulty.

If we mutually accumulate the outlooks about perfect human told above, following conclusions come into existence:

— Perfect human — most perfect, kind and most wise one among the people.

Perfect human is a person between the God and the people; he is a patron who delivers the divine task, the secrets of the heaven (*Ghaib*) to the simple people.

> — Perfect human is equal to *Aqli kull (Aqli avval)* on the grade. Allah created first of all Aqli kull, *i.e.* perfect human, then other creatures was created because of him.

— The spirit of the perfect human has been clear since very ancient times.

> — Perfect human is a presence, who accumulated absolute divine peculiarities with these qualities, although he is seen as a form of a simple person, he is always vigilant person who occupied the Universe spiritually and a person who informed all the events.

— On this grade he becomes a *khalifa* of Allah.

> — Perfect human is an honorable person who comes from the society of the people. He achieved the perfectness on the process of mental-spiritual pureness. His grade was not obvious from the beginning.

> — So each person who is pure, well-bred, lover of the Beloved may strive to the perfectness and get a share on this way.

> — The highest sign of perfectness is to live on the way of the God, and to make profit for people. If a person makes profit for the people with his words, practical doings and intentions and summons the bad people for the correct way and devotes himself on the way of the God, he becomes a real perfect human.

Although these outlooks seem to be against to each other, according to the essence and originality they are close to each other. That is, following conceptions are mutual concerned with each other such as the perfectness of the human, admitting the greatness, human and Universe, human and the God, human and Presence. The difference among the outlooks consists of following matters, according to the conception of the people of *sharia,* the ability and inclinations of the human have been obvious since very ancient times, Allah outlined the fate. The spirits of the prophets, holies and wise men were obvious in the high world from the beginning, the grades of those spirits were outlined in advance, say the people of *sharia'*

But according to the people of wisdom (the philosophies and Sufi people), human was given a will (intention, want) in order to attempt, he may achieve his intentions, become a perfect human by his attempt. Sheikh Aziziddin Nasafi in his work called *Zubdat ul khaqayiq* (The cream of realities) writes: "There are no outlined measures beforehand for the words and attempts of people. Possessing knowledge and wealth are combined with the attempt of the human: the more the human tries the more his knowledge and wealth increase".

CHAPTER 16

Sufism in Karnataka: An Analysis of Shishunala Sharif's Songs

Varada M Nikalje

As one mellows, and gains deeper understanding of concepts, layers of meaning begin to emerge. So it is with songs, poetry and literature. My early childhood memories are of the songs heard from a local temple. Soulful and melodious like the early morning sunrays, they reached all homes. They were effortlessly imbibed into one's wakeful consciousness . Years later, I realized the qualities portrayed in the songs—universal fraternity, expression of truth and purity of thought.

These songs were the inspired creations of Sant Shishunala Sharif known as Karnataka's Kabir—the first Sufi saint to use the Kannada language. Sharif's secular upbringing, the powerful influence of his Brahmin teacher, and his own inner spiritual experiences blurred artificial distinctions of Hinduism and Islam. It is situated in the context of everyday life, his songs established an immediate connect with the common people, and came to represent a hyphen between the mundane and the metaphysical. This paper is an attempt to analyze the startling images and the technique of paradox used in the songs that helped to create a sense of wonder, bringing forth the fundamental harmony that is the essence of all religions.

Sufism in Karnataka: An Analysis of Shishunala Sharif's Songs

As one mellows, and gains deeper understanding of concepts, layers of meaning begin to emerge. Many of the notions which we would usually regard as the basic 'givens' of existence are actually fluid and unstable things, rather than fixed and reliable essences.[1] Texts exist in time and space; they use language (oral or written) and are placed in a continuum of a literary tradition. In the mosaic of literary traditions in south India, the Bhakti movement and Sufism were significant in recreating philosophy through vernacular language and folk music. In 19th century Karnataka, the Sufi saint Shishunala Sharif enriched an understanding of the subtleties of spiritualism through his songs.

Shishunala Sharif, Pencil portrait of Shishunala Sharif.
Image @ www.poemhunter.com

Shishunala Sharif was born around 180 years ago, in Shishunala village, Haveri district, Karnataka in South India. His father's name was Imam, his mother was Hajmuna. They were poor but belonged to a cultured family. As a boy, Sharif was bought up in an atmosphere that combined the best of both Hinduism and Islam. In addition to reading the Quran, Imamji had studied astrology and the Hindu *puranas*.

Imamji often narrated the Ramayan and the Mahabharat to the young boy. In fact, Imamji own teacher was Hajresha Khadri, who had obtained Linga deeksha a religious ceremony followed by Veerashaiva Pundits. He had a deep knowledge of Hindu traditions and was known as Khaddar Linga. He had associated with Allama Prabhu and other Shivasaranas. The turning point in Sharif's life came with the advent of Shri Govind Bhatta. Govind Bhatta hailed from the village next to Shishunala. Govinda Bhatta was highly respected for

Sufism in India and Central Asia

his scholarship and wisdom, but was known to be a maverick. In an era of rigid caste lines, Govinda Bhatta was equally at ease in the homes of high caste Brahmins or those of the untouchable caste, and shared a hookah with anyone regardless of societal wrath.

When Govinda Bhatta reached Shishunala, people flocked to meet him and seek his blessings. Imamji too, took his son Sharif along. He stood before Govinda Bhatta and requested him to accept Sharif as a disciple. Govinda Bhatta gestured to the young boy to come nearer, and asked him, "Who is your father?" Sharif answered, "Your father is my father." The unexpected, and to some ears, somewhat rude reply, took everyone by surprise. But Govinda Bhatta could discern the true meaning of the boy's words: we are all children of One Father, and the essence of all religions is the same. Govinda Bhatta instantly said, "The soil is fertile. The seed is right. Let the boy be with me."

Orthodoxy, bordering on fanaticism, could not bear to see Govinda Bhatta and the young Sharif becomes inseparable 'like milk and sugar' as the Kannada phrase goes. Govinda Bhatta had to all practical purposes, adopted Sharif as a son. "If you consider him as a son," sneered of the jealous ones, "Why don't you invest him with the sacred thread?" The sacred thread (janivara) ceremony is conducted for Brahmin boy's *i.e.* young men belonging to the highest caste in Hinduism. In those days, the janivara was ceremoniously bestowed on a disciple to his teacher or priest. Without a second thought, Govinda Bhatta took off his own sacred thread and put it over Sharif's head and across his left shoulder, leaving the on lookers dumb founded. Sharif spontaneously burst into song:

"Hakida janivara va

Sadgurunatha, hakida janivara va"

"My revered teacher has bestowed on me The sacred thread

With his blessings.

Liberated me from earthly shackles

Thus advancing me on the path of knowledge."

My early childhood memories are of the soulful and melodious songs heard from a local temple which, like the early morning sunrays, reached all homes. They were effortlessly imbibed into one's wakeful consciousness. Years later, I realized the qualities portrayed in the songs—universal fraternity, expression of truth and purity of thought.

Rooted in the life and beliefs of the common people, using similes from their everyday existence, the songs had a universal appeal. The songs begin with a literal meaning, situated in a particular time and place. One famous lyric describes a leaking roof:

Sorutihudu maneya maligi

The roof of the house leaks

It is leaking all over

Due to ignorance

The roof is leaking

No one to repair it

In this utter complete darkness

I dare not to climb up.

These words, ordinary and unremarkable in themselves, acquire a deeper meaning as the concept begins to unfold in its multiple layers.

The roof is leaking.

The thatched roof is torn

Its fibre mixed with mud and dirt,

Red ants that bite are crawling all over it.

The metaphor makes a qualitative leap from the prosaic description to a deep spiritual experience. The awareness of ignorance in itself becomes the first step towards realization.

The roof is leaking.

With no one to guide me

I cannot climb up

Sufism in India and Central Asia

The roof is leaking.

O beloved, in such chaos

A steadfast belief in God

Will be my shelter

He alone is my Saviour.

The idea of a steadfast belief in God is found in both Sufism and the Bhakti movement. Both emphasize direct communication with God, with the ultimate aim being personal establishment of a relationship with God. An anecdote about Sharif illustrates this point. Once, Govinda Bhatta and his disciples were on their way to a temple dedicated to Mother Kali, the guru had slippers on his feet, while the disciples were barefoot. They took a shortcut to across a field, which had a fence of thorny bushes set close together. Since Govinda Bhatta had slippers, his feet were protected from the thorns. Having crossed the fence, he put the slippers on the fence, so that his disciples could wear them and cross the fence one by one. To most of the disciples, however, it presented a dilemma. All of them, except Sharif, said, "We hold our guru in such reverence; how can we pick up his slippers? We are his disciples, and as such, we are unfit to touch his slippers, leave alone, wearing them". Sharif, on the other hand, did not hesitate. He took the slippers, put them on and crossed the fence. One interpretation of the above narrative, of course, is that, in life, one should not be so immersed in formality as to forget the practical. A deeper meaning is that ritualistic reverence should be rejected in order to move ahead on the path of righteousness. This is the essence of Sufism and Bhakti-casting away the restrictions legalized by orthodoxy in favour of a direct and personal relationship with God.

In one of his songs titled *Biddi abbé, muduki, Biddi abbé*, (Take heed not to fall), Sharif describes how an old woman is jostled in a crowd at a fair. Pushed here and there in the sea of humanity, she almost falls, but recovers her balance. The song beautifully captures the context:

Take heed, old mother,

You have seen many days

Many weeks, many years,

Take heed, and be careful,

You are presently in a village fair

In the midst of a crowd

Let not your basket tilt.

Sharif once again uses the context of everyday life, local dialect and familiar idiom, and the song establishes an immediate connect with the common people. It moves to another level:

After all, you are old

Getting on in years;

Not in robust health,

With unclear vision,

There are all kinds of people

Around you in the fair

Do not move ahead

Unmindful of yourself,

Take heed old mother

Take care not to fall.

The song expresses compassion for the old woman, but at the same time, enjoins her not to neglect the possibility of a fall. Each listener could interpret a common core of symbolic and cultural elements within his/her religious framework. The symbol of the fair/*mela* to represent the tumult and noise of the world is not a new one. However, here the world is not condemned. While co-existing with the rest of the world, the seeker of truth should not falter. A verse from Basavanna, the Veerashaiva saint is similar:-

Live with the world

Yet away from it,

As the lotus bud

That is rooted in water

Yet rises above it

As the soft tongue

Exists, in the midst of

Thirty-two gnashing teeth.

It is comparatively easier to speak of God after having given up the world and leading a monastic existence. It is much more difficult to sustain an unshaken belief in God while living in the society, amidst life's ills and sorrows. The death of his beloved wife was deeply felt by Sharif, and the tragic experience brought forth an extremely poignant song:

"Mohada hendati teerida balika

Maavana maneya hanginyako..."

When the wife called lust

Is dead, and no more,

One need not have obligations

To one's father-in-law.

When the love for material possessions

Is dead, and no more

One is not obliged to even listen

To the words of the world.

The tragic experience expressed in the song uses highly compressed syntax: very few words, but a swarm of associations. The central concept of 'loss' begins to take on various shapes and meanings, and ultimately it is no loss at all but a moving away from the fatal attraction of worldliness. The song is an illustration of how textual understanding moves beyond the actual text to include metaphor, social relationships, philosophy and much more. Another song, and one of my personal favourites, uses all the elements of language that contribute to acoustic and rhythmic effects. There is wonderful use of alliteration, repetition, and exploitation of oral subtleties that makes the song linger in one's mind.

> *"Kodugana Koli nungitha*
>
> *Kodugana koli nungitha"*
>
> The monkey was swallowed by the hen,
>
> The goat ate the elephant;
>
> The wall sucked in the whitewash;
>
> The seeds ate the pounding stone;
>
> The thread swallowed the loom;
>
> The ant swallowed the cave;
>
> The cave had, by then,
>
> Swallowed the mountain.

The pairing of seems the opposites results in highly unlikely circumstances--in this case, the larger entity being swallowed by the smaller one. The whole song is a paradox, contrary to perception, belief and expectation. The song continues the apparent contradiction.

> A complete being
>
> Was swallowed by the feet
>
> O sister, Govinda Guru's feet
>
> Have completely consumed me.

Touching the feet of a teacher or an elder is a tradition in India, symbolizing respect and reverence. Sharif here refers to Govinda Bhatta, his teacher and mentor, but it can also be interpreted as a complete surrender to the Almighty. The song thus moves from the bringing together of incongruous elements to a blinding flash of spiritual insight. It is generally acknowledged that great works of art and literature are timeless. Shishunala Sharif's voice too is an expression of the culture, history and experiences of his time, yet addresses what is constant in human nature. As the critic T.S. Eliot wrote, "A poet must embody a whole lot of literature, a representation of a kind of historic timelessness, and at the same time, express his/her contemporary environment". In the context of Sufism, it re-emphasizes that elements such as

Hindu philosophy, folk traditions and local dialects were not mere 'add-ons, they were fused in form and content.

This is illustrated in the following song titled 'Snake'.

Haavu tulidene, malini

Haavu tulidene

I stepped on a snake,

Listen, O friend,

I inadvertently stepped on a snake.

I leaped up in fear

My three entities

Wanted nothing

Except succour in God.

The three entities refer to the physical body, the soul in the body, and the cause for the existence of the soul in the body. The song describes the role of the snake in Hindu mythology: it is the soft bed on which Lord Vishnu reclines; it is the coiled ornament on Lord Shiva's neck, it supports and carries Mother Earth. As the song continues, the snake becomes the symbol of the easily distracted mind. Nothing can happen without the will of God. So it is with the grace of God that the snake of fickle-mindedness has been stepped on and squashed on the way to spiritual understanding.

As mentioned in the beginning, this article is inspired by my cherished memories of the songs of Shishunala Sharif, who, to my mind, is the embodiment of Sufism in Kannada. There is a shrine, dedicated to him, at his birthplace, and I believe, a religious ceremony is held there annually. He had a daughter who died early in childhood. No lineage exists. A Google search provided limited information; and only one of his numerous songs could be found translated into English-and that was an extremely bad translation. A few scholars have done research on Sharif's life and songs, but there is no institutionalized Sufi trust or centre.

Idol of Shishunala Sharif

On the whole, the sad fact is that his songs, with their unique combination of simplicity and complexity, remain relatively unknown. The startling images and the technique of paradox used in the songs are help to create a sense of wonder, bringing forth the fundamental harmony that is the essence of all religions. It is hoped that this article would lead to a re-kindling of interest in the works of Shishunala Sharif. Sharif's songs, still sung in homes, temples and mosques, espouse qualities of universal fraternity and purity of thought, and blur artificial distinctions between Hinduism and Islam. One who has given the world such songs should not remain unsung.

Reference

[1]This is one of the recurring and underlying ideas of literary theory. A detailed explanation is found in *Beginning Theory* by Peter Barry.

Bibliography

Abbas, Shemeem Burney, *The Female Voice in Sufi Ritual: Devotional Practices of Pakistan and India*, University of Texas Press, 2003.

Ahmad, Aziz, *Studies in Islamic Culture in the Indian Environment*, Oxford: Clarendon Press, 1964.

Alhaq, Shuja, A *Forgotten Vision: A study of human spirituality in the light of the Islamic tradition*. Minerva Press, 1996.

Ara, Matsuo, *Dargahs in Medieval India; A Historical Study on the Shrines of Sufi Saints in Delhi with Reference to the Relationship between the Religious Authority and the Ruling Power*. 3 vols. Tokyo: University of Tokyo, Institute of Oriental Culture, 1977.

Bang, Anne K., *Islamic Sufi Networks in the Western Indian Ocean* (c. 1880-1940): Ripples of Reform, Brill, 2014.

Bayly, Susan, "Cult Saints, Heroes, and Warrior Kings: South Asian Islam in the Making," in *Religion and Public Culture: Encounters and Identities in Modern South India,* ed. Keith E. Yandell and John J. Paul Richmond: Curzon Press, 2000.

Bellow, H. W., "*Kashmir and Kashghar: A Narrative of the Journey of the Embassy to Kashghar,* Delhi, reprint. 1989.

Chittick, William C, Travelling the Sufi Path. A Chishti Handbook from Bijapur," in L. Lewisohn & D. Morgan, edited, *The Heritage of Sufism*, vol. 3, Oxford: 1999, pp. 247-264.

Dahlavi, Shaikh Jamali, *Siyarul-Arifeen,* Delhi, A. H.1311.

David Gilmartin, 'Shrines, Succession, and Sources of Moral Authority', Barbara Daly Metcalf (ed.), *Moral Conduct and Authority: The Place of Adab in South Asian Islam,* Berkeley, 1984.

Dehlawi, Sadiq Muhammad, Kashmiri Hamadani, *Kalimat al-Sadiqin,* ed., Muhammad Saleem Akhtar, Islamabad: Iran Pakistan Research Centre, 1988.

Dhar, Shivji, *"Tarikh-i-Kishtwar"* (Persian), Jammu, 1962.

Eaton, Richard M., (ed.) *India's Islamic Traditions 711–1750,* Delhi: Oxford University Press, 2006.

Eaton, Richard M., *Sufis of Bijapur 1300–1700: Social Roles of Sufis in Medieval India,* Princeton: Princeton University Press, 1978.

Elizabeth E. Bacon, *Central Asians under Russian Rule, A Study in Cultural Change,* London, reprint 1994.

Ernst, Carl W., *Eternal Garden: Mysticism, History, and Politics at a South Asian Sufi Center,* SUNY Series in Muslim Spirituality in South Asia. State University of New York Press.1992.

Ernst, Carl W., and Bruce B. Lawrence, *Sufi Martyrs of Love: Chishti Sufism in South Asia and Beyond,* New York: Palgrave Press, 2002.

Faridabadi, Sad, Sadullah, *Shah Farid-ud-din Baghdadi* (Urdu), Doda; 2000.

Fazl, Abul, *"Ain-i-Akbari, Vol. II,* Eng. Tr. by Jarret, Corrected and further annotated by Sir J.N.Sarkar, Low Price Publication Delhi. 1994

Green, Nile, *Indian Sufism Since the Seventeenth Century: Dervishes, Devotees and Emperors,* Routledge, 2006.

Green, Nile, *Making Space: Sufis and Settlers In Early Modern India,* New York: Oxford University Press, 2012.

Hanif, N., *Biographical Encyclopaedia of Sufis: South Asia,* Vol. 3. Sarup & Sons, 2000.

Hasan, Sijzi, *Fawaidul-Fuad,* Neva, Kishore Press, Lucknow, 1885.

Hussain, Fatima, *The War that Wasn't: The Sufi and the Sultan,* Delhi;

Munshiram Manoharlal Publishers, 2009.

Islam, Riazul, *Sufism in South Asia: Impact on fourteenth century Muslim society*, Oxford University Press, 2002.

Jackson, Paul, *Shaikh Sharafuddin Yahya M Aneri; The Way of A Sufi*, Delhi; 1987.

Khaki Dawood, Baba, *Rishi Nama*, Srinagar, ff. 60–85 ab.

Khan, Ishaq Mohammad, *Sufis of Kashmir*, Srinagar, India: Gulshan Books, 2011.

Khan, Zafarullah Mirza, *Tazkirah-i-Bemisal, Rajgan-i-Rajour* (Urdu), Jallandhar.

Khatoon, Zohra, *Muslim Saints and their Shrines,* Jammu; 1990.

Khusrau, Amir, *Qiran al-Sadayn,* Lucknow: Newal Kishore, 1875..

Lakhnavi, Molvi Hashmatullah, *Mukhtasar Tarikh-i-Jammu wa Kashmir* (Urdu), Jammu; 1992.

Lawrence, Bruce B. (Editor, Translator), *Morals for the Heart: Conversations of Shaykh Nizam Ad-Din Awliya Recorded by Amir Hasan Sijzi*, (Classics of Western Spirituality), 1991.

Lawrence, Bruce B., *Notes from a distant flute: the extant Literature of Pre-Mughal Indian Sufism,* Imperial Iranian Academy of Philosophy, 1978.

Louw, Elisabeth Maria, *Everyday Islam in Post-Soviet Central Asia*, USA: Routledge; 2007.

Maini, Dil Khush, *"Ziarat-I-Sayyid Baba Ghulam Shah Badshah, Shahdara Sharif"* (Urdu), Jammu; 2002.

Maulvi Zafar Hasan and J.A. Page (eds), *Monuments of Delhi Lasting Splendour of the Great Mughals and Others*, Vol. III, Mehrauli Zail, Aryan Books International, New Delhi.

Munshi, Salahuddin, *Muslim Monuments of Gulbarga: A Cultural Study (14th Century A.D. to 17th Century A.D.)*, Dharwad: Karnatak University, 1997.

Nanji, A., 'Shariat and Haqiqat: Its Continuity and Synthesis in the Nizari Ismaili Muslim Tradition' in K Ewing (ed), *Shariat and Ambiguity in*

SouthAsian Islam, University of California Press, Berkeley; 1988.

Nasriddin, Muhammad, *Al-Khanafi al-Khasani al-Bukhari. Tukhfat Az-Zairin*, edited by Kh.Turaev. // IFEAC № 2. 2003. – P.17, 2003, (In Russian Language).

Nirmohi Shiv, *Duggar Ke Darvesh* (Hindi), Udhampur; 2005.

Nizami, Ahmad Khaliq, *Some Aspects of Religion and Politics in India during the thirteenth Century*, Idarah-i-Adabiyat, Delhi; 1974.

Nizami, Khaliq Ahmad, *Religion and Politics In India during The Thirteenth Century*, Oxford University Press, USA, 1961.

Pinto, Desiderio. *Piri-Muridi Relationship: A Study of the Nizamuddin Dargah*, Delhi, Manohar Publishers & Distributors, 1995.

Qalandar, Hamid, *Khairul-Majalis*, (ed.), K. A. Nizami, Aligarh, 1959.

Rai, Mridu, *Islam, Rights and History of Kashmir, Muslim Subjects*, Delhi; 2004.

Richard M. Eaton, *Essays on Islam and Indian History*, Delhi, 2000.

Rizvi, Saiyid Athar Abbas. *A History of Sufism in India. 1. Early Sufism and its history in India 1600 AD*. MunshiramManoharlal, 1978.

Rizvi, Saiyid Athar Abbas. *A history of Sufism in India*. Vol. 2. New Delhi: Munshiram Manoharlal, 1983.

Roy, Olivier, *The Failure of Political Islam*, Cambridge, Mass.: Harvard University Press,1994.

Roy, Olivier, *Globalised Islam: The Search for a New Ummah*, New York: Columbia University Press; 2004.

Schimmel, Annemarie (1986), *Malfuzat Khwan-i-Pur Nimat*, compiled by Zain Badr Arabi and translated in English by Paul Jackson S J, Delhi.

Schwerin, Kerrin G.V., 'Saint Worship in Indian Islam: the Legend of the Martyr Salar Masud Ghazi,' in Imtiaz Ahmad, ed., *Ritual and Religion among Muslims in India*. Delhi; Manohar, 1981.

Shah, Hassan, *T'arikh-i Hassan*, Urdu tr., Moulvi Ibrahim, *Tarikh-i Kashmir*, Srinagar; 1957.

Shaw, Robert, *"Visit to High Tartary and Kashghar,"* 1867--69 *Chinese Central Asia,* New Delhi, reprint, 1996.

Siddiqi, Muhammad Suleman, *The Bahmani Sufis,* Delhi; Idarah-iAdabiyat, 1989.

Singh, Nagendra, *Islamic Mysticism in India,* South Asia Books, 1996.

Steinberger, Petra, "Fundamentalism in Central Asia: Reasons, Reality and Prospects," In *Central Asia: Aspects of Transition,* London,2003.

Subhan, John A., *Sufism, Its Saints and Shrines: An Introduction to the Study of Sufism with Special Reference to India and Pakistan.* Lucknow, Publishing House, 1960.

Taylor, Bayard, *"Travels in Cashmere, Little Tibet and Central Asia," 1876–81,* New York, 1892.

The Holy Qur'an," eng. tr. of the Meanings and Commentary, Revised and Edited by the Presidency of Islamic Researches, IFTA, Kingdom of Saudi Arabia, 1413 Hijra/ 1988 AD., Madinah Munawarah.

Tolman, Charles, *Psychology, Society and Subjectivity: An Introduction to German Psychological Critique,* London: Routledge, 1995.

Trimingham, J. Spencer, *The Sufi Orders in Islam,* Oxford University Press, 1998.

Troll, Christian W., (ed.), *Muslim Shrines in India: Their Character, History and Significance.* Oxford University Press, 2003.

Vohra, N.N. (ed.), *Culture, Society and Politics in Central Asia,* Delhi, 1999.

Wani,Ashraf Muhammad (2004), *Islam in Kashmir (Fourteenth to Sixteenth Century),* Srinagar,2005..

Zarcone, Thierry, 'Central Asian Influence on the Early Development of the Chishtiyya Sufi Order in India,' in Muzaffar Alam (ed.), *The Making of Indo-Persian Culture,* Delhi: Manohar, 2000.

Zutshi, Chitralekha, *"Language of Belonging, Islam, Regional Identity, and the Making of Kashmir,* Permanent Black, Delhi, 2003.

Articles

Ahmad, Aziz, "The Sufi and the Sultan in Pre-Mughal Muslim India," *Der Islam; Zeitschriftfür Geschichte und Kultur des Islamischen Orients* 38 (1963): 142

Akbari, Mehdi, "Role of sufism in the Social Transformation of Bahmani Kingdom," in *Afro Asian Journal of Anthropology and Social Policy* 2. 2 (2011): 105-112.

Alam, Muzaffar, "The Mughals, the Sufi Shaikhs and the formation of the Akbari Dispensation," in *Modern Asian Studies* 43, no. 01 (2009): 135-174.

Algar, Hamid, "The Naqshbandī Order: A Preliminary Survey of its History and Significance" in *Studia Islamica*, vol. 44 (1976), pp. 131-154.

Anjum, Tanvir, "State-Sufi Confrontation in Islamicate South Asia: A Causal Typology," in *Journal of Asian Civilizations* 37. 1 (2014): 149.

Buehler, Arthur F., "Currents of Sufism in Nineteenth-And Twentieth-Century Indo-Pakistan: An Overview," in *The Muslim World* 87, no. 3-4 (1997): 299-314.

Buehler, Arthur, "The Naqshbandiyya in Timurid India: The Central Asian Legacy," in *Journal of Islamic Studies* 7, no. 2 (1996): 208-228.

DeWeese, Devin. "Women Mystics and Sufi Shrines in India by Kelly Pemberton." *Journal of Islamic Studies* (2012): ets086.

Eaton, Richard M. "Sufi folk literature and the expansion of Indian Islam," in *History of Religions* 14, no. 2 (1974): 117-127.

Eaton, Richard Maxwell, "Sufi Folk Literature and the Expansion of Islam in India" in *History of Religions*, vol. 1412 (1974), pp. 117-127.

Elias, Jamal J. "Sufi saints and shrines in Muslim society: Introduction." *The Muslim World* 90, no. 3/4 (2000): 253.

Elias, Jamal J., "Sufism," in *Iranian Studies* 31, no. 3-4 (1998): 595-613.

Ernst, Carl W., 'From Hagiography to Martyrlogy: Conflicting Testimonies to a Sufi Martyr of the Delhi Sultanate,' in *History of Religions* 24.4 (1985):308–27

Freitag, Ulrike, "Hadhramaut: a religious centre for the Indian Ocean in the late 19th and early 20th Centuries?," in *Studia Islamica* 89 (1999): 165-183.

Gafoor, Syed, and S. S. Sarvodaya, "Sufi's Monuments/Architecture of Gulbarga and Bidar," in *Journal of Biological Chemistry* 1. 9 (2012).

Green, Nile, "A Persian Sufi in British India: The Travels of Mīrzā asan afī Alī Shāh (1251/1835-1316/1899)", in *Iran* 42 (2004): 201-218.

Green, Nile, "Emerging Approaches to the Sufi Traditions of South Asia: Between Texts, Territories and the Transcendent," in *South Asia Research* 24. 2 (2004): 123-148.

Green, Nile, "Geography, empire and sainthood in the eighteenth-century Muslim Deccan." *Bulletin of the School of Oriental and African Studies* 67. 2 (2004): 207-225.

Green, Nile. "Migrant Sufis and Sacred Space in South Asian Islam," in *Contemporary South Asia* 12, no. 4 (2003): 493-509.

Green, Nile. 'Emerging Approaches to the Sufi Traditions of South Asia: Between Texts, Territories and the Transcendent', in *South Asia Research* 24.2 (2004):123–48.

Haq, M. M., "The Shuttari Order of Sufism in India and Its Exponents in Bengal and Bihar," in *Journal of the Asiatic society of Pakistan* 16 (1971): 167-175.

Ibrahim, W. "Ata, The spread and influence of Sufism in India–Historical development," in *Islamic Culture* 54, no. 1 (1980): 43.

Johns, A., "Aspects of Sufi thought in India and Indonesia in the first half of the 17th century," in *Journal of the Malayan Branch of the Royal Asiatic Society* 28.1, (1955): 70-77.

Kaw, A. Mushtaq, "Kashmir and Chinese Turkistan-A Study in Cultural Affinities", *Hamdard Islamicus*, XXVII (3) (Karachi), July–September. & *Journal of Pakistan Historical Society,* LII (3) (Karachi), July–September, 2004.

Kaw, A. Mushtaq, Popular Islam in Chinese Central Asia, *Central Asiatic Journal*, Vol. 50 (2), 2006.

Mate, M. S., "Urban Culture of Medieval Deccan (1300 AD to 1650

AD)."*Bulletin of the Deccan College Research Institute,* 56 (1996): 161-217.

Narayanan, Vasudha, "Shared Ritual Spaces: Hindus and Muslims at the Shrine of Shahul Hamid in South India," in *Religious Studies News* 13. 1 (1998):

Nizami, Khaliq Ahmad, "Early Indo-Muslim Mystics and their Attitude towards the State," in *Islamic Culture* 22, 4 (1948): 387-99.

Nizami, Khaliq Ahmad, "Impact of Sufi Saints on Indian Society and Culture," in *Islamic Culture* 58 (1984): 33.

Nizami, Khaliq Ahmad, "Sufi Movement in Deccan," in *History of Medieval Deccan* 11 (1974): 181.

Nizami, Khaliq Ahmed, "The Shattari Saints and their attitude towards the State," in *Medieval India Quarterly* 1, no. 2 (1950): 56.

Parveen, Babli, "Muslim Mysticism and Conversion in Medieval India: A Look at the Role of the Sufis," in *Journal of the Institute for Research in Social Sciences and Humanities* (2014): 125- 137.

Peeran, S. L., *The Essence of Islam, Sufism, and Its Impact on India,* in *Islamic Wonders Bureau,* 1998.

Rizvi, S., "Faith Deployed for a New shiê¿i Polity in India: The Theology of SayyidDildar 'Ali Nasirabadi," in *Journal of the Royal Asiatic Society* 24.3 (2014): 363-380.

Sarao, K. T. S., "Sufi Mysticism and Indian Religions," in *Religious Thoughts* (2012): 5.

Siddiqi, Muhammad Suleman, "Sufi-State Relationship Under TheBahmanids (AD 1348-1538)." *Rivistadeglistudiorientali* 64, 1/2 (1990): 71-96.

Umashankar, R. R., "Metropolitan Microcosms: The Dynamic Spaces of Contemporary Sufi Shrines in India, in" *South Asian Studies* 31 (1): 127-143, 2015.

Zarcone, Thierry, "Turkish Sufism in India: The Case of the Yasawiyya," in *Confluence of Cultures* (1995): 41-51.

Index

A

Abdul Hamid Lahori 9

Abdul Haq Muhaddis Dehalvi 53, 55, 57

Abdul Kasim Jili 22

Abdullah Khan Tura 43

Abd-ur-Rahman Jami' 10, 11, 171

Abul Fazl 9, 55, 103

Abusaid Abul Kahir 21

Afaq Khodja

Afghanistan 1, 6, 27, 32

Agra 9, 96, 104

Ahmedabad 9

Ain-e-Akbari 55, 59, 74

Ajmer 4, 9, 55, 71

Ajodhan 4, 55, 71

Ajzūbān-iHaq 63

Akbar 2, 9, 55

Akbarnama/Akbar Namah 9, 59, 103

Akbar-ul Akhyar 55, 56, 59

Akhi Sirajud Din Badayuni 125.

Alauddin Khilji1 2, 54, 197

Al-Badaoni 106

Ali Hujwiri 3, 124, 173

Aliquli Amir-i Lashkar 46, 48, 49

Allah 1, 61, 62

Amir 96, 215

Amir Ali 196

Amir Hasan Sijzi 56, 88, 94

Amir Khaidar 44, 45

Amir Khurd 18, 55, 62

Amir Khusaro 12, 86, 87

Amir Muwiyah 201

Amritkunda 10, 135

Amroha 12

Anatolia 1, 94

Ansari 10, 150, 152

Arabic 1, 10, 135

Ashraf 131

Ashram 10

Assam 4

Index

Aurad-e-Fatiya 29, 33

Awarif-al-Ma'arif 4

Ayyubid Dynasty 5

Azerbaijan 3

B

Baba Farid 4

Baba Fariduddin Ganj Shakar 4

Babur 41, 42, 195

Badakshan/Badakshani 28, 96

Badaon 19

Badaruddin Samarkhandi 8, 18, 19

Baghdad 4, 18, 75

Bauls 10, 123, 124

Bengal 4, 6, 9

Beshik Khan 42

Bhujar Brahmin 10, 135

Bihar 4, 20, 21

Bijapur 8, 81, 83

British/Britain 2, 8, 39

Buddhism/Budhist 10, 21, 25

Bukhara 3, 28, 30

Bukhari 28, 45, 46

Bulbul Shah 26, 74

C

Caliph 4

Caliph 5, 58, 153

Cambay 3

Chakkinama 8, 72

Chausa 58, 64

Chinggis Khan 17

Chingisism 144

Chiragh Dehalvi 53, 56

Chiragh-e- Delhi 4

Chishti/Chishtiya/Chishtia 4, 6, 9

D

Dalil al-Arifin 90, 92

Dargah 2, 3, 7

Darvesh 57, 216

Dataganj Bakhsh 4

Deccan 3, 4, 110

Delhi 4, 6, 8

Delhi Sultanate 3, 17, 18

Deoband 2, 31

Dervish 3, 93, 147

Devendranath Tagore 10, 135

Dhikr 7, 29, 129

Diwan-e-Hafiz 10, 135

E

Egypt 5

F

Fakhrad-Din Iraqi 10, 150, 154

Fariduddin Nagauri 113

Fatwa 2, 21

Fawaid-ul-Fawad 3

Sufism in India and Central Asia 243

Fawayid-u-Fuad 19, 21, 56

Fergana 40, 41, 43

Firdausi/Firdousi/Firdausiya 6, 8, 17

Firoz Shah Kotla 53, 58

Firoz Shah Tughlaq 23, 58, 89

Folk Islam 26, 34, 144

Futhat-i-Malkuiya 9.

G

Gauhar 18

Ghayaspur 53, 56

Ghazal 12, 173, 175

Ghazali 91, 173, 180

*Ghazaliyat*198.

Ghiasudin Tughlaq 12

Gitanjali 10, 123, 135

Gopal 12

Gujarat 3, 9, 103

Gulam Rabbani 49

Gulbarga 3, 81

Guru Nanak 80, 81

H

Hadith 13, 88, 98

Hajj 42

Hamiduddin Rehani 9, 102, 112

Hamiduddin Nagauri 9, 72, 101

Hanafi 6, 41, 142

Hansi 12, 55

Hauz al Hayat 10, 135

Hazrat Sheikh Abdullah 3

Hazrat Abul Hasan Ali Hadrami 3

Hazrat Nizamuddin Aulia 3, 4, 11

Hindu 2, 10, 21

Hindukush 7, 25

Hujviri 10

Hussain Nagauri 113

I

Ibn Khaldun 171

Ibn-al-Arabi 22, 97, 98

Imaduddin Firdousi 56, 60

Imam Abu Hanifa 30, 206

Imam Rabbani Akhmad al-Sirkhindi 7, 39, 44, 45

Imdadullah Muhajir Makki 2

Iran/Iranian 1, 27, 42

Iraq 11, 114, 185, 196

Ismailia 3

Istanbul 47

J

Jadidist 30

Jahangir 9, 45, 89, 205

Jahangir Khan Tura 45

Jahanian-I-Jahangasht 19

Jaisingh 8

Jalaluddin Tabrizii 18, 19, 124

Jalaludin Rumi 12, 124, 135

J

Jalalussin Khilji 12, 197, 198

Jamaat-e-Ahli-Hadis/Ahli- Hadis Movement 33

Jamali Dehlavi 18, 88, 94

Jammu 8, 71, 73

Jammu and Kashmir 39, 71, 74

Jawami-ul-Kilim 55, 61

Jiyarat 8

Juybar 47

K

K A Nizami 19, 54, 72

Kabir 2, 132, 223

Kafir/Kufr 2, 204, 205

Kaiqubad 56

Kalimat-us-Sadiqin 8, 55, 58

Kannada 13, 223, 225

Karamth 18, 64, 79

Karimov 30, 31

Karnataka 13, 223, 224

Kashf-ul-Mahjoob 4

Kashghar 28, 173

Kashmir 6, 7, 25

Kazak/Kazakh 6, 46, 144

Khair-ulMajālis 55, 56, 57

Khaja Education Society 2

Khaja Bandanawaz 3

Khan 42, 45, 46

Khanate 39, 40, 41

Khankah/Khanqah 1, 2, 3

Khodja Akhrar 45

Khodja Bek 40, 48, 49

Khoqand 8, 39, 40

Khoqand Khanate 7, 39, 40

Khuda Baksh Library 12

Khudayar Khan 47

Khurasan 6, 21

Khutbuddin Bhaktiar Khaki 18

Khwaja Moinuddin Chishti 4, 5, 9

Khwaja Qutubuddin Bakhtiyar Kaki 4, 54, 61

Khwan-i-Pur Nimat 21

Khwarazm Shah Ala Uddin Muhammad 5

Khwarizm 17, 53

Kirghiztan 40

Kirgiz 6

Kishwar Qadri 8

Kubrawi/Kubrawiya 6, 17, 18

Kuliyab 29, 30

L

Lahore 3, 48, 49

Langar 53, 56, 80

Lori Nama 72

Lorinama 8

M

Ma'sum Khan Tura 45

Madrasa 41, 171

Makhdumi A'zam 45

Makhmud II 47

Maktaba 13, 171

Maktabat-i-sadi 20, 22

Maktubat 4

Malfuz/Malfuzat 4, 19, 20

Malfuzāt 59, 64, 73

Malik al-Adil 5

Manāqib-ul Asfiya 54, 56, 61

Margilan 43

Marxism 30

Masthnavis 12

Mecca/Macca 2, 42, 43

Mehbub-e-Ilahi 4

Ming 42, 48

Minhaj-us Siraj 56

Mirsad al Ibad 151, 152, 154

Miththa 8

Miyan Khalil Sakhibzada 7, 8, 39

Mohammad Afzal 12

Mohammad bin Munavvar 10, 150

Mongol 5, 17, 185

Muhammad Ali-Khan 39, 44, 45

Muhammad Ali-Khan 8, 39, 44

Muhammad Anwar Khan 44

Muhammad Yunusjan
   Shigovul 46, 48

Muhammed bin Tuglaq 23, 92, 113

Muhammed Sadiq Hamadani 26, 55,

Mulana Abul Kalam Library 12

Multan 18, 74, 81, 103, 109, 110

Murad 2

Murid 7, 12, 17

Murshid 1, 95

Musa Khan Dakhbedi 43

Mystic/Mystical/Mysticism 1, 3, 5

N

Nafs 11, 189, 211

Nagaur 9, 101, 102

Najibuddin Kubra 6

Najibuddin Firdousi 20, 59

Najmuddhin Kubra 17, 18, 19

Najmuddin Razi 10, 11, 150

Najmuddin Sughra 17, 18, 19

Naqshbandi/Naqshbandia/Naqsh-
bandiya 4, 7, 28

Naqshbandiyya-Mujaddidiyya 7, 39

Nathism 10, 127

Nayman-say 41

Niyaz Muhamad Khuqanti 44

Nur QutbAlam 10, 125

Nuruddin Ismail Nur Satgarh 3

O

Oltin Beshik 30, 41, 42

Ottoman 41, 42, 46

P

Pak Pattan 4.

PamirPlateau/Pamir 7, 25

Panipat 11, 12, 89

Persia/Persian 3, 7, 10

Pir1, 3, 8, 20

Prophet Muhammed 21, 200

Punjab 4, 8, 71

Puritan Islam 31, 34.

Q

Qadri/Qadriya 4, 73, 75

Qalader 12

Qasba 9, 101, 106

Qasi Ashrafudhin 21

Qayumi 44

Qazi Hamiduddin Nagauri 9, 107

Qazi Nazrul 10, 123, 136

Qazi Shamsuddin 58, 64

Qur'an/Quran/Koran 13, 21, 22

Qutabin–din Mubarak Shah 12

R

Rabindranath Tagore 10, 123, 135

Rajasthan 9, 101, 102

Rajgir 22

Ramayan 12, 224

Rauza/Rauzat 57, 93

RauzatulArifin 8, 77

Rishi/Rishis 7, 26, 28

Rukn-Al-Din-Samarqandi 10, 135

Ruknuddin Firdousi 18, 20, 56

Russia/Russian 7, 39, 40

S

S A A Rizvi 19, 54, 73

Sadr 19

Saifuddin Baqarzi 18, 20, 53

Saint 1, 2, 4

Salafi 31

Salat-I-Kabir 94

Salat-I-M'akus 21

Salik 12, 13, 219

Sama 20, 53, 54

Samarqand 3, 28, 30

Sanskrit 10, 135

Santiniketan 10, 135

Sarai 9, 58, 102

Sayyid Ali Hamadani 26, 77

Sayyid Khan 49

Sayyid 49, 79, 28

Seljuk 5, 91

Shadinama 72

Shadinama 8

Shaerali Khan 48

Shahjahan 9

Shaikhul Islam 17, 18, 19, 23

Shams Siraj Afif 55, 58

Shamsuddin Iltumish 17, 18

Sharafuddin Yahya Maneri Firdousi 20, 21, 23

Sharfuddin Bu Ali Qalander Panipati 11, 195, 196

Sharia'/Shariate 18, 95, 98

Shattari 54, 63

Sheikh Akhi Siraj 10, 123

Sheikh Husain Zanjani 3

Sheikh Ismail 3

Sheikh Sadquallah Panipati 12

Shiah 42

Shihabuddin Suhrawardi 4

Shishunala Sharif 13, 223, 224

Shrine 5, 6, 7

Siddi Raja 3

Sikh 4, 80, 81, 83

Silk Route 7, 25

Silsila 4, 6, 8

Singola/Singhola/Sinkola 53, 56, 58

Siyar-ul-Arifin 88

Siyar-ul-Auliya 55, 57, 59

Sonargaon 21

South Asia 3, 27, 33

Soviet 3, 37, 30

Suhagnama 8

Suhela 8

Suhrawardi/Suhravardi/Suhrawardi-ya 4, 9, 17

Sunni 2, 6, 42

Surdas 2

Syed Anas Mashhadi 9, 102

Syed Jalal Bukhari 9

Syed Mohammad Tahir 9, 102

Syed Nisar Shah 3

Syed Roshan Ali 9, 102

Syria 3

T

Tabriz 75

Tajik 6, 30, 185

Tajikistan 5, 28, 29

Taliban 32

Tanhid 22

Tantric 10, 127, 128, 135

TarikhiAliquli Amir-i-lashkar 46, 48

Tarikh-i-FirozShahi 55, 58, 88

TarikhiShakhrukhi 44

Tariqat 46, 148, 188

Tasawwuf 13, 20, 22

Tash Khodja Sudur 40, 48, 49

Tashkent 40, 48, 49

Timurid 5, 96, 173

Transoxiana 21

Trichinopoly 3

Tughlaq 85, 92

Turkey 1, 6

Turkic 6, 144, 145

Turkish 108, 124

Turkistan/Turkestan 28, 40, 41

Turkmen 6

Turkmenistan 5, 28, 177

Turks 6, 9, 102

U

Ulema 21, 39, 40

Umar-Khan 45

Upanishad 9, 123

Upasana 10.

Uzbek 6, 32, 41

Uzbekistan 5, 28, 31

V

Veerashaiva 224, 228

W

Wahabi 30, 31, 130

Wahdat-al-Wujud 22, 80, 9

West Asia 4

Y

Yamuna 56, 58, 60

Yarkand 28, 173

Yemen 3, 96

Yoga 10, 21, 134

Yogi 10, 21, 23

Yogic 123, 134, 135

Yogini 32

Z

Zakirat-ulMuluk 33, 200

Zeyarat 5

Zikr 26, 95, 96, 128, 151, 216